D0262078

823.
2
DRA

1909287329

The Drama of the Renaissance

The Drama of the Renaissance: *Essays for Leicester Bradner*

EDITED BY ELMER M. BLISTEIN

Brown University Press

PROVIDENCE, RHODE ISLAND 1970

Standard Book Number: 87057–117–6
Library of Congress Catalog Card Number: 72–91653
Brown University Press, Providence, Rhode Island 02912
© 1970 by Brown University
Published 1970
Printed in the United States of America
By the Crimson Printing Company
On Warren's University Text
Bound by Stanhope Bindery, Inc.
Designed by David Ford

Contents

Foreword

To honor Leicester Bradner for his influence and enthusiasm as a teacher is necessary; to honor him for his wide-ranging contributions to literary scholarship is essential; to honor him with a *Festschrift* is inevitable. What does not seem inevitable—at least on the surface—is the subject matter of this particular homage volume.

Customarily when a colleague or an old student thinks of honoring a teacher-scholar with a *Festschrift,* the name of the person to be honored carries with it, almost automatically, the subject matter of the essays, the title of the volume: *Essays in Neoclassical Literature for J. Q. Black; Studies in the Victorian Novel, a* Festschrift *for Algernon White; Spenserian Studies in Honor of Walter Brown.* Obviously, Black is a neoclassicist, White's field is the Victorian novel, Brown is a Spenserian. Yet, when a colleague and a department chairman (both terms apply to one man; they are not necessarily mutually exclusive) suggested to this old student that a *Festschrift* in honor of Leicester Bradner might be in order, no automatic subject matter, no automatic title, trailed along with his name. Nevertheless, any of the three subject matters in the hypothetical titles listed above could have come to mind when Leicester Bradner's name was mentioned, but then so could another dozen or so titles, another dozen or so subject matters.

For most often when a man has taught and has been a productive scholar for over forty years, his name and one field are inextricably linked. With Leicester Bradner, such is not the case. The title of this volume and the subject matter of these essays were not arrived at immediately or instinctively. An immediate reaction might have suggested a volume dealing with grand opera or with Gilbert and Sullivan, for while music has always been one of his interests, words *and* music have been his passion. An instinctive reaction might have suggested a volume dealing with—of all things—baseball, for he has spent many a spring and summer and fall afternoon, watching, playing, and talking about that game. He is, quite clearly, multifaceted. So, the briefest way to explain the reason behind this volume's title and this volume's subject matter is, paradoxically, an indirect way.

The sober facts may be recited soberly. Upon receiving his A.B. from Yale in 1920, Leicester Bradner taught for a year at the Los Alamos Ranch School. He went back to Yale for graduate study, and received his A.M. in 1923 and his Ph.D. in 1926. During the academic year 1924–25, he served as an instructor in English at Union College. In 1926 he came to Brown University as an instructor in English. By coming to Brown, he was returning to Providence, Rhode Island, a city in which he had spent most of his boyhood days, most of his adolescent years. More than alliteration made Brown and Bradner *simpático:* he has spent the rest of his academic career at that university, becoming an assistant professor in 1930, an associate professor in 1934, and a professor in 1945.

During these years of teaching at Brown, he has been both specialist and generalist. Like other young men, before him and since, he began by teaching the customary courses in rhetoric and composition, in the history of literature, in the genres. Many teachers of English literature like to refer to themselves as utility infielders, able to step into any course and teach it brilliantly and even adequately. Leicester Bradner, without talking about it, is that rare type, the specialist who is, at the same time, the genuinely competent utility infielder. Occasionally because of an emergency, but most often because of enthusiasm and desire, he has taught courses in Chaucer, Sidney, Spenser, and Shakespeare; he has taught courses in the fifteenth, sixteenth, seventeenth, eighteenth, and nineteenth centuries; he has taught courses in poetry, in the novel, and in drama; he has taught such specialized courses as Literary Periodicals of the Eighteenth Century, Anglo-American Literary Relations in the Eighteenth Century, The Continental Backgrounds of English Literature, Man's Faith and Fate, Bibliography, and Sixteenth-Century Satire. He does not seem ever to have taught Anglo-Saxon, and he seems to have taught American literature and twentieth-century literature only as aspects of other courses, but these three areas aside, he has taught the entire spectrum. That is one reason why it was not easy to fix on a subject matter for this volume.

Although the variety of courses he has taught is extremely wide, equally various have been the doctoral dissertations which he has either directed or helped to direct. Such dissertations range from "The Kingis Quair" and "Purity" to Charles Dickens and Edith Wharton, and include such literary figures as Jonathan Swift and Anthony Trollope, William Dean Howells and Bishop Francis Atterbury, George Peele and John Donne, William Davenant and John Crowne, Shakespeare and Milton, Spenser and Sidney, Edward Cave and John Shirley, George Herbert and William Dunbar. He has been helpful to young scholars as they have written on the decline of the occult and supernatural in England during the neo-classical period, sixteenth-century narrative poetry, *The New England Courant,* the development of Edinburgh as a literary center in the eighteenth century, music for the English drama from the beginnings to 1642, expressions of cultural nationalism in early American magazines, American verse from 1783 through 1799, and English satire of the sixteenth century. And this list by no means is exhaustive; nor have masters' essays been included. It is little wonder that many have argued that Leicester Bradner is at his best when dealing with graduate students—even though many undergraduates would dispute that point. At any rate, this great variety is but another reason why it was extremely difficult to determine a subject matter for this volume.

If a third reason for the difficulty in determining the focus of this *Festschrift* is required, one need look only at Leicester Bradner's bibliography at the end of this volume. Others may have written more books, more pamphlets, more articles, and more reviews, but few scholars' bibliographies indicate an interest and enthusiasm in so many different fields. An additional proof of the catholicity of his interests is provided by his memberships in learned societies. He is a member of Phi Beta Kappa, the Modern Language Association of America, the Bibliographical Society (London), The Malone Society, The Index Society, the Guild of Scholars of the Episcopal Church, and the Modern Humanities Research Association. He is a founder member of the Renaissance Society of America, has been a member of the board of directors and president of the Faculty Conference in Theology, and chairman of the Committee on Renaissance Studies of the American Council of Learned Societies. He is extremely active in his church and, curiously enough—or perhaps not curiously at all—Leicester Bradner has been an active and assiduous director of the Legal Aid Society of Rhode Island for over thirty years.

Since the man we honor with this volume has such a wide range of interests, has such a multifaceted personality, it is little wonder that it was difficult to arrive at the subject matter for this *Festschrift*. Finally, his own current interest, his own current enthusiasm (despite his neoclassical attitudes, it is hard not to use that word in speaking of him) determined the subject matter. He is now engaged in writing a history of Renaissance drama. What could be more appropriate than to offer him a homage volume on the same subject? Hence our volume is entitled *The Drama of the Renaissance: Essays for Leicester Bradner*.

When a scholar thinks of Renaissance drama, one writer's name springs immediately to mind. It is not strange, then, that studies of Shakespeare as a dramatist and as man comprise over half of the essays in this volume. In "The Significance of Hamlet's Advice to the Players," Roy W. Battenhouse argues cogently that the advice is characteristic of Hamlet's credo, but not necessarily of Shakespeare's. Indeed, says Mr. Battenhouse, "the play as a whole implies a criticism of Hamlet's taste and theorizing." Hamlet's advice becomes, hence, a double irony: "For, on the one hand, we watch a Hamlet who violates his own rules, and on the other hand, we realize what intolerable drama we would be stuck with if he didn't."

Fredson Bowers, writing on "Theme and Structure in *King Henry IV*, Part 1," gives an extremely close reading to that much-read play.

He points out that Shakespeare has created in a sense a "structural paradox, because Hal, who is to become the true protagonist of the play (in that the spire of meaning rises from him), transfers from the under- to the main plot to create the climax." So far as theme is concerned, Mr. Bowers argues that Prince Hal achieves the "ultimate definition" of honor, a definition that goes beyond Falstaff's materialistic attitude, King Henry IV's sense of the expedient, and "Hotspur's fatal distortion."

While Mr. Bowers deals with a noun, Madeleine Doran bends her attention to a conjunction, and Paul A. Jorgensen is concerned with "Shakespeare's Dark Vocabulary." Many readers of *Othello* have noticed the frequent occurrence of the conjunction *if* in the play, and now in "Iago's 'if': An Essay on the Syntax of *Othello*" Miss Doran points out not only the frequency but also the function of the conjunction. She demonstrates persuasively that "syntax is the most intimate way to show movement of mind; it is the dramatist's most refined tool in shaping monologue or dialogue." It is, then, not at all strange that the subtle Iago would use as the most subtle of his grammatical and logical tools "the conditional sentence expressing a condition assumed to be possible." And when Iago's *if*s are over, we finally arrive once more in the "world of fact, monstrous but true. At last a crime has been committed, and it is Othello's."

In his essay, Mr. Jorgensen believes "the vocabulary, even more than the imagery," helps us to understand a play. Yet he points out that "the vocabulary of *Hamlet* is not amenable to the extraction of dark words," however amenable *Titus Andronicus* and *Macbeth* may be. And while *Macbeth* has a quality which "defies a vocabulary study. . . . the dark vocabulary does—more so than discussions of sleep, clothes, and procreation—make us more nearly adequate to appreciating fully Shakespeare's skill with his most important tools: words."

S. Schoenbaum asserts in "Shakespeare the Ignoramus" that Shakespeare was many men: "a husband and father, a provincial, a poet, a playwright, an actor, a shareholder in a theatrical company, a real-estate investor." Despite the long line of detractors from Francis Beaumont and Ben Jonson to Sidney Lee and A. L. Rowse; despite the Droeshout engraving with its vacuous expression; despite the Janssen bust ("The mouth gapes open; the poet is in the throes of composition—or is it indigestion?"); despite all these men and things, Mr. Schoenbaum believes that William Shakespeare is definitely "an intellectual, not an ignoramus."

M. A. Shaaber reminds us in a fine epigrammatic phrase that Shakespeare's characters are not heretics but "Laodiceans in the religion of love." For this, as well as for many other reasons, Mr. Shaaber believes that we should stress the noun and not the adjective when we call Shakespeare's comedies romantic comedies. His argument that "the comic view of life in these plays is largely a comic view of love," tends to support his contention. "Shakespeare's comic view of love is based . . . on the acceptance of all of it, its component of folly as well as its component of glory." Since Shakespeare so often sets up affectation of all kinds as his object of satire, it is little wonder that affectation in love would be one of his favorite targets.

A study of William Gager's plays would be welcome in any collection of essays on Renaissance drama, but in this particular volume it is many times welcome. After all, C. F. Tucker Brooke, Leicester Bradner's mentor and friend, wrote a seminal essay on Gager. Then, Leicester Bradner's interest in neo-Latin poetry and drama is profound and abiding. And finally, all lovers of drama are indebted to Dr. Gager for his spirited defence of stage plays in his arguments with Dr. John Rainolds, the student of ascetical theology. In his essay, "William Gager's *Meleager* and *Ulysses Redux*," Mr. J. W. Binns contends that Gager is successful in depicting character because his dramatis personae are not merely mouthpieces for tedious disquisitions on trite themes or static feelings. Unlike the characters in many Latin plays, Gager's characters belong to the world of drama, not to the world of epic. And, he concludes, although Gager wrote in Latin, he was "nonetheless an Elizabethan dramatist, who wrote in one of the greatest periods of English literature."

Discussing "Tragedy in the Spanish Golden Age," C. A. Jones suggests that the tendency of many contemporary critics to find signs of classical tragedy in the works of the Spanish dramatists of the Golden Age may well be mistaken. He feels that "as a dramatist at least, Calderón followed the tradition associated with Lope de Vega, a tradition which looked to the audience rather than to the rule book." And he concludes that the creators of Golden Age Spanish drama "were more interested in the 'whole truth' than they were in the creation of tragedy."

Because relatively little attention has been paid to Calderón's comedies, Kenneth Muir feels that this neglect should be remedied, and does so in "The Comedies of Calderón." By examining several of the plays (using his own English versions), Mr. Muir decides that Calderón was at his best in his ability "to exploit a dramatic situation so as to extract from it the maximum of entertainment."

"*La Venexiana* in the Light of Recent Criticism," by Bodo L. O. Richter, presents us with a fine example of bibliographical, esthetic, textual, historical, and interpretive criticism of a "small masterpiece" too little known and, probably for that reason alone, too little appreciated. Mr. Richter's study should do much to rescue *La Venexiana* from neglect. A knowledge of dialectology is essential for a proper study of the play, because it is written in "Venetian dialect, with a strong sprinkling of Bergamask." As interesting as the close reading Mr. Richter gives this play is the information he provides on its dating and sources.

These ten essays, diverse in approach, varied in subject matter, make up a volume which is a tribute to a man and a scholar. The contributors and the editor can only hope that the *Festschrift* attains to Leicester Bradner's extremely high standards of scholarship and humanity.

E.M.B.

The Drama of the Renaissance

The Significance of
Hamlet's Advice to the Players

ROY W. BATTENHOUSE

Can Hamlet's views on the actor's art and the purpose of playing be equated with Shakespeare's? Many modern critics have blithely assumed so. George Brandes, writing in the 1890s, remarked that Hamlet's speech of advice gives us "what we should scarcely have expected—an insight into Shakespeare's own ideas of his art as poet and actor"; and this opinion has been widely echoed, not only around 1904 by A. C. Bradley and A. H. Tolman, but much more recently by at least a half-dozen other commentators.[1] Some of them, one suspects, have been conditioned as Brandes was by a prior belief that Shakespeare "merged himself in Hamlet" throughout the play. S. L. Bethell, however, has a more guarded explanation, arguing only that in this particular instance the dramatist got so caught up in writing his own ideas that "he half forgot Hamlet in writing them." That is, he here suspended characterization in order to express himself. But is this likely? Would Shakespeare thus fracture dramatic illusion? Moreover, would it not be somewhat presumptuous of him to give instruction, even in this indirect way, to members of his own profession, who might well resent being lectured on their craft?

Michael Redgrave, while supposing Hamlet's advice to be Shakespeare's, nevertheless admits that in a life situation the speech "would seem somewhat insulting to even a mediocre actor"; and similarly Cecile de Banke finds it surprising that Hamlet should "step right out of character to carry coals to Newcastle." The uneasiness these critics feel as to Hamlet's procedure ought to have led them, I think, to doubt whether Shakespeare wishes in any way at all to identify himself with this speaker's advice-giving. The

Elsinore players, we may note, respond to it deferentially but coolly. Is not Shakespeare suggesting that they find it actually of little help but tolerate it as being in character for Hamlet the amateur theorist?

To sharpen our question further, some mention must be made of a few critics who have not followed majority opinion. The literary historian J. W. H. Atkins, while noting that Hamlet's "mirror" concept goes back to Plato, has added the comment that Shakespeare's own dramatic theory, although embodied in all his practice, remains "unformulated" in statement.[2] And W. F. Trench, in raising (as long ago as 1913) some important disagreements with Bradley, vigorously insisted that Hamlet's lecture to the actors is introduced entirely to suit Hamlet's outlook. "We should be strangely perverse," he wrote, "were we to suppose the dramatist to have turned aside from his dramatic purpose for the sake of an opportunity that has occurred for conveying to us through Hamlet's lips his own views upon elocution! Shakespeare had no desire whatever to instruct us unless it be in the lineaments of Hamlet's mind and character."[3] Lecturing on art is particularly congenial to Hamlet, Trench went on to say, because having found himself unable to reform life as it is lived, he would now turn to reforming the art which represents life—and would invoke for this the same abstract principles. The perfect art Hamlet has in mind is to be compounded of a tempestuous passion tempered by "discretion," just as (in the episode with Horatio which immediately follows) the perfect life is defined as a commingling of blood and judgment. Trench's point, that a balancing of emotion by reason is Hamlet's whole ideal, alike for life and for art, seems to me quite correct; and it furnishes convincing grounds for regarding Hamlet's advice to the players as being characteristic of *his* credo—not necessarily of Shakespeare's.

The ideal of equipoise is plainly a Stoic one. Should we suppose that Shakespeare was giving it his unqualified endorsement? While associating it with Horatio, the dramatist shows this representative of "antique Roman" temperament trying at the play's end to commit suicide—and being withheld by a Hamlet who asks merely that he delay for awhile this "felicity" for which Hamlet too has been long-ing. Suicide, as we know from *Julius Caesar,* is in Roman eyes a paradoxical proof of self-mastery. But surely for Shakespeare this version of life's consummation, and the judgment that it is ulti-mately the way to prove oneself not Fortune's slave, must have seemed a questionable kind of discretion—one which the Hamlet of Act I knew to be contrary to heaven's canon. When Horatio attempts suicide, should we not infer either that he is here failing to commingle judgment and blood, or else that he is mingling these well by a Stoic ideal but that this ideal is itself of dubious validity? This is the case similarly, it seems to me, as regards Hamlet's ideal of dramatic art. For here too the announced standard is a main-taining of the "modesty" of nature; yet how modest actually is the First Player's speech in Act II, which Hamlet so fulsomely has com-mended? We may either say, as some readers of *Hamlet* have said, that this speech is really all bombast and rant, a thinly veiled parody by Shakespeare of the style of his theater rivals;[4] or else we may regard it as modest enough by Senecan standards, yet intended by Shakespeare to reveal the delusive grandeur of neo-Senecan rhetoric and, implicitly, the tragedy of Hamlet's addiction to such art.

The second of these two ways of reading seems to me the more comprehensive. That is, Shakespeare may be indicating for us the defective ideals, alike in the area of esthetics and in the area of ethics, which contribute to Hamlet's tragedy by misleading him with hollow versions of self-nobility. If Shakespeare's play is to effect a catharsis in us, these ideals need to be presented in such a way as to tempt our admiration, yet be recognizable (when we ponder them) as having served to feed in the hero superficial understanding and sterile pretensions. The Player's speech is no doubt regarded by Hamlet as free of rant, but Shakespeare is show-ing that its Senecan art substitutes bombast for insight and reduces tragedy to melodrama. A good part of Shakespeare's irony lies in the fact that Hamlet does not realize how puerile such art is—how in fact it will suggest, in his own case, an experiment in boyish drama not unlike the kind which Rosencrantz has reported as fascinating the "elite" gentlemen of the city. Although Hamlet has thought it strange that "little eyases" should in the city be applauded for berattling the stage and has commented that "their writers do them wrong" to thus run down their careers, will not he himself engage, after listening to the Aeneas speech, in "much throwing about of brains" and turn to producing a play which he hopes will berattle Claudius—but which results, ironically, in running down his own future career? Tragedy, Shakespeare seems to be saying, arises typically from a misuse of the intellect on the part of a civilization's intelligentsia—whether in Denmark or in Elizabethan England or anywhere else.

My concern in the present essay is to focus chiefly on the dramatic function of Hamlet's advice to the players, yet my discussion of this must involve also some reference to the Player's speech and to the Gonzago playlet. I wish to show, first, how Shakespeare's play as a whole implies a criticism of Hamlet's taste and theorizing; and, secondly, how Hamlet's views reflect canons typically neoclassical, especially those by which Ben Jonson was attempting, around the year 1600, to "reform" the theater. In an indirect way Shakespeare is more than glancing at the so-called war of the theaters. He is covertly suggesting how coterie drama (such as Jonson was turning to, after having played earlier in *The Spanish Tragedy*) could tend toward tragic consequences in life for anyone who, like Hamlet, dotes on Senecan and then Italianate tragedy unaware of how shallow its intellectual premises are.

I

That Shakespeare's understanding of the art of acting was (to say the least) of a range much larger than Hamlet's, we can easily discover by asking one simple question: Can the actor who plays Hamlet in Shakespeare's play do so without abridging the rules laid down in Hamlet's advice? Consider, for instance, the scene at Ophelia's grave in Act V. As Hamlet there engages in a quarrel with Laertes, he cries out:

'Swounds, show me what thou't do.
Woo't weep? woo't fight? woo't fast? woo't tear thyself?
Woo't drink up esill? eat a crocodile?
I'll do't. . . .

Surely no actor can speak these lines "trippingly on the tongue." Rather, they obviously require a "mouthing" such as the earlier advice had denounced. Moreover, Hamlet had scorned vulgarity of accent; yet here his own diction is lapsing into a repeated use of "woo't."[5] For here he is caught up, not in a passion of grief, as Laertes had been, but by a desperate desire to deflate Laertes' expression of love for Ophelia. We see Hamlet becoming extravagantly self-defensive after Laertes retorts, "The devil take thy soul!"; for this cry calls in question Hamlet's cherished self-righteousness. To escape self-examination, he then whirls into an attack on Laertes' sincerity: "Nay, an thou'lt mouth, / I'll rant as well as thou." The Queen rightly characterizes Hamlet's behavior here as madness. Later he himself will apologize for it to Laertes, attributing it to "sore distraction." But plainly it has been an instance of the very noise and bellowing which Hamlet had supposed players should and could avoid. The Shakespearean actor of Hamlet can not avoid it, we may say, because he must imitate the *real* psychic action of Hamlet, not the ideal of self-controlled action to which Hamlet's rules would confine the art of acting. In genuine tragedy, the actor of the hero's role needs to be able to imitate truthfully the unintended self-contradictions of self-divided man.

Tragedy's irony depends on there being a gap between the hero's premises and his practice, and also between his vision and that of other observers. Long before we hear Hamlet insisting on propriety of "gait" in an actor, Shakespeare has reported to us Hamlet's own outlandish mode of walking from Ophelia's chamber, and has shown us on stage Hamlet's capering with a ghost. In acting that cellarage scene, Hamlet has employed not temperance of utterance but what Horatio calls "wild and whirling words." Further, is not the nunnery scene likely to occasion some sawing of the air with the hand? (Indeed, in the advice speech itself, Hamlet must saw the air in order to imitate what he is denouncing—which is Shakespeare's hint as to the inadequacy of Hamlet's rules.) Ophelia's comment at the end of the nunnery scene, "O heavenly powers, restore him," highlights for us her sense of Hamlet's eccentric behavior. Not a whirlwind passion acted with smoothness, but a *reason* "Like sweet bells jangled, out of tune and harsh" is her impression of Hamlet. And that is the quality, similarly, of his behavior in the bedroom scene. Here an actor playing Hamlet must represent to us a man who struts noisily, gesticulates feverishly, and stabs wildly, yet who imagines himself as behaving temperately. "My pulse as yours doth temperately keep time / And makes as healthful music" is Hamlet's reply when Gertrude upbraids his "ecstasy." But the spirit underneath his lines tells us otherwise, as do also Gertrude's reference to his "tongue in noise so rude" and her alarm at speech that "roars so loud and thunders in the index."

All told, no fewer than seven attacks of "ungovernable agitation," as Dover Wilson terms them in counting them up, mark Hamlet's behavior in the course of the play.[6] Can any of these be acted effectively without tearing a passion to tatters? Particularly notable is the out-Heroding of Herod which emerges in the dramatically superb third soliloquy—which Shakespeare places, surely for deliberate contrast, immediately after the ultrasmooth tempest of passion enacted by the decorous and discreet First Player in his tale of Aeneas. That player was enacting a declamatory recitative of Senecan style. A far different style is required for a Hamlet of truly tragic passion:

> Am I a coward?
> Who calls me villain? breaks my pate across?
> Plucks off my beard and blows it in my face?
> Tweaks me by th' nose, gives me the lie i' th' throat
> As deep as to the lungs? Who does me this, ha?
> 'Swounds, I should take it! for it cannot be
> But I am pigeon-liver'd and lack gall
> To make oppression bitter, or ere this

I should have fatted all the region kites,
With this slave's offal. Bloody, bawdy villain!
Remorseless, treacherous, lecherous, kindless villain!
O, vengeance!

If the actor of this speech suits his action to the words, is he not likely to do some strutting and rakish sawing, and to speak not trippingly but with abrupt plosives, which escalate into noisy bellow and end, a moment later, with the mouthed explosive of "Fie upon't! foh!"? The very rhythm of the language would so require.

Hamlet's theory that a player who struts and bellows is to be censured for imitating "humanity so abominably" overlooks a point basic to the art of acting. The actor's task is to imitate, we may reply, not some mode of ideal humanity, but rather the action of some believable individual man—who in moments when he is giving way to the passion of revenge can not be expected to behave other than ab-hominably, since revenge is no neutral passion but one which takes a man away from himself, distracting him from his human essence. Shakespeare's realism on this score can be said to accord with the insight of Aquinas. Aquinas had observed that "the gait of a man shows what he is," in that his outward movements are signs of an "inward disposition" (*S.T.* II–II.168.1); but that when the inward disposition is one of intemperate anger, its features are those listed by Gregory the Great: indignation, a swelling of the mind with heated imaginings, the clamor of injurious words, blasphemy, contumely, and quarreling (*S.T.* II–II.168.7). In the action of such a man, there is inevitably a "privation of mode, species, and order" (*S.T.* I–II.85). This privation, I would say, is what Shakespeare intends us to see in Hamlet's action; and therefore any actor who plays Hamlet intelligently must present that kind of action.[7] The audience—even those groundlings whom Hamlet belittles—must be given signs for recognizing that Hamlet, after all, has the spirit of a Herod. The audience can thus enjoy, ironically at Hamlet's expense, a kind of theater fare which his aristocratic theory has forbidden. Doubtless the Globe's groundlings were quite "capable" of appreciating, not solely the noise displayed, but what it signified—a Hamlet of genuinely tragic passion.

The lines Aeneas was given to speak presuppose a detached, almost Olympian observer, engaged in scene painting a tragedy outside himself. Such a speaker's presentation of the behavior of Pyrrhus, Priam, and Hecuba is wholly by external description. As Harry Levin has remarked, "We might almost be listening to the play-by-play account of a sporting event." [8] To guide our responses, the reporter then comments with a noble Stoic tirade:

> Out, out, thou strumpet Fortune! All you gods,
> In general synod take away her power;
> Break all the spokes and fellies from her wheel,
> And bowl the round nave down the hill of heaven,
> As low as to the fiends!

It is as if this speaker were himself on a hill of heaven and allied to the gods he invokes. And a moment later, after picturing Hecuba's plight, he turns to imagining how this scene would affect anyone who viewed it. It would arouse, he says, a venomous-tongued denouncing of Fortune. But note that his own rhythms of speech here lack any spirit of venom. Instead, he is proceeding to speculate that the scene would have caused the gods, very likely, to turn milky-eyed in a passion of grief. While describing these hypothetical responses, the player is evidently accompanying them with an activity of voice and face to match the passion he is imagining. But does such activity imitate the psychic action of a believable Aeneas?

What impresses Hamlet, let us note, is the player's ability to

>   force his soul so to his own conceit
> That, from her working, all his visage wann'd,
> Tears in his eyes, distraction in's aspect,
> A broken voice, and his whole function suiting
> With forms to his conceit....

Here we see that the chief result of this player's acting has been to call attention to his own technique. The illusion of a believable Aeneas has not been created. One reason is that the text of the drama has provided no interaction between Aeneas and Dido. Dido has faded into a nonentity, while Aeneas has become depersonalized into a *nuntius*. There has been no indication of an Aeneas who feels grief because Hecuba was the mother of his own beloved Creusa. Rather, the grief seems impersonal or superpersonal, and we may suspect the shed tears to have been more manufactured than felt. Even Hamlet asks, "What's Hecuba to him, or he to Hecuba, / That he should weep for her?" And then his own action turns to a coveting of the player's art, rather than to any sympathy for the putative human being in the character named Aeneas. We may sense a Shakespearean irony in Hamlet's terming the tale he has just heard a "nothing," a mere fiction; for we know that Shakespeare's own drama of Hamlet is also a fiction—but one importantly different in that Hamlet is so lifelike that we can sympathize with *him,* rather than with the actor playing Hamlet. Moreover, we sense a paradox in Hamlet's present situation: whereas he is feeling angry with himself for not being able, like the player, to suit his action of body and voice to his own "conceit"—that is, to his imagining of how he ought to behave—we are aware, at this very moment, that he is very capably revealing through body and voice his inner motivation, a desire to emulate the player.

Not stopping to ask why this player's style of acting has brought no moisture of tears to Hamlet as spectator, Hamlet turns to imagining how this player would act if only he had Hamlet's "cue for passion." He would then, says Hamlet, "drown the stage with tears," cleave the ears of auditors with horrid speech, and madden guilty souls. Here Hamlet is projecting for himself a role—one which we will see him fulfilling in his later moments of hysteria, except perhaps in one respect: there will never be any tears shed by him, because in a human being tears depend on a feeling of compassion, which Shakespeare knows to be incompatible with

Hamlet's basic attitude. However, we will see Hamlet on many occasions tearing a passion to tatters and, in this respect, fulfilling the kind of acting he has here projected. This kind of acting is obviously not in accord with his own later advice to the players. Why, then, do we find him longing for it? Is it not because, at this moment, he has forgotten about his ideal of exercising "discretion," so absorbed is he in expressing a very personal inner desire, namely, a revenge urge to bring a judgment of flood and thunder on guilty neighbors? The First Player had assumed a godlike stance; Hamlet is longing to supply that stance with his imagined motivation—that is, with what he calls "my cause" and understands as being the world's iniquity done *to him* and therefore felt as real—whereas Shakespeare is showing Hamlet's real motivation as being, in effect, a desire to play god as revenger, a motive for which Hamlet's "cause" is merely the occasion or cue. That is why the more Hamlet focuses on "my cause," the more he forgoes all temperance. His utterance and action give vent to what is his real passion, a revengeful indignation which, on finding itself balked of satisfaction, ends up cursing "like a very drab." It becomes thus far different from the mannerly passion of the First Player.

But at the end of his outburst, Hamlet recognizes that he has become asinine in his passion, and therefore he calls on his brain for a turnabout. He will make a new start, to overcome his "weakness." He will produce a public play, cunningly devised to resemble his father's murder, and thereby he will prove the guilt of a man in the audience. This is a curiously twisted view of drama's traditional purpose of catharsis. It involves, moreover, something more than is stated to be the "purpose of playing" in the advice speech. There, a showing of the "very age and body of the time" is claimed as drama's *raison d'être:* but here we see the secret purpose of setting a mousetrap. To help the trap go off, a producer soon finds himself stepping into his play as unofficial chorus and interrupting its staging with intrusive program notes. The result is a ruined and abortive play, one which hoists Hamlet with his own petard. He has in effect broken his "mirror" by pointing a dagger, through his

naming of Lucianus as "nephew"; and through his own impetuous-
ness he has become, as H. C. Goddard notes, an ironic instance of
those clowns who speak more than is set down for them.[9]

Does not such playing raise a laugh from some "barren"
spectator or "unskilful" critic? Ironically, yes—in that Hamlet himself turns out to be the critic-spectator who unskilfully chortles
over the hit the play has made. In this case, are not the "judicious"
auditors—at Elsinore, or in the Globe Theatre—those who sense
in Hamlet's play-production a villainous and pitiful ambition on
his part? In a way unsuspected by Hamlet, the whole situation
mocks the meaning Hamlet had in mind when uttering his gen-
eralizations to the players.

And such an outcome, it seems to me, is analogous to the fate of
Polonius and his equally famous advice speech. That is, both he
and Hamlet (in different contexts, of course) parade superficial
maxims which turn ironical in the light of the play's action. The
Polonius who warns against lending is soon seen to be a practicer
of ruinous advice-lending, just as the Hamlet who warns players
against indiscretion himself produces a bad play through indiscreet
antics. Moreover, Polonius as little understands the true basis of
friendship as does Hamlet the true secret of dramatic art. Shakespeare has made tandem use of the two advice speeches to highlight
the analogous blindnesses which give structure to *Hamlet* as a developing tragedy.

But what are we to think of the literary quality of *The Murder
of Gonzago,* quite apart from the twist Hamlet gives it? Clearly, it
is in itself an instance of neoclassical style, but at an opposite end
of the spectrum from the style of the Aeneas tale. It is written entirely in rhymed couplets, a verse form such as one finds used for
passages of *sententia* in *The Spanish Tragedy* or *Sejanus* or *Bussy
D'Ambois.* The image of Phoebus' cart in the opening lines can
be traced to Seneca's *Agamemnon* (ll. 627–28), but here it is being
used with other decorative mythology in the style of Lyly's or
Jonson's courtly drama. Every sentiment in this playlet is elegantly
graceful and ideal. But also the sentiment strikes us as trivial, and

the verse is spineless. As Alice Walker has shrewdly remarked, it reads as if Shakespeare were here mimicking "underdone" writing —of a style tame and "come tardy off"—just as he had mimicked in the Aeneas tale a style of overdone writing.[10]

It is hard to see, indeed, how any of the actors in *The Murder of Gonzago* would need Hamlet's warning against strutting and bellowing. The very rhythm of the lines has reformed that altogether. Only when Hamlet himself noisily cries, "Come, the croaking raven doth bellow for revenge," do we get an echo of the older Senecan style. There then follow smooth lines by the Lucianus Player, lines utterly lacking in tension. Revenge, as he speaks it, is a tinkling incantation suggestive of the ritualized activity of a puppet. This player has made some prefatory "damnable faces" —presumably in order to fit his action to the words he will speak —but neither such action nor its matching words have any inner, psychological realism. As drama the scene is empty of convincingness, the action being as automatic as the fatalism voiced earlier by the superficial Player King.[11] And as for the Player Queen's elegantly phrased exclamations of eternal fidelity, they are so rotely repetitious as to justify Gertrude's judgment that "The lady doth protest too much, methinks"—just as, in the midst of the earlier tale of Aeneas, Polonius was quite justified in commenting, "This is too long." Shakespeare, by offering in both these cases a homespun common sense through persons whom Hamlet has been belittling, achieves two things at once: a critical remark which can provide a word for the wise, but also an opportunity for Hamlet-obsessed spectators blindly to override it as coming from a supposedly "unworthy source." Shakespeare thus maintains for *his* drama both irony and tension, whereas the set neoclassical play-pieces have none.

The two neoclassical insets would bore us if listened to and watched outside of Shakespeare's context. For despite the lavish scene painting and magnificence of the one, and the neatly packaged didacticism of the other, both lack a verisimilitude to real experience. In both cases the actors no doubt measured up to the plaudit Polonius gives the First Player: "Well spoken, with good accent and good discretion." Yet accent and discretion, Shakespeare implies, need something to serve beyond themselves, namely, believable action on the part of some lifelike personage. On this score, the dramatic text of the two insets has shortchanged the actors. These pieces can hold our attention only in relation to the responses of Hamlet, who by his use and abuse of their puerile dramaturgy finds indirect direction for his revenge. What fascinates and rewards our attention is Shakespeare's enveloping framework, through which we can see how the neoclassical rhetorical drama provides its devotee, instead of self-knowledge, a spur to ambitions for revenge, thus forwarding tragic disaster in the personal life of Hamlet.

The Player Queen's sentiments, we may further note, reflect a concept of wifely duty which is neoclassical rather than Christian. Chapman's *Sir Giles Goosecap* (dated 1600 by C. W. Wallace; 1602 by T. M. Parrott) has eulogized such a concept in the person of Lady Eugenia, who in speaking of her union with Clarence calls on Heaven to witness "the knot of our eternity, / Which Fortune, Death, nor Hell shall ever loose" (V.ii.220–21). Plainly, in this view, any second marriage would be of the devil. And Chapman further emphasizes this doctrine by having bystanders exclaim over her "marriage made for virtue, only virtue . . . A wonder . . . and withal / A worthy precedent for all the world" (V.ii.310–13). Chapman's *The Widow's Tears* (1602, Wallace; 1605, Parrott), based on the well-known story of the widow of Ephesus in Petronius, likewise preaches this same ideal: "That to wed the second was no better than to cuckold the first" (II.iv.30). But in this play the widow's betrayal of her ideal provides occasion for satire, and for a concluding rhetoric of tragical declamation over the fall into "Lust, impiety, and hell" of this professed votress of widow-constancy, this "mirror of nuptial chastity" (V.i.114–23). Clearly, Hamlet's sensational diatribes against Gertrude belong to the same school of thought. He, like Chapman, has a neoclassical idea of marriage.

It is interesting to observe, moreover, that *The Murder of Gonzago* is a tragedy which Hamlet also refers to as a "comedy"

(III.ii.269). Like Chapman and Jonson, Hamlet has an ambivalent, or hybrid, sense of genre, because his underlying predilection is for Graeco-Roman satire. Drama in this vein, instead of arousing an audience to pity, employs a didacticism to stimulate scorn by pitting the author's ideals of virtue against images of vice.

II

Glynne Wickham has described sixteenth-century thought as a "constant struggle for predominance between two rival philosophies of life." On the one hand, he discerns "a popular, native tradition that is fundamentally medieval"; on the other hand, a group of new intellectuals "attempting to force a complete divorce from this 'barbaric' native tradition in favor of a new marriage with 'civilized' Hellenistic culture." Shakespeare was writing within the native tradition, says Wickham, the one inherited from the Middle Ages, whereas Ben Jonson was especially representative of the neoclassical school which in England ranges from Sidney to Dryden and beyond. To Jonson, "form" was the cardinal virtue in art—form understood as an elegancy of manner imitative of Horace. To Shakespeare, on the other hand, the "narrative" was itself the poet's form for revealing significance through the shape of its action.[12] Alongside this ground of contrast, we may recall also Nevill Coghill's well-argued point that Shakespeare's comedies are basically romances, with an action moving from misery to joy in accord with medieval Christian premises, whereas Jonson's comedies are directed, in neoclassical fashion, to the ridicule and punishment of vice.[13] Alfred Harbage, in his general study of rival traditions within Elizabethan times, has given further evidence for regarding Shakespeare as the mainstay of popular drama, while of Jonson he writes: "The Prologue to *Cynthia's Revels* repudiates the popular drama entire, *Poetaster* ridicules Shakespeare's own company, and the Prologue to the revised *Every Man in His Humour* points scornfully at Shakespeare's own plays."[14]

Shakespeare aimed to please Everyman. His themes were of broad interest; and in developing them he often found occasion to give his groundlings, as Sir John Squire has remarked, "full measure of that Billingsgate vituperation, the torrential flow of which, from angry man, habitual railer, or (best still) virago, always delights an audience."[15] Jonson, on the other hand, proudly advertised his own fastidiousness. His Prologue to *Cynthia's Revels* (1600) appeals to an audience of "judgment," disdaining "every vulgar" brain. And in the Dialogue appended to *Poetaster* (1601), in which we are told of his intent to write a tragedy next, Jonson says he will be satisfied if one understanding spirit approves—"So he judicious be; He shall b'alone / A Theatre unto me." Sophisticated auditors of Shakespeare's *Hamlet* around 1602, must have sensed an echo of this in Prince Hamlet's disdain of "the million" and in his declaring that one "judicious" hearer must "o'erweigh a whole theatre of others." Moreover, on seeing Hamlet give his lengthy advice to the players, would not these auditors be somewhat reminded of Jonson's habit of lecturing about theater matters through a prologue or induction? The Induction to *Cynthia's Revels,* for instance, had brought on stage an actor who, after announcing that he was now speaking for the author, proceeded to list practices he objected to: "the immodest and obscene writing of manie in their playes"; the promoting of wit gleaned from "common stages"; plays in which ghosts walk the stage to frighten spectators; and critics who esteem the old Hieronimo play as the best penned play of Europe. We know that these jibes of Jonson's had not gone unnoticed by other playwrights. Marston in *Histriomastix* (1600?) had satirized, in the person of Chrisogonus, Jonson's disdain of "the common sort / Of thickskin'd auditors," and his claim to having "A Turtle's eye within an Aspic head," and his preaching of Stoic fortitude. As a further caricature of Jonson's pretensions, the *Satiromastix* (1601) of Dekker and Marston had introduced a character named Horace. This Horace was portrayed as being an ex-bricklayer and ex-player, who had ranted in Hieronimo's part and borrowed from other writers, but who now, having degenerated from scholar to satirist, was spitting at those who attacked him.[16]

Shakespeare's unfavorable opinion of the entire group of satirists had been indicated, without satire, through his portrait of the melancholy Jaques in *As You Like It*.[17] Jaques was depicted as admiring the pessimism of the rustic Touchstone, while unaware that Touchstone was merely parodying the philosophy of Jaques. Even a country fellow, Shakespeare implies, is able to see through and gently mimic the world view of this courtier. Hence the good Duke of the play need waste no time on Jaques beyond a brief reprimand for his "Most mischievous foul sin, in chiding sin." And as over against Jaques' theory of life's ages and end, we see embodied in the faithful servant Adam a choosing of pilgrimage as life's proper end.

In the melancholy Hamlet we have an echo of the Jaques type of character, but now as part of Shakespeare's larger story of a tragic prince who chooses to engage in mischievous scourging and who uses, as one of his means for this, an Italianate kind of theater fare. Accompanying such a use of drama there is also, we may note, Hamlet's use of bawdy innuendo in taunting Ophelia—in this respect a merriment not unlike that which Jaques found in voicing a ripe-and-rot view of life. Hamlet would justify being merry in this way by terming himself a "jig-maker," even though earlier he has derogated "jig and a tale of bawdry" when ascribing to Polonius a lowbrow taste. Why such a contradiction? Is Shakespeare, perhaps, glancing at some of the satirists of his day and implying that their claims to an elitist taste merely cover over a penchant for jig making, although in versions of this popular art form which twist it to bitter uses? Moreover, by tying Hamlet's purpose of scourging through drama to his having communed with a ghost, Shakespeare may be hinting that Jonson's "new" drama is less free of ghosts than he supposes. The Ghost in *Hamlet* can strike us as analogous to the Horatian spirit which Jonsonian drama seeks to serve and justify. Jonson's ghosts have been, in effect, Horace and Juvenal.

Jonson as a critic was outspoken against those who "fly from all humanity with the *Tamerlanes,* and *Tamer-Chams,* of the late age, which had nothing in them but the scenical strutting, and furious vociferation, to warrant them to the ignorant gapers"; [18] yet Jonson himself is, as T. S. Eliot and other recent critics have remarked, a recognizable heir of Marlowe in that his own tragedies scene-paint Tamburlaines of vice for didactic edification. Sejanus, in Jonson's tragedy of 1603, has been described by Herford and Simpson as "an artist in crime, ambitious of renown for unheard-of prodigies of wickedness"; and they remark further that this hero's colossal brag "belongs to the Marlowesque phase of tragedy." [19] Much more indeed than was Marlowe's practice, Jonson draws his characters from the outside. By leaving unprobed their recesses of soul, Jonson is less a popular artist, less in the medieval tradition than Marlowe. Whereas Marlowe was able to dramatize conflict of conscience in Faustus, and in the dying Tamburlaine the anguish of desires thwarted by an interior sickness, Jonson in his drawing of Tiberius overlooks, as Herford and Simpson note, even the touches of inner torment which Tacitus had reported in Tiberius. "Jonsonian tragedy suffers from an inner poverty in the humanities of the heart"; it lacks any attempt to portray "the delusions which jangle and overthrow a noble nature." [20] One reason for this, surely, is the Olympian moral stance Jonson adopts—a correlative, we may suppose, of his remark in the *Discoveries* that "our whole life is like a Play" in which the few good men of the times are its stars, planets, and spectators. Placed "high on the top of all vertue," he says, these men have always "looked down on the Stage of the world and contemned the Play of Fortune." [21]

Essentially, is this not a stance like that of the First Player in the Aeneas tale, which Hamlet thought modest and "as wholesome as sweet"? Shakespeare's Aeneas Player voices a Stoic outlook which we can recognize as basically akin to that of Arruntius in Jonson's *Sejanus*—or, likewise, that of Crites in *Cynthia's Revels,* to whom Jonson ascribes a balance of the four humors and "a most perfect and divine temper." It is understandable that C. W. Wallace should think the Aeneas passage "characteristic of Jonson in his nobler vein," [22] and that other critics have judged it Marlovian or Chapmanesque. [23] Shakespeare was no doubt epitomizing a general heritage of neoclassical style, from streaks of it in Marlowe to Jonson's omnipresent practice, and was using this to image the esthetic and ethical values which attract Hamlet. By following up this passage, one act later, with a playlet through which Hamlet by innuendo verbally stabs at Claudius, Shakespeare may have been indicating the continuity between Senecanism and the later half-Horatian, half-Juvenalian art of Jonson and other neoclassicists turned satirists.[24]

Hamlet's comment on the success of his remodeled Italianate tragedy is: "Would not this, sir, . . . get me a fellowship in a cry of players, sir?" The tone of self-congratulation here might be compared, I think, to Jonson's boasting in the Epilogue to *Cynthia's Revels:* "By God, 'tis good." I am not saying that Hamlet's remark constitutes an allusion to the earlier play's Epilogue; rather, that Shakespeare may be implying a glancing analogy. Shakespeare seems to be providing, moreover, a sober estimate of Hamlet's elation by having Horatio (the Horace of *his* play?) express rather little enthusiasm over Hamlet's dramaturgy. Understandably so; for Hamlet is proceeding to judge Claudius an ass (compare Asper's jibing at "an *Aristarchus* or starke-asse" in the Induction of *Every Man out of His Humour*); and this penchant, after being heightened by exercising it on Polonius, can lead Hamlet (when Horatio is not at hand to model restraint) to soliloquize that now he could "do such bitter business as the day / Would quake to look on." Although Hamlet here retains, still, enough traditional Roman conscience to disapprove of Nero's behavior, yet he is resolving on verbal daggers, and in a subsequent scene we see him using these with a rising hysteria which involves him in the half-accidental slaying of Polonius. This consequence I take to be Shakespeare's portrayal of the potential destructiveness of classical "reason" when let loose satirically to pursue its didactic dreams. (Also there may have been in Shakespeare's mind the recollection that both Marlowe and Jonson, in their actual lives, had got themselves in trouble with the law by killing a man in a duel.)

The Elizabethan satirists commonly defended their art by arguing that innocent auditors have no cause to be troubled by seeing the guilty taxed and that anyone who objects is thereby betraying guilt. This argument, borrowed from Horace, is voiced by Jonson in his *Discoveries*[25] and also through Asper in the Induction to *Every Man out of His Humour*. In *Hamlet* we see the hero using it to justify a "Mouse-trap" drama. "Let the galled jade wince, our withers are unwrung." Moreover, Hamlet's reasons for resorting to satire notably resemble those of Jonson's Asper. The earth is so "crackt with the weight of sinne," says Asper, "Who . . . can check his spirit, or reine his tongue?" Because Asper hates "the time's condition," which he claims to know rightly, he feels impelled to scourge it by turning "an Actor and a Humorist" under guise of the persona Macilente. In doing so he is confident that "Good men, and virtuous spirits, that loathe their vices, / Will cherish my free labours, love my lines." At the end of the play when he puts off his disguise, he explains that his spleen is no longer needed now that the wicked have been brought to repentance. Jonson thus implies that the "played" role of Macilente, although characterized by railing and the humor of envy, has been justified as the mouthpiece for a moral nemesis, through which the guilty are scourged into renouncing their sins on seeing them in the satirist's mirror.[26] At the same time, Jonson seems to think he has kept Asper's true self free of malice by assigning all the vituperation to a disguise-self. This tactic is rather like the one Shakespeare's Hamlet adopts. We hear Hamlet arguing that not he, but Heaven, is responsible for the things he does when the "madness" of scourge playing takes him away from himself. But Shakespeare, unlike Jonson, is implying no approval of such reasoning. He lets us see the evasiveness and moral double talk in it.

In *Cynthia's Revels* and in *Poetaster,* Jonson had somewhat revised his tactics in the hope of clearing himself, completely, from the imputation of railing. He had there created heroes intended to have only admirable qualities as satirists. The Crites and Horace of these plays are declared to be well-balanced and temperate judges. Their role is to observe and comment on abuses of satire by other poets, using only "sharp, yet modest rimes" to bring them to recant. The result here, however, as Alvin Kernan has remarked, is that Horace and Crites become rather vapid as satirists, since they spend too much time explaining the beauties of their own character and have no function "except to serve as an apology for Jonson's own satiric activities."[27] They become exemplars of a toned-down, and therefore supposedly virtuous use of satire. Yet their stance of ethical superiority scarcely hides an egotism and polite scorn. What Shakespeare seems to suggest in *Hamlet* is that the method of a Crites is unstable, because temperate only in a superficial sense. Hamlet planned, we may say, to use only genteel satire in his play-let; yet because of his lurking eagerness to vindicate his neoclassical vision of his neighbors, he easily lapsed into moments of antic truthtelling, like a Macilente. And although Hamlet would justify such moments as a "put-on" role, they are actually motivated by his impulse to use art revengefully. What is this, then, but old Hier-onimo in a new guise?

In *The Spanish Tragedy* a concluding Interlude had served as the catastrophic medium. Did the *Ur-Hamlet,* similarly, perhaps have as its catastrophic medium the staging of something like a Gonzago playlet at the very end—but with Claudius cast to play Gonzago, Gertrude as Baptista, and Hamlet as Lucianus pouring a literal poison? Did Shakespeare then remodel this Interlude and transpose it to his play's middle, there juxtaposing it to an Induction (the sequence of theater discussion beginning in Act II, scene i, and concluded with advice in Act III, scene iii) loosely like the inductions which Jonson and Marston had been using for polemic purposes in their plays? J. M. Nosworthy offered this conjecture in an article some years ago but presupposed on Shakespeare's part a somewhat different intent than I have been suggesting. Nos-worthy supposed that Shakespeare, by way of answering his rivals' jibes at the "musty fopperies" of Globe theater fare, was indicating that he too liked the new style of interlude and deplored overacting and was offering through Hamlet "a sort of pendant to Jonson's plea for the reform of dramatic endeavors."[28] My objection to this interpretation is that it sees Shakespeare as meekly seconding the taste of Jonson. I see, rather, an answer to Jonson which echoes his interests, but by using them to characterize Hamlet's taste and its misconceptions.

There can be no doubt that Hamlet's theory of the purpose of playing—to "show virtue her own feature, scorn her own image, and the very age and body of the time his form and pressure"—is a characteristically Jonsonian idea. Asper in *Every Man out of His Humour,* before he turns Actor, tells us that his purpose is to provide a mirror in which to see "the time's deformitie / Anatomiz'd in every nerve and sinew"; and later in this play Cordatus declares that comedy is *"Imitatio vitae, Speculum consuetudinis, Imago veritatis;* a thing throughout pleasant, and ridiculous, and accommodated to the correction of manners." These definitions focus, like Hamlet's, on a picturing of the body of an age, its manners and postures of virtue or vice, rather than on imitating the action of a human psyche. On this score, the poetic is a typically neoclassicist one. That is why Dover Wilson, quite rightly, could claim that Hamlet's theory is the same as Sidney's and Chapman's, and could gloss Hamlet's "both at the first and now" to mean both in the time of Horace and Seneca and now in Elizabethan times.[29] Hamlet's theory, Roman in its lineage, had a large following in Shakespeare's day.

Wilson is less right, however, in thinking that Shakespeare's own theory is "not altogether unlike" that of the neoclassicists. For they, one and all, misread Aristotle's concept of *mimesis* to mean a "speaking picture" of virtues and vices, set as foils to each other —an interpretation which, as various historians of criticism have shown,[30] twists Aristotle in a didactic and rhetorical direction favored by Plutarch and Quintilian. Plutarch's analogy of poetry to painting ignores, as Shakespeare surely did not, Aristotle's idea of poetic movement. Yet Plutarch's stress, because seconded by Horace and practiced in Senecan drama, was accepted by Renaissance Italians such as Scaliger and adopted by Sidney and Jonson. In place of Aristotle's important doctrine of unity of action, there was substituted a mechanical kind of unity centering about a decorum of social convention and seemliness. It is not surprising, therefore, that Jonson's plots have often been criticized as little more than contrivances for juxtaposing type characters in situations where they can exhibit moral features. "What he imitated in life," Herford and Simpson remark, "was above all its heterogeneous sequence, its motley kaleidoscopic disarray," instead of starting out where drama ought to start, with action or the imitation of a piece of life.[31] The same can be said, I think, of what Hamlet gives us to see of *The Murder of Gonzago.* This playlet is episodic and mechanically strung together. And why does Hamlet prepare his players for this tragedy by citing an ancient formula for comedy? Because, I think we may say, the matter of genre was likewise of little concern to neoclassicists such as Chapman and Jonson, who, whether in comedies or in tragedies, focused centrally on manners, ethical instruction, and elocution.[32]

Arruntius and Sabinus in *Sejanus,* like the earlier Crites or Horace, are Jonson's proxies for the man of virtue denouncing vices of the times. Arruntius never gets carried away into sore distraction, as Hamlet does; for Jonson has made Arruntius behave in accord with his stated admiration for "the soule / Of god-like CATO" (I.90). And Sabinus, when indignant at the "filthy lusts" of Caesar, is nevertheless shown rejecting a proposal to redeem Rome by violence. "No ill should force the subject undertake / Against the sovereign" (IV.iii.71) is the pious, and essentially Tudor, reasoning by which he assures us of his Stoic virtue. Shakespeare's Hamlet, by contrast, is a good deal more than an observer of a tragedy outside himself. He is a man caught between a desire to escape the world and a felt duty to set it right. He would like to be a Stoic who "in suffering all, suffers nothing"; yet in trying to live this Horatian ideal he finds himself falling into antic actions which he half regrets but resigns himself to. Here is the tragedy of a hero who wounds his own name by his self-contradictions.

In commenting on Jonson's concept of tragedy, J. A. Bryant has remarked: "Shakespeare was more apt to emphasize rebellion and

disorder as overt manifestations of man's innate proclivity to dis-
obedience; Jonson, to emphasize them as symptoms of civil decay,
which he interpreted as the result of man's unwillingness to live
by reason and to assume responsibility."[33] But what does it mean
to "live by reason"? The "good" characters in *Sejanus* do little more
than deplore vice while displaying in themselves a contempt of
fortune and a nobility of demeanor. The one responsibility they
assume is that of voicing an abhorrence of avarice and debauchery.
The "bad" hero, on the other hand, secretly glories in defying all
morality until his excesses of ambition bring a sudden ruin. The
focus of such drama is on exemplifying character traits; for in
Jonson's view what is required of a poet is "the exact knowledge
of all vertues, and their Contraries, with ability to render the one
loved, the other hated, by his proper embattling them."[34] Jonson's
theory suffers from an inability to understand Aristotle's concept
of action. But Shakespeare, if we may accept Milton B. Kennedy's
well-argued conviction, was "either consciously or unconsciously
Aristotelian" in his poetic.[35]

It was by using principles more Aristotelian than Senecan that
Shakespeare restored to drama the primacy of action and of plot.[36]
I see his Hamlet as a hero in accord with Aristotle's sense of tragedy:
a man neither villainous nor eminently just, who is brought to
misfortune by an error of judgment. The process and progress of
Hamlet's misjudging constitutes the action which the play as a
whole presents, through a series of incidents ordered by Shakespeare's sense of probability. One sequence of incidents, probable
for a man of Hamlet's educational background, has been the
subject of my present essay.[37] It has to do with Hamlet's turning
to neoclassical models of theater fare, by which he exposes his
imagination to a melodramatic view of life, and is then tempted
to think that by turning dramatist he can both justify his vision
and find out his course. What actually he discovers is a stimulus,
merely self-convincing, for doing "bitter business." Then when this
stalls, because a praying Claudius does not fit his stereotype of a
villain he can damn, he substitutes a play-acting of his vision to

Gertrude, by holding up a "glass" in which he picture-paints the hellishness of her alleged infidelity to a godlike first husband.

Here Hamlet has become the satirist, using a mirror of rhetoric. Indignantly he pronounces ethical judgments which he supposes to be temperate and virtuous, but which Shakespeare shows to be rancorous, wild, and blind to the viciousness of his own wayside stabbing and noisy bullying. Thus while Hamlet is pursuing *his* notion of drama's didactic purpose, and intending thereby to make virtue loved and vice hated, Shakespeare is dramatizing the inner and real tragedy of Hamlet's self-delusion and thereby is engaging our pity and fear, which is the properly Aristotelian purpose of *his* drama. Hamlet's theories, through their outcome in action, are being placed and tested within the orbit of the play's total story. And that test, interestingly, makes double irony of Hamlet's advice to players. For, on the one hand, we watch a Hamlet who violates his own rules, and on the other hand, we realize what intolerable drama we would be stuck with if he didn't. Shakespeare's play, if it obeyed Hamlet's advice theory, might be as lifeless as *Sejanus*.[38]

William Gager's *Meleager* and *Ulysses Redux*

J. W. BINNS

As a Renaissance dramatist, William Gager, the leading writer of academic Latin drama at Oxford in the late sixteenth century, claims our attention for two plays, *Meleager* and *Ulysses Redux*.[1] Of his other plays, *Rivales,* which probably led Francis Meres to include his name in the list of "the best for Comedy amongst vs" has not survived;[2] while *Dido,* a close adaptation from Vergil of the story of Dido and Aeneas in *Aeneid* IV, and considerably shorter than both *Meleager* and *Ulysses Redux,* bears many marks of haste in composition. Large parts of *Dido* consist merely of Vergilian hexameters recast as iambic senarii, and the play only rarely succeeds in breaking away from its source to achieve a life of its own. *Meleager* and *Ulysses Redux* however demonstrate the full range of Gager's powers as a dramatist. *Meleager* was first performed at Christ Church, Oxford, in February 1581/2; it was revived in January 1584/5 for performance before the earls of Pembroke and Leicester and Sir Philip Sidney, who were visiting the University, and it was printed in 1592/3.[3] *Ulysses Redux* was performed at Christ Church on February 6, 1591/2 and was printed shortly afterwards, in May 1592.[4] *Meleager* is a dramatization of the classical legend of the hunting of the Calydonian boar, while *Ulysses Redux* is adapted from Homer's *Odyssey* and tells of the return to Ithaca of Ulysses and his reunion with his wife, Penelope.

The plays written in Latin by Englishmen during the sixteenth century are an interesting episode in the history of the Elizabethan drama. At the universities of Oxford and Cambridge, plays in Latin were written and performed often enough during the reign of Queen Elizabeth for us to be justified in regarding them as part of the potential theatrical experience of most men who were then at University.[5] The best university Latin plays possess a good deal of the vigor and exuberance typical of the Elizabethan drama of the popular stage; at the same time they reflect the attitude toward drama of the educated men of the times, men who knew the plays of Seneca, Plautus, and Terence, and who were aware of dramatic theory, and who were able to write balanced and coherent plays which often foreshadowed later developments in the popular drama.

William Gager himself displays this sophisticated dramatic awareness. He was a thoughtful and careful dramatist, and when *Meleager* and *Ulysses Redux* were printed, he prefixed to the text of both plays a discussion of his ideas. In *Meleager* his discussion shows that he was acquainted with previous treatments of the legend in Greek and Roman poetry and drama. He justifies his emphasis of various traits of character in his dramatis personae and explains his omission from the play of the episode in which Meleager's sisters are changed into birds on the grounds that this would have detracted from the tragic effect. In *Ulysses Redux,* in his "Ad Criticum," Gager defends the play against certain criticisms that he anticipated: namely, that the play was not truly tragic because it offended by the beggarliness of its subject matter, because its style was largely comic, because it aroused laughter in the person of the beggar Irus, because the deserved death of the suitors and handmaidens did not arouse tragic emotion, and because the play had a happy ending. Gager concedes that there may be some truth in these objections, and he justifies himself partly by an appeal to precedents set by various classical dramas. However, he also claimed for himself artistic freedom and refused to be shackled by unchanging rules:

> Nam ut vivendi, sic etiam scribendi ratio mihi inprimis probatur ea, quae est paulo liberior ac pene dissolutior, quaeque non tam doctissimis, quam imperitis placeat. . . . Equidem ego hanc sive tragaediam, sive fabulam, sive narrationem historicam, sive quicquid eam dici ius fasque est, non ad exquisi-

tam artis poeticae tanquam aurificis stateram, sed ad popularis iudicii trutinam exigendam proposui.[6]

[For I approve especially of that way of writing, as also of living, which is a little freer and almost unrestrained, and which may give pleasure not so much to scholars as to the unlearned. . . . For I indeed set forth this tragedy, or fable, or historical narrative, or whatever it is right and lawful to call it, to be judged not on the exact goldsmith's balance, as it were, of the Art of Poetry, but on the scales of popular judgment.]

Gager there affects an unwillingness to define precisely the type of play he has written. We today would be inclined to call *Ulysses Redux* a tragicomedy, principally because the play ends happily. Gager's suggestion that the play may be a "fabulam" or "narrationem historicam" is however borne out by the play's expansive structure. It presents to us in a series of tableaux Ulysses witnessing and experiencing the debauchery and riotous behavior of the suitors: he sees them wasting the substance of his household, he is insulted by them in his disguise as a beggar, and he observes their importunate behavior toward Penelope. The pace of the play is leisurely and allows time for Gager to include episodes such as the fight between Ulysses and Irus the beggar, the feasting of the suitors, and the love affair between Eurymachus, one of the suitors, and Melantho, chief of Penelope's handmaidens. The mingling of comic and tragic scenes, and the transitions from "low" scenes in which Ulysses is insulted as he begs food from the suitors' table to scenes in which Penelope suffers the emotions of high tragedy, contribute to the rich variety of the play. However, *Ulysses Redux* is never too diffuse. The play is carefully constructed. Ulysses himself is the center of attention in Act I and Act V, the suitors in Act II and Act IV, and Penelope in Act III, so that a certain symmetry is achieved. Furthermore a background of dramatic irony unifies the play. For most of the play, only the audience and Telemachus know that Ulysses has at last returned to Ithaca, and that for Penelope salvation is at hand, for the suitors, retribution. Gager exploits this situation to the full, for it adds another dimension to the play. Ulysses makes many oblique allusions to the difference between his real and pretended position. Thus when he is begging scraps of food from the suitors at their feast in Act II he says:

Habui ipse quondam divitem certe domum,
Et mille servos, quaeque mortales solent
Facere beatos, multa possedi bona,
Et saepe tenues stipe donavi hospites.

[sig. B8ʳ]

[To be sure, I myself once had a wealthy household, and a thousand servants; I possessed many blessings which usually make men happy, and I often bestowed alms upon needy strangers.]

Again, in Act III Ulysses, hiding in a corner, is discovered by Melantho while Eurymachus makes love to her. Ulysses asks her for mercy and reminds her that her master may return home one day, but her only response is to insult him. We are always conscious of the pervasive presence of Ulysses throughout the play. He himself had said:

Sequar, procisque semper astabo comes,
Lustrabo iuvenum scelera, scrutabor domum,
Et instar umbrae, singulis adero locis.

[sig. C3ʳ]

[I will follow, and always stand by the suitors as their companion, I will observe the crimes of these youths, I will explore the household, and like a shadow I will be present in every place.]

The most movingly effective use which Gager makes of Ulysses' double identity occurs in the scene in which Penelope meets Ulysses in his disguise as a beggar. As he answers her questions about her husband, almost every line is poignant with a double significance. Gager uses dramatic irony in a similar manner in *Meleager,* which is acted out against the foreknowledge by the audience that the royal house of Calydon is doomed, for in the very first scene of the play the Senecan figure of Megaera arises from the underworld to foretell this. This device intensifies the tragic mood; however, the plot arises naturally out of the action of the characters. Megaera does not appear again, and the characters are not mere puppets whom she manipulates. *Meleager* is a more tightly constructed play than *Ulysses Redux.* There is no subplot and each act unfolds a definite advance in the action. The first act of *Meleager* sets the scene and is focused on the figure of Meleager and his love for Atalanta, which provides the genesis of the tragedy. Act II is dominated by the proud figure of Oeneus, king of Calydon; Act III deals with the boar hunt and its aftermath, the killing by Meleager of his uncles, Plexippus and Toxeus. Act IV centers on Althaea, torn apart by conflicting loyalty toward her dead brothers and toward her son Meleager who has murdered them. Act V is concerned with the remorse of Oeneus and Althaea, and with their deaths. The mood is unvaryingly tragic. The formal structure of *Meleager* and *Ulysses Redux* is emphasized in both plays by the choruses which conclude each act; each of these sums up the theme of the preceding act, while the final chorus sums up the theme of the whole play. For example, the chorus at the end of Act IV of *Meleager* comments on the anger of which women are capable—which the act has just illustrated in the person of Althaea.

The taut structure of *Meleager* increases the intense and torrid atmosphere of the play, which is permeated by Fate and a sense of inevitable doom. Gager uses supernatural elements, visions, and dreams to add a somber color to the play, and to suggest that dark and ominous forces are at work beyond the powers of men. The first words which Althaea, queen of Calydon, utters when she enters concern a dream which had come to her the previous night, when in the moonlight the figure of her dead mother entered her bedchamber to warn Althaea of the impending disaster that would destroy the royal household. The Soothsayer prophesies an evil he is unable to define, and Althaea, Oeneus, and Meleager all experience visions before they die. The demented Althaea, steeling herself to the death of her son, sees the bloody and violent images of her brothers demanding revenge, until, as they kneel before her, she complies with their demand. Meleager, on the point of death, likewise sees Plexippus and Toxeus inciting a band of Furies to his destruction. Meleager rushes upon them and wildly tries to send those who are already dead to a new death. Oeneus, too, before he dies, sees the Furies let forth from the underworld, his trial at the hands of the gods, the implacable Diana urging ferocious punishments, and the coming of Chaos. Death alone can free Meleager, Althaea, and Oeneus from their sufferings.

In *Ulysses Redux* the tragicomic mood predominates. The probity of Telemachus, the purity of Penelope, the honest worthiness of Ulysses' retainers, Eumaeus and Philoetius, are contrasted with the debauchery of the suitors, the wantonness of Melantho, and the opportunism of the beggar Irus. The discord of the play is resolved at last in the calm happiness of the closing scenes. That the play will end happily is, for the audience, implicit in its well-known story: but within the play as well, the suggestion that Ulysses will return is ever present, stressed partly by his own insinuations, and partly by Penelope's constant conviction that her husband will return. The minstrel Phemius and the choruses at the end of Act I and Act II also express a longing for Ulysses' return. The disharmony of the play, its potential for tragedy, reaches its climax in the plans of the suitors to murder Telemachus, plans which are forestalled only by the greater violence with which Ulysses and his followers ruthlessly kill the unarmed suitors and their hangers-on, sparing only Phemius the minstrel for the sake of his music and Medon who had loved Telemachus when the latter was a child. The massacre of the suitors is followed by the hanging of Melantho and eleven more of Penelope's handmaidens whom the suitors had made love to. Both episodes seem cruel to modern taste, but Gager had implied in his "Ad Criticum" that an audience of his day would have considered that the suitors deserved to die because they were wicked, and the handmaidens because they had become whores. In any event, the violence is overlain by joy when Ulysses and Penelope, each of whom has suffered so much, are reunited in the final scene of the play.

In *Meleager* and *Ulysses Redux,* Gager is adapting for the stage stories that are well known from other sources, and to some extent this circumscribes his freedom of characterization. But the plays are not a mere retelling on the stage of their original sources. Gager succeeds in bestowing upon his characters an identity of their own within the drama, so that our interest is aroused in, say, the Meleager of the tragedy, not in the Meleager of narrative epic. In the medium of drama, the relationship of the characters to one another is thrown into sharper definition. No single character in *Meleager* stands out as the hero of the play. The tragedy involves all the members of the royal house of Calydon—Meleager, Oeneus, Plexippus, Toxeus, and Althaea. The interest of the play shifts from one to another of these characters, and their relationship to one another and to the other characters in the play is brought out. Perhaps the most powerfully drawn character in *Meleager* is Oeneus, king of Calydon, and he must serve here as an illustration of Gager's abilities in this direction. Gager presents Oeneus as a man proud, vaunting, and arrogant almost to madness, as his first words indicate:

> Par diis suberbis gradior, et caelo tenus,
> Inter tyrannos, arduum caput effero.
>
> [sig. B6ʳ]

[I go my way the equal of the proud gods, and I raise my lofty head heaven-high among kings.]

Oeneus recalls all his reasons for happiness: his wealth, his fortune, his family, his prosperous kingdom. In words which bode ill, he boasts that he can never be unhappy—words full of irony, for they are an adaptation of Niobe's speech in Ovid's *Metamorphoses*,[7] shortly before all her children were killed:

> Faelix vocor; nam quis neget? faelixque ita
> Semper manebo; nulla me miserum dies
> Videbit unquam; quis dubitet istud quoque?
> Copia beatum fecit; en sedeo altior,
> Quam cui nocere, velle fac, casus queat.
>
> [sig. B7ʳ]

> [Happy am I called. Who can deny it? And thus happy will I always remain. No day shall ever see me wretched. Who can doubt that too? Abundance has made me blessed. See, I sit too high for chance to harm me, even if it should wish to.]

He rejects counsel from the Old Man, his confidant, who warns him that pride such as his will not pass unpunished by the gods. Oeneus' only response to these warnings is to say "Sum maior ipsa sorte" ("I am greater than Fate herself" [sig. B7ᵛ]). In the following scene Oeneus is shown first deriding the prophetic dream of his wife Althaea and then dismissing the warnings of the Sooth-sayer. His folly is demonstrated by the misfortunes which befall his household, but even after the death of Meleager, he is defiant in the bitterness of his humbled pride and upbraids the gods. At last, virtually mad, he sees himself as leader of the Titans waging war against the gods themselves:

> Nunc nunc furentes arma Titanes ferant,
> Me duce, secunda bella cum Superis gerant.
> . . . .
> Iamque ecce fugiunt: hoc petam montis iugum
> Aequale caelo, detraham Superos polo.
>
> [sig. E4ᵛ–E5ʳ]

[Now, now, let the raging Titans take up arms, and under my leadership wage favorable battles with the gods. . . . See, now they flee. I will seek this mountain ridge, on a level with the sky, and pluck down the gods from the heavens.]

Oeneus finally kills himself by leaping from a lofty tower. As F. S. Boas points out,[8] Gager anticipates Marlowe in his portrayal of this Tamburlaine-like figure, colossally proud, defying the gods and ready to make war on them. In *Ulysses Redux,* the characters are naturally based on Homer. Gager shows considerable skill in his handling of a vast crowd of characters: Ulysses himself, his son Telemachus, and his faithful retainers Eumaeus and Philoetius; the goddess Minerva; the soothsayer Theoclymenus; the beggar Irus; Phemius the minstrel; the beautiful character of Penelope, whose presence can be felt throughout the play; her nurse Euryclea; Melantho and Eurymachus; the crowd of suitors themselves, among whom Antinous and Amphinomus stand out, the former as the most vicious—callous to Ulysses in his disguise as a beggar and a leading advocate of the murder of Telemachus—the latter as the kindliest of the suitors. By the manner of her death, Melantho makes herself one of the most interesting characters in the play. When Ulysses regains control of his household, Melantho is led out to her death, her neck in a noose, because she had been defiled by accepting the love of Eurymachus. Earlier in the play, she had appeared as an unsympathetic character because of her insults to Ulysses, but she now behaves with great composure in the face of Philoetius' unfeeling jibes and dies with quiet dignity, lamenting her past way of life. Her final speech is a poignant adaptation of the Emperor Hadrian's dying hymn:

> Animula, quae mox dulcis invises loca,
> Pallidula, tremula, nudula? haud posthac dabis
> Ut ante ludos, vagula, petulans, blandula,
> Non veste molli gesties, non tu dapes

> Gustabis ore, dulce non vinum bibes;
> Furtiva nullus oscula Eurymachus dabit.

[sig. E5ᵛ]

[O my sweet little soul, what places will you soon visit, pale, tremulous, and naked? After this, you won't make yourself ridiculous as you did before, wandering away now, saucy and charming. You won't be happy in soft garments, you won't taste feasts, you won't drink sweet wine. No Eurymachus will give you stolen kisses.]

The success of Gager in depicting character can perhaps be explained by the fact that his dramatis personae are not the mere mouthpieces for wordy expressions of static feeling or for tedious disquisitions on trite themes such as the fickleness of Fortune. In *Ulysses Redux* as in *Meleager,* the characters belong to the world of Elizabethan drama, and not to Homeric epic or to a remote legendary past.

Gager's command of poetry enhances the balance and coherence of *Meleager* and *Ulysses Redux.* It is perhaps difficult for a writer of Renaissance Latin drama really to distinguish himself as a poet. Consciously striving to imitate the latinity of the Roman poets, the dramatist has less scope for impressing a definite style of his own upon the language and sustaining this at length. Gager's verse in these plays is, however, fluent and elegant. His iambics are a flexible medium which can render good service in all the varying moods of the play. There is the formal, elaborate language adapted from Catullus[9] in Act I of *Meleager,* where Atalanta and Meleager exchange stylized conceits. Atalanta compares virginity to a rose:

> Quam mulcet aura, sol fovet, pluviae rigant,
> Multae puellae, multi eam pueri expetunt;
> Eademque ab ungue carpta, ubi defloruit,
> Nullae puellae, nulli eam pueri expetunt.

[sig. B4ʳ]

[Many maidens, many youths seek after a rose which is caressed by the breeze, cherished by the sun, and bedewed by the rains. But when that same rose has been plucked by the nail, when it has withered, no maidens, no youths desire it.]

Meleager however compares it to a vine:

Ut vitis agro vidua quae nudo iacet,

. . . .

Radice summam prona claviculam implicat,
Nulli coloni, nullae eam curant manus,
Eadem sed ulmo cum maritata est suo,
Multi coloni, multae eam curant manus.

[sig. B4^r–B4^v]

[No husbandmen, no hands, care for a vine which lies unwedded in the barren field, entwining its topmost tendril with its root down on the ground; but when the same vine is married to its elm, many husbandmen, many hands care for it.]

There is the laconic, witty language of the passages of stichomythia in which Meleager discusses with Philemon whether to carry Atalanta away by force, or in which Amphinomus urges marriage on Penelope in Act III of *Ulysses Redux*:

Amphinomus. Lenimen animi dulce, cur credis malum?
Penelope. Quoties venenum, melle sub dulci, latet?
Amphinomus. Formam iuventae singuli carpunt dies.
Penelope. At castitatis fama perpetuo viret.

[sig. C6^v]

[*Amphinomus.* Why do you think the mind's sweet solace to be evil?
Penelope. How often does poison lurk beneath honeyed sweetness?

Amphinomus. Every day that passes devours the beauty of
youth.
Penelope. But the glory of chastity is forever fresh.]

And there is the controlled rant in which the devotees of the academic no less than the popular stage delighted—such as Ulysses'
exultancy when he sees the slaughtered suitors:

O nuptialis thalamus! o sponsi inclyti!
Iuvat videre sanguine aspersas dapes,
Sanie fluentes aspicere mensas iuvat.

[sig. E4^r]

[What a bridal chamber! What splendid bridegrooms! I am delighted to see the feast bestrewed with blood, delighted to behold the tables flowing with bloody matter.]

Gager's most graceful poetry is undoubtedly to be found in the
lyric interludes which occur from time to time during the plays.
In *Meleager,* when the huntsmen return successfully from hunting
the boar, they sing happily of its death, ending each stanza of their
song with the triumphant lines, "Tota deducat Calydon superbum
/ Laeta triumphum" ("Let all Calydon happily celebrate a proud
triumph" [sig. C5^v]). In contrast, at the end of the play, there is
the beautiful elegiac lament of the Matres Calydonides over the
dead Meleager:

Ingens terrae decus Aetolae,
Columen rerum, spes Calydonis,
Iuvenum gloria, flos, et lumen,
Ille ille apri domitor saevi
Occidit, . . .

.   .   .   .
Meleagre, domus decus Oeneae,
Generosus ubi est ardor, et oris

Decor egregius? periere ista;
Reliquum nihil est, praeter luctus,
Lachrymasque graves.

[sig. E5ᵛ]

[Great glory of the Aetolian land, our mainstay, the hope of
Calydon, the flower, glory and light of our youth, the con-
queror indeed of the cruel boar has fallen. . . . Meleager, glory
of the house of Oeneus, where is your noble ardor, and the
outstanding beauty of your countenance? They have perished,
and naught is left save grief and heavy tears.]

In *Ulysses Redux,* there are three lyric interludes: in Act II, when
the minstrel Phemius sings a song in praise of Ulysses; in Act III,
when Hippodamia exalts the virtues of chastity; and in Act V, when
Phemius sings again in praise of music and of his deliverance from
Ulysses' vengeance. The lyric interludes in Gager's plays are formal
and ceremonious. They are a device for dwelling on and intensifying a particular mood. The action of the play stops, and the attention of the audience is drawn to the lyric. The lyric is set apart
from the rest of the play not only because it is written in a lyric
meter which is different from the iambic senarii of the rest of the
play, but also because it was generally meant to be sung. The stage
direction accompanying the chorus of huntsmen in *Meleager* is
"Canunt in Scena" ("They sing on the stage"), and from the
documents of Gager's controversy with Dr. John Rainolds, a prominent opponent of academic drama at Oxford, we learn that the
lyrics in *Ulysses Redux* were also sung during the performance,
although this is clear anyway from references in the text of the
play itself.[10] In the fifth scene of Act III of *Ulysses Redux* another
song, to be sung by Melantho, the words of which are not given,
is called for by the stage direction "Dulce aliquid ad lyram canit"
("She sings something sweet to the lyre"). All these lyrics enrich
the texture of the play.

Music indeed was particularly important in the performance of

Ulysses Redux. It would have accompanied the dancing of the suitors with which Act II opens; the stage direction at the end of the second scene of Act II calls for a "Symphonia" inside the inner part of the stage; another "Symphonia" is called for by a stage direction at the beginning of the second scene of Act V as Ulysses and Telemachus take up their positions for slaughtering the suitors; Ulysses orders a drum to be beaten in order to drown the cries of the suitors as they are being shot down with arrows, and the signal for his final attack is to be given on a trumpet.

In order to form a just estimate of Gager's abilities as a dramatist, one has to try to appreciate the effect of his plays in performance. This was of great concern to Gager, as his very full stage directions show.[11] At the beginning of Act II of *Meleager,* a long stage direction calls for a ceremonial procession of the hunters from one side of the stage, where the king's palace was, to the other side, where the temple of Diana was situated. The Soothsayer is to march alone in the middle with the sacrificial victim and all the paraphernalia of the sacrifice. In Act IV of the play there are detailed stage directions which govern Althaea's preparations for the death of Meleager: a fire is prepared on an altar "in remotiore Scenae parte" ("in the more distant part of the stage")—on what was presumably an inner stage. In the third scene of Act IV, Meleager is shown to be consumed with inward fire, which after first abating, finally kills him, while corresponding stage directions indicate that Althaea is moving the brand on which Meleager's life depends in and out of the flames. In *Ulysses Redux* there are numerous stage directions which not only provide detailed information about the way in which episodes such as the suitors' archery contest and Ulysses' massacre of the suitors were managed, but which also ordain certain reactions for the actors. For example, when Penelope and Ulysses are united in the final scene of the play, the stage direction reads: "Penelope aspectu Ulyssis obstupescit" ("Penelope is struck with amazement at the sight of Ulysses"); and when Eumaeus and Philoetius bring in Ulysses' bow and quiver for the archery contest in the third scene of Act IV, the stage direction reads: "ex eorum aspectu lachrymantur" ("at the sight of them, they weep"). One of the most visually striking episodes in *Ulysses Redux* must have been the dance of the suitors at the beginning of Act II. The stage direction reads: "Proci primum larvati alicunde prodeunt, saltantque in scena, deinde exeunt in conclave" ("The suitors, wearing masks, first come out from somewhere on to the stage and dance on it, and then depart into the dining-room"). We learn from a letter of Dr. John Rainolds to Gager that the suitors danced with Penelope's handmaidens, and that those who played the part of the handmaidens sat amongst women in the audience and were only known to be men when they rose to dance: "Howe many did obserue, and with mislike haue mentioned, that *Penelopes* maides did not onely weare it, [i.e., women's raiment] but also sate in it among true wemen in deed, longer then *David* woare *Sauls* armour? neither were more knowne to them to bee men, then *Achilles* was at firste to *Deidamia;* vntill they suspected it seeing them entreated by the wooers to rise and danse vpon the stage."[12] In a discussion of the masque, E. K. Chambers points out that this is perhaps the first instance in a play of the "taking out" by personages in a drama of spectators who were also personages in the same play.[13]

William Gager's plays unfold a panorama of character and incident to which music, song, poetry, spectacle, and stage action all contribute. Much of his success as a dramatist lies in the fluid manner in which he composes his plays from these disparate elements. His sense of theater does not falter, whether in the great public scene in Act III of *Meleager,* surely one of the play's *coups de théâtre,* when Althaea rushes joyfully on to the stage to greet her brothers, who now lie murdered by the daggers of her son, or in the private serenity of the scene in which Ulysses and Penelope are reunited at the end of *Ulysses Redux*. William Gager wrote in Latin at a time when that language was slowly being supplanted, but he is nonetheless an Elizabethan dramatist, who wrote in one of the greatest periods of English literature.

Theme and Structure in *King Henry IV*, Part I

FREDSON BOWERS

The popular history play of Elizabeth's reign was likely to be a chronicle history. The name is applied not just because the history in the play was taken from the chronicles, but because it was dramatized in the chronicle manner. History is not an Elizabethan literary form. Some few examples of relatively coherent history exist, as in Sir Thomas More's account of Richard III or Bacon's of Henry VII, but these are exceptional. A coherent history is written from a point of view; it concerns itself as much with the *why* of an action as with its *how*. It delves into causes and carefully traces their effects. It looks to men and to the influence of their characters on action. It relates the event to the whole. It sets the details of its narrative in proportion against one another so that motivation and causality are apparent. In short, true historical writing shapes events to a higher purpose of ultimate truth than simple factual narrative that has not been analyzed to show the underlying purposes of affairs.

On the contrary, the favorite Elizabethan form was the chronicle history, which has something to say about each year of a reign, seldom in any pattern of coherence, and often attempts little more than a report of what seem to be the important events of that year, whether the birth of a five-legged calf, the rise of a civil war, the fall of hailstones in July, the onslaught of the plague, or the death of kings. Any notable event from a vast miscellany of choices is grist for its mill.

When Shakespeare first attempted the history, as in the *Henry VI* plays, one may watch him struggling to free himself from the dramatization of the chronicle—what happens next, what happens next. He was not immediately successful. Some attempts at a focus of events in the person of a single man may be seen in Talbot, of Part 1, for example; but the efforts never succeed in making out of historical fact what can be described as a plotted play. The focusing of events in one person reached its limit in *Richard III,* but this elementary though successful technique could not be indefinitely repeated in all circumstances because the central factors of plot were missing. That is, an all-purpose plot requires conflict between two relative equals, action and counteraction of like weight, leading to a crucial decision put into action, and then its working out in inevitable terms to the final untying of the knot. This is how Elizabethan plays were ordered if they were true dramas, not dramatic representations.

However, sophisticated technique in plotting is useless unless the action is shaped to form something larger than itself in total effect. Literature cannot be literature if the dance is not of greater import than the dancer. *Significance* is a word viewed with a certain distrust today largely because of the simplistic view that it can be inserted on demand, as if Milton had written *Paradise Lost* and then put in the theology. *Meaning* may be a little better, although it is more neutral. Any writer except a hack must feel that the cumulative connections established between a series of events builds into a design that gives them a meaning they would not have without this correlation. At what may often be a relatively high level of sophistication in drama, this sense of a pattern placed on the chaotic raw material of life may be enough, if it is so understood and so imaginatively presented by the playwright that it is transmitted as what seems to be true experience to his audience. Critics have not notably succeeded in finding much more than this in *Hamlet.*

But in literature of another order, what we may call a "theme" that shapes events may prove useful. Themes are not confined to less sophisticated forms of literature than *Hamlet,* of course. The theme may be so powerful and universal as to soar above any possible limitations that might else have been placed on the imagination, as may be seen in *Paradise Lost,* and with more art, in *Samson*

Agonistes. Or what appears to be a theme may prove to be only the gateway to an experience that transcends the ostensible theme, as occurs in *King Lear.*

In his history plays, however, Shakespeare was to learn that the unifying force of a single central character was not adaptable enough to constitute a substitute for true plot. In the somewhat experimental play *King John* he found that too powerful a force, like the Bastard, could disrupt a play if he were not the central character or if he were not integrated into the plot. In its conventional definition, plot did not make a real history play (barring the case of *Richard III*) out of the chronicles until *Richard II.* *Richard II* brought the intractable material of history closer to the powerful shaping of a fictive imagination even though it was not an entire success in the meaningful presentation of action and counteraction generalized to what Galsworthy called "a spire of meaning."

Shakespeare's most perfect English history play, *King Henry the Fourth,* Part I, succeeds magnificently, where *Richard II* had partly failed, in the examination in dramatic terms of kingship, which is to say of power and its control. The title of a history play by convention is assigned to the name of the king in whose reign the events took place. But the king may or may not be the protagonist, even though the play is called after him. In a chronicle sense, the subject of the first part, and perhaps even more of the second part, is King Henry's suppression of a rebellion, thus ending the threat to the establishment of the Lancastrian dynasty to be carried on by his son. In any other sense, this is also what the play is really about. Richard II had let power slip from his careless hands; in contrast, Henry uses whatever means are suited to the situation to nurse his power; and he succeeds in imposing his will by breaking the back of a strong opposition to the extension of royal authority. On his death, his son can inherit an uncontested throne. Of all the history plays this one is most clearly and directly concerned with a theme close to Tudor hearts: the triumph of order through the imposition of centralized royal power as against the disorder of the fragmented rule of the nobles under the feudal system.

In that it is Henry who accepts the first challenge in this conflict, who is the sole and vigorous leader of his part, who orders and fights the war, the play may be said to be about him. The main plot is certainly structured on this central action, and in it Henry is the protagonist. Who, then, is the antagonist? The easy answer would be Hotspur, but this is wrong. Important as Hotspur is to the action, it is not he who initiates the conspiracy against Henry, gathers together the aid of Mortimer and Glendower, and in the end precipitates the Battle of Shrewsbury. The true antagonist is Worcester, as Westmoreland in the first scene shrewdly declares: "This is his uncle's teaching, this is Worcester, / Malevolent to you in all aspects" (I.i.96–97). Both at the start and at the end Hotspur is his uncle's factor (as unwittingly he becomes Hal's), almost his pawn.[1] Henry could have dealt with Hotspur, but not with Worcester, whom he recognizes as his true opposite in the parley before Shrewsbury.[2]

The rise and fall of the rebellion, then, is a contest essentially between Henry and Worcester. This is certainly the framework of the play's action; but no audience would agree that it comprises more than the background for the central interest, which rests without question on the opposition of Hotspur and Hal. The result is a sophisticated plotting in which the two elderly men who hold the reins of power associate with their action and counteraction two strong young men to whom, in personal terms, the audience gives its main attention. Shakespeare had tentatively tried something like this in *King John* but had failed to unify the plot interest and the true issues involved in the action. The Bastard has no more future than Talbot of *Henry VI,* Part I, except as the supporter of a king. The more independently he acts, the more in a sense he usurps the king's power without being able to supply a permanent solution to the troubles of the realm. But a firm unity is imposed in *Henry IV,* Part I, for Hal is himself the future and the solution. As the next king he will inherit Henry's power and continue the struggle against the divisive forces that endanger royal authority. Thus he thoroughly typifies the royal side of the struggle,

and indeed represents it better than his father. He is the wave of
the future, not the last struggle of the past. He is to be the hero
king, Henry V, who united England and conquered France.

Unlike Faulconbridge, who had no true opponent, Hal's proper
antagonist is Hotspur, who typifies the virtues of the feudal nobility as Hal typifies the virtues of the centralized monarchy. The
elders are essentially schemers; the younger are men of action. The
contrast of Hal and Percy comes to be central in the play as the
power of each side swells to the conflict and to the meeting at
Shrewsbury. It is an indication of the importance of these men to
the central action that in a very real sense the battle is won and
the rebellion broken by one episode alone, the single combat between Hal and Hotspur to which the whole play moves. Hal and
Percy, then, are the true principals in the resolution of the play, its
denouement. In it past does not meet past; but future, future. It is
no accident that both Hal and Percy are carefully kept apart from
that action of the past whose consequences are being worked out in
this play. Henry's seizure of the throne from Richard was aided
by Northumberland and Worcester. Hotspur, indeed, has to be told
of the events before he knows their details. The antagonisms of
the past, then, center on Henry and Worcester. In their development
these antagonisms bring in two active young men who had no
part in the original episode. The rights and wrongs of this episode
are so ambiguous, and moreover are so further obscured by the
present scheming of the elders, that no clear issue can be drawn
from a conflict of Henry and Worcester. Right and wrong dissolve
into expediencies. But with the younger men the case is different,
for they are dissociated from this coil of the past. When, after Vernon's praise of Hal and a prophecy of the future greatness of England if he survives the battle,[3] Hotspur's sole reaction is the promise
to kill the Prince,[4] something is being said that transcends past
wrongs and battles long ago. Correspondingly, when Hal challenges
Percy on the battlefield—"Why then I see / A very valiant rebel of
the name" (V.iv.61–62)—an issue is being drawn that has little

relation to whether Worcester and Northumberland were suitably rewarded and whether Henry broke his promise to them.

Both Henry and Worcester are too tainted, we may say, to be fit representatives for what becomes the central issue of the play—the shape and meaning that arise from the action—for which the rights and wrongs of Henry's claim to the throne have no true relevance. On the contrary, Hal and Hotspur can represent this issue. They have not met in the web of the dark past. They alone crystallize in their purest form the opposing principles of the power struggle in English history that was not to meet its resolution, according to the Tudor myth, until the crowning of Henry VII. In the turbulence of English history as Shakespeare, at least, saw it, the theme was the endlessly repeated struggle between what came to be the modern Tudor principle of national patriotism resting on centralized royal authority, and the old system of diffused authority and personal loyalties represented by the feudal nobility.

Nowhere is this struggle more clearly pointed as a theme that illuminates the real significance of events than in *King Henry IV*, where it controls the major structure of the plot and dictates the characterization. When on the field of Shrewsbury Hal challenges Hotspur,

> I am the Prince of Wales; and think not, Percy,
> To share with me in glory any more.
> Two stars keep not their motion in one sphere,
> Nor can one England brook a double reign
> Of Harry Percy and the Prince of Wales.
>
> [V.iv.63–67]

the issue is clearly joined. In Shakespeare's best dramatic manner, history has been concentrated in terms of men.

This principle behind the struggle for power between nobles and throne is what the history in the play is about. Like any good Elizabethan, Shakespeare saw the Tudor concept of kingship as allied with law and order; the challenge to this authority stems from fear and incipient chaos. It is no accident that though the rebels are brought together initially in the name of Mortimer, the least of their concerns is to put him on the throne of England. The country is marked up into three parts, and Mortimer is fortunate to secure a third. If the rebels were to triumph, before long Wales and Hotspur's new kingdom would be at war. The chaos of *Gorboduc,* of *King Lear,* would be repeated, and France would gobble up the weakened and divided realm. Shakespeare emphasizes the contrasts between the two parties. The King's party are united in a common cause under their lawful sovereign. Their councils are in agreement, no personal differences ruffle the accord. Shirley, Stafford, Blunt bravely sacrifice their lives to keep their king from danger. In contrast, the rebels bicker even in the meeting at which they seal their compact. The father Northumberland sacrifices his son by a diplomatic illness. Glendower is overruled by prophecies and breaks the compact, the powerless Mortimer with him. Hotspur and Douglas warily disguise the antagonism of Englishman and of Scot under effusive compliment, though the ancient enmity breaks out in Vernon. The council before the battle is angrily at odds, and indeed the battle is joined only because of a lie: every indication exists that Hotspur would have accepted Henry's composition if it had been truly reported. The bad cause corrupts the men. Vernon, who had protested to the Douglas that "If well-respected honour bid me on, / I hold as little counsel with weak fear" (IV.iii.10–11), swallows his honor and agrees to support Worcester's false report of the King's offers: "Deliver what you will, I'll say 'tis so" (V.ii.26).

This lack of conscience about the effect on others as long as their own nests are lined is characteristic of the rebels. Worcester brings on the holocaust because he fears that Hotspur will be forgiven, but he and Northumberland will suffer if peace is made; and Vernon has no thought of the men who will die to protect Worcester's personal welfare. Not so the King. It is one of his most royal characteristics that he holds himself responsible for the lives under him. His chief accusation directed at Mortimer's defection is that Mortimer deliberately engaged in a battle he intended to lose in order to be captured, and thus was the cause of the death of many English subjects. Before Shrewsbury, Hal's offer of a single combat is generously intended to prevent the slaughter. In condemning Worcester and Vernon to death, Henry in effect calls them murderers. Just as an evil king proverbially could not rule well, so an evil cause cannot produce good actions, and Worcester is a child of the times.

This is the significance of the history, and it is a sound one. But ideas must be incorporated into men. Henry and Worcester—though technically the principals—cannot embody the ideas of this play, and instead history comes to rest in the persons of Hal and of Hotspur, who represent the great opposing forces with which the drama is essentially concerned. This contrast is sharpened by making Hotspur of Hal's exact age, although in reality he was a contemporary of the King. The opposition of the two young men is handled with skill and suspense. Hotspur is early won to the conspiracy, and the action assigned him is devoted exclusively to this main line of the plot. Hal is brought over late: his official entrance into the main plot does not take place before the climax of the play. In fact, his joining his father to put down the revolt becomes his first *action* in opposing Hotspur, and since it is made the turning-point of the drama, it is thereby given major significance. The terms of this decision are such as to narrow the future action and to lead it inevitably to the single combat on the field of Shrewsbury, another of Shakespeare's inventions to emphasize the concentration of the play on these two figures, like the reduction in Hotspur's age. (History does not record how Percy died.)

In technical terms of the plot, the significance of this climax is profound. The implication is that the King alone may not be able to conquer the rebels; and indeed this doubt is emphasized when but for Hal the Douglas would have killed Henry in the battle and won the day. The entrance of the Prince into the main action, therefore, is the decisive factor that tips the scales. If the opposition had begun early—if, say, Hal had moved to counter Hotspur the moment the rebellion was formed—the peculiar effect of this climax intervention would have been lost. As it is, the structure of the plot identifies Hal as the most powerful person in the play, on whose decision in the climax—the interview with his father—the form of the catastrophe, that is to say, the outcome of the play, will depend.

The dramatic effect of Hal's late coming to the main action emphasizes the strength of the future Henry V and, technically, adds a new interest to the events between climax and denouement. The new interest depends in some part on the audience now having a clear-cut choice between two figures—Hal and Percy—within the same action. This is a little different from the choice that was latent previously, between an active Hotspur and an inactive Prince, each in a different plot. Before the climactic interview with his father, Hal existed as a potential force, only. After the climax-interview, Shakespeare rapidly builds the young Henry V to-be toward his fulfillment at Shrewsbury. This process is managed with considerable economy, for rather more lines are assigned to Hotspur's side, but it is perhaps the more effective because of the economy. In the interval the audience must detach its natural sympathy with Hotspur and transfer it to Hal. Shakespeare orders this process brilliantly. The more faulty the management of the rebels' cause and the brighter the prospects of the King's party from the union of son with father, the more impossible it becomes to accept any justice in the rebellion when contrasted with Hal's right to the throne and his acceptance of the engagement to defend it. Any sentimental leaning to the ideology of rebellion is now impossible; but as this sympathy is detached, Shakespeare carefully replaces it by building up the more admirable side of Hotspur's personal character. The frenetic choler, the inability to control his tongue, the abrasive effect of his pride on his companions exist no longer; and for the first time we glimpse the careful general, conscious of the relation of his words and actions to the morale of his soldiers, and so cautious of defeat that he would probably have composed with

Henry if he had not been fatally deceived by Worcester. Thus as Hotspur's cause dwindles in its rectitude, until it reaches the nadir of Worcester's false report, Hotspur the man rises. By this means there is pity and justice in Hal's summation, first, "Why, then I see / A very valiant rebel of the name" (V.iv.61–62), and after the combat,

> Adieu, and take thy praise with thee to heaven!
> Thy ignominy sleep with thee in the grave,
> But not rememb'red in thy epitaph!
>
> > [V.iv.99–101]

It was a pity that for one especial weakness a brave young man had been so misled as to seek the destruction of his country. The forces of law and order must strike him down when he threatens the public safety and will not be reconciled. The audience is brought into the right attitude of the *lachrimae rerum,* the pity of things in this mixed human condition of right and wrong. But the personal sympathy one may feel for Hotspur is detached from the ideological. One may admire his bravery, but he must not be allowed to kill the future Henry V to whom the divine right of rule will descend.

On the other hand, the delay in the association of Hal with the main plot presents some technical problems. If Hal were not to be introduced until the climax, or shortly before, the audience would be unacquainted with him, and a transfer of interest from a powerful Hotspur to the newcomer would be difficult to effect. Clearly, Hal must be a part of the play from the beginning; but if he cannot join the main action until the middle of the third act, Shakespeare must provide some other action for him and motivate it in a manner that will hold the audience's interest. This he does by emphasizing Hal in his potential aspect only, and by rationalizing the old stories of Hal's wild youth—the Bear's Son archetype traditional for a hero. The action representing Hal's wild youth, on quite another plane from the crudities of the old play *The Famous Victories of Henry the Fifth,* leads to the invention of Falstaff.

The emphasis on Hal's potential is then rationalized by his relations first with Falstaff, then with his father, and finally with Hotspur. In the process of realizing his potential the progression moves Hal from his initial planned idleness with Falstaff to the climax of his decision to join the King, and on to the single combat with Percy at Shrewsbury. This is the shape of the action. But all three relationships are present from the start and are integral in Shakespeare's justification of Hal's idleness. We may summarize this rationalization by saying that Shakespeare puts tension into the tavern scenes when he transforms Hal's withdrawal from the responsibility of his position as Prince to make it, instead, a waiting period of preparation for his future greatness. This preparation takes the form of tests which Hal applies to each of the three ways of life he is under pressure to adopt. In the end, he chooses neither one nor the other—neither Falstaff's hedonism, Henry's political manipulation, nor Hotspur's crude ideals of honor—but rises superior to each by combining the best of all three to form a new synthesis of conduct that will guide the higher royalty of the Henry V to come.

Tests is too conventional a word to apply, perhaps. Three ways of life do indeed present themselves to Hal, dramatized in the persons of Falstaff, the King, and Percy, and what each one stands for. I suggest that there is a rising scale of difficulty here—it is hard to avoid the use of the word *temptation*, but its implications cast a false light on the picture. *Attraction* is perhaps better—a rising scale of attraction. I do not mean to imply that the attractiveness of any one of these ways is increased in the course of the action. I mean only that given the kind of man Hal is, the high place designed for him by his birth, and the higher by his ambitions, the attractiveness of certain elements in what Hotspur stands for is greater than what Falstaff stands for as a way of life.

All progression must be from lesser to greater, and thus it is appropriate to consider Falstaff first. Despite the fact that he is the least of the magnets that might pull the Prince from the fixed course of his future, the action devoted to his relations to Hal takes up more space than the others. This imbalance was forced on Shakespeare because the action involving the Prince and the King could not appear until the climax of the play, in the middle of the third act, and Falstaff must occupy Hal for roughly a half of the play. Hence Shakespeare forms of Hal and Falstaff the underplot, a device that involves a structural paradox, because Hal, who is to become the true protagonist of the play (in that the spire of meaning rises from him), transfers from the under- to the main plot to create the climax. At this point the underplot loses its structural identity; and though its characters continue in the action, they are now—from Hal to Bardolph—merged in the central action, the suppression of the rebellion.

The action of the underplot is exclusively concerned with the Gadshill robbery and its aftermath. This action has no independent ideological significance in itself, but in Shakespeare's usual manner it is brought into the larger unity as a form of parody of the main plot. In the mimic world of the underplot an action is initiated against royal law and order, in earnest on the part of Falstaff but in jest on the part of the Prince. That the Prince is in but not of the Gadshill plot means that he can guide it, soften its impact, and ultimately, by the restitution of the stolen money, heal the wound given to the commonwealth. The conclusion of this jest coincides with the father's summons to Hal; thereafter no further action arises from the underplot, and its persons are absorbed into the main plot—Hal to take a pre-eminent part in its denouement, Falstaff to continue the function of parody begun in the Gadshill affair.

Since the underplot—although complete in itself—parodies the main action of the rebellion in its war on law and order, it is not conducted without reference to the larger issues that are still in suspense. The parody of Hal's forthcoming interview with his father serves to bring the whole of the jest to a focus, and indeed its conclusion, or denouement, marks the moment of Hal's decision to forsake the way of life that Falstaff represents. We shall come to this presently. In the interval a less clear-cut incident in the under-plot needs analysis, for it contains the equivalent parody of the part that Hotspur represents.[5]

As Falstaff owes his invention to a technical necessity of the action, so this scene—as important in its purpose as the mock father-son interview—has its origin in the need to bridge Falstaff's roaring exit from Gadshill and his entrance into the tavern where the Prince and Poins are prepared to round off the jest by his humiliation. To while away the time the Prince and Poins agree to bewilder poor Francis, the drawer, and they succeed so thoroughly that he becomes as transfixed as a rabbit. Poins dimly sees that this jest —which sentimental critics have rebuked for its assumed cruelty —must have some ulterior purpose, but his inquiry is riddlingly put aside by the Prince with the indirect answer that it was his humor, or whim. But when Francis returns, still in a daze, and runs off to answer what is only the echo of a summons in his ears, the truth comes out. If the actor of Hal has correctly played his part up to this point, he will have displayed no merriment in the conduct of the jest, but rather boredom and impatience, a bitter-tinged irony directed against himself, as in his satiric comment to Poins after his description of the drinking with the apprentices, "I tell thee, Ned, thou hast lost much honour that thou wert not with me in this action" (II.iv.22-24).[6] Now the disgust breaks out in a speech that has the privacy (and also the dramatic illumination) of a soliloquy. He begins—"That ever this fellow should have fewer words than a parrot, and yet the son of a woman! His industry is upstairs and downstairs, his eloquence the parcel of a reckoning" (II.iv.110-13). There is a bitter comment under the joke that the son of a woman, a sex noted for its loquaciousness, should yield to a parrot in the scope of his vocabulary. What Hal is remarking is the fact that Francis's training and occupation get nowhere and result in no more useful purpose than, say, an animal serving on a treadmill. The human activity that Francis's divine spark motivates is expressed in upstairs and down, the height (or depth) of futility for an "action." His speech, by which his godlike reason (next to the angels') should be exhibited, is lower than that of a mimic bird. This is what happens to the son of a woman—that is, a human being—when his activity is not rationally motivated and his occupation becomes a soulless one.

Hal then makes an important connection, when he continues:

> I am not yet of Percy's mind, the Hotspur of the North; he that kills me some six or seven dozen of Scots at a breakfast, washes his hands, and says to his wife, "Fie upon this quiet life! I want work." "O my sweet Harry," says she, "how many hast thou kill'd to-day?" "Give my roan horse a drench," says he, and answers "Some fourteen," an hour after, " a trifle, a trifle." I prithee call in Falstaff. I'll play Percy, and that damn'd brawn shall play Dame Mortimer his wife. "Rivo!" says the drunkard. Call in ribs, call in tallow. [II.iv.114–25]

We are not here dealing with a humor, or whim, either, but with a coherent continuation of Hal's line of thought about the "action" of the drinking bout and the subhuman activity of Francis as an expression of the depths to which rational man can sink when governed only by his animal nature. "I am not yet of Percy's mind." This ironic "not yet" divorces Hal from Hotspur's way of life in two respects. In the first, Hal is not yet prepared to win his reputation merely in the slaughter of the battlefield. The numerical listing of Percy's victims by which Hotspur has gained his fame as England's first soldier is then linked by this "not yet" to the commentary on Francis. Francis was the son of a woman: he belonged to the human race. But the up-and-downstairs activity of his trade is certainly no better than that of a beast. And his speech, instrument of his rationally guided judgment, is inferior to the mimic sounds of a bird. Withal, Francis is so stupid that he never thinks of breaking his indentures and running away to a better life: his "mind" is content with his trade.

When Hal rejects this concept of life as one without the operation of human reason, he simultaneously rejects Hotspur's "mind," which is—given only the difference in the plane of activity—identical with Francis's. Hotspur's slaughter of the Scots in private pursuit of the mere word *honor,* which as Falstaff remarks is only air, is fundamentally no more a rational, or noble, occupation than Francis's treading the staircase in his endless rounds. Since the Elizabethans measured intelligence, or wit, by speech, and esteemed eloquence as the mark of wisdom, so Hotspur's inarticulate responses to his wife's breakfast-table chitchat compare no more favorably as evidence for the operation in him of a human reason than Francis's "Anon, anon, sir." If we laugh at Francis, we must laugh at Hotspur. His "mind," or inclination, or ideals, is not that of the balanced and rational man whom Hal can respect as a full equal. Percy has been placed in his right perspective beside Francis, whose industry was "upstairs and downstairs" and "his eloquence the parcel of a [tavern] reckoning," no different from the itemizing of a parcel of some fourteen dead Scots. Hal is "not yet of Percy's mind," nor will he ever be.

The tavern parody of the King's interview with Hal is more obvious and thus less in need of discussion. What it does do, however, is to provide clear evidence that we do not need to wait for the famed rejection scene that ends Part 2 on Hal's return from his coronation. He rejects Falstaff here in the tavern, and all he stands for, no less decisively—and Falstaff knows it. Before this scene Hal's concentration of interest has been on Falstaff, but after it he turns to Percy, and Falstaff—though still entertaining him —is on the periphery of his real concerns.

This is not the place to discuss the complex relations of Falstaff to Hal except to remark that the conventional picture of an ancient Vice tempting an innocent young man is wide of the mark. Although we should not underestimate Falstaff's delight in Hal's wit —for his own followers are lamentably deficient in stimulating him to anything but abuse—the chief attraction of the young Prince is his position. Underneath the combats of wit, Falstaff is earnestly working to make himself so indispensable to the Prince that he will be protected and raised to high position when Hal inherits the throne. "When thou art king" comes to be something of a re-frain, and the suggestion is more than casual that Falstaff has his eye on the office of Lord Chief Justice. For Hal the attraction is also the wit, which does not flower on his side of the fence either. This wit is more than the breaking of a few puns. On the one hand it is related to eloquence in its mastery of rhetorical devices and its comic inversion of logical modes of thought; on the other it is related to wisdom in the realistic view it takes of human imperfec-tion, and in its satiric unmasking of inflated pretensions, as in the private joke about the Douglas and his marksmanship, all the more wise because its termination foreshadows the aftermath of Shrews-bury.

> *Falstaff.* Well, that rascal hath good metal in him; he will not run.
> *Prince.* Why, what a rascal art thou then, to praise him so for running!
> *Falstaff.* A-horseback, ye cuckoo! but afoot he will not budge a foot.
> *Prince.* Yes, Jack, upon instinct.
>
> [II.iv.383–89]

In defeat the Douglas's instinct is to flee. Instead of running "a-horse-back up a hill perpendicular" as in the joke, he

> fled with the rest;
> And falling from a hill, he was so bruis'd
> That the pursuers took him.
>
> [V.v.20–22]

The equation is most apt.

In Hal's hands this wit is to become constructive, a sign of his superior intelligence applied to the welfare of his kingdom. In Falstaff's hands, however, it is essentially destructive since it serves chiefly to disguise self-seeking as in his determined efforts to bind

Hal to him for his own profit. What happens to the kingdom is of no concern. It may be funny to accept bribes to relieve able men from military service and to cull out such dregs of the countryside as provoke Westmoreland's protest, "Ay, but, Sir John, methinks they are exceeding poor and bare—too beggarly" (IV.ii.74–75)— or to wear a bottle of wine into battle instead of a pistol. The one could lose a battle, and the other could kill Hal in his need. This abuse of wit therefore by a levity in dealing with serious situations —its failure indeed in an almost existential manner to recognize any action or human motive as necessarily serious even in emergency conditions—this distortion inherent in Falstaff's way of life under its surface charm is the very reverse of wisdom. In plain terms, Falstaff is as much an internal danger to law and order in the kingdom as Percy is an external danger. Neither can be permitted. As long as Falstaff can be controlled under suitable conditions, as when Hal is prince, Hal will tolerate him and will pretend to be deceived about Falstaff's true intentions, though all the time defending himself by the exercise of his superior wit against the imposition of Falstaff's will. When Hal is king, the danger to the commonwealth by association with an incorrigible force for internal dissension cannot be tolerated.[7]

Throughout the first acts Hal defends himself from "when thou art king," and in the mock interview his warning is fairly given and fairly understood. Pretending to be Henry speaking to his dissolute son, represented by Falstaff, Hal turns Falstaff's self-praise into a diatribe on "That villanous abominable misleader of youth, Falstaff, that old white-bearded Satan" (II.iv.508–9). Falstaff defends his hedonism and ends with the plea to banish all companions but himself, for "Banish plump Jack, and banish all the world!" (II.iv.526–27). To this the Prince responds, "I do, I will." Properly acted this can send a shiver through the audience as its significance is recognized. Falstaff's "banish all the world" would instantly, in context, recall the constant association of the *world* with *vanity*, that is, with an excessive regard for the pleasures and rewards of mundane life. Hal's response is to that proposition as much as to

Falstaff. He is forsaking the life of the taverns—in which he had sought refuge, as well as pleasure, according to the terms of the important "I know you all" soliloquy (I.ii.219-41)[8]—and is taking up the life of duty required by his birth. One must realize that when the fatal words sound, "I do, I will," Hal is only in small part playing the role of his father. He speaks in his own person directly to Falstaff, who knows it.[9]

As a final comment, it is proper to note that though Hal forsakes the taverns, he does not turn his back on what had been of value there, the pleasure-loving principle divorced from vanity. He is not a puritan like Hotspur. The well-rounded Renaissance ideal man should be deficient in no side of experience or appreciation so long as it was carefully kept under the control of reason. Falstaff's devotion to pleasure was so extreme that in any position of real authority he would have endangered the kingdom. To that extent he is irrational and governed by his passions. On the contrary, Hal—appreciating pleasure but in control of its excesses—is a supremely rational Renaissance man. His wooing of Katherine of France shows how he had learned his lesson in London.

The actual interview with the King offers a problem. Henry is as intent on forcing a code of conduct upon his son as Falstaff had been. It is a legitimate inference that Hal's unwillingness to live by his father's code had been a primary factor in his flight from the court to the taverns, where he could be his own man in private life until the opportunity came to be his own man in public life. He is not Henry's image in temperament or in conviction. If he had lived as Prince of Wales, he could not have influenced his father's policy and thus would have been tarred with the same brush. It was easier to make a fresh start in imposing his own image on the kingdom by removing the false picture of himself as a ne'er-do-well than the false picture of himself as the Machiavellian son of a Machiavellian father.

Henry's mistake is a natural one. He rules, and most successfully, too, according to the terms of his own temperament. What he does not realize is that his formula does not fit all kings, and that Hal must rule according to the terms of *his* temperament and also the conditions he will encounter, which differ from those with which Henry must deal. On the evidence of Part 2 possibly Henry would have seen the distinction, since he recognizes that Hal will inherit a peaceful kingdom in contrast to the civil wars that beset him. But in Part 1 he is obsessed with his fear that Hal is another Richard II and will be overthrown by another Bolingbroke. Point by point, almost, his lecture to Hal has been refuted in the "I know you all" soliloquy, which has provided a blueprint to the audience for the plan of Hal's future actions. The son must listen, but he cannot agree that Henry's course is right for him.

At the end of the tavern scene that concluded the Gadshill jest, Hal had recognized the altered part he must play now that Percy had made his move against the throne: "I'll to the court in the morning. We must all to the wars . . ." (II.iv.595–96). Henry may think that he is pleading with a hostile son to join his party, but the decision has already been made. If it is the union of son and father that spells the failure of the rebellion, and if after this scene Hal joins the main plot as the great opposite to Percy, the spearhead of the menace to his kingdom, the decision made in this scene must form the climax or turning point of the action. A few years ago I analyzed the scene from this point of view and argued that it was a climax that was not a climax. Indeed, that Shakespeare had constructed it so in order to make a dramatic point to the audience not easily contrived by another means. That is, Henry thought that by his last calculated insult he had won over an enemy son to his side; and thus he had every right to be pleased with the successful outcome of the highly calculated speech that had done the job. But the audience knew that Henry was deceived, that Hal had been won over all the time, and that the moment had come, in Hal's view, to thrust aside the dark obscuring clouds and reveal the sun of his royalty. That Hal throughout the play was in perfect control of every situation, that he was thoroughly his own man, and that this was the point of the play, I suggested, was demonstrated by the nonclimax. A true victory for his father would have implied a malleable son, and a conversion. But Hal had never needed conversion, as shown by the "I know you all" soliloquy. All he needed, as he there recognized, was the arrival at some future time of the proper conditions in which he could step forward as himself.[10]

I think that this view is still substantially correct, but I will offer one modification that should have been presented before. That is, it is true that Hal's decision has been made on the rational, or intellectual, plane before the interview. The audience can be in no doubt that the King does not persuade Hal to join him, for no persuasion is needed. It seems to me now, however, that more emphasis should be placed on the implications of the really decisive part of the interview containing the King's calculated insult: "Why, Harry, do I tell thee of my foes, / Which art my nearest and dearest enemy?" (III.ii.122–23). This reference to Hal as his "enemy" is an obscure one to us, but not to the Elizabethans, who knew the whole story. It is referred to when Hal cries, "God forgive them that so much have sway'd / Your Majesty's good thoughts away from me!" (III.ii.130–31), but again, just as obscurely. We do not, in fact, find the true reference until Hal rescues his father at Shrewsbury from the onslaught of the Douglas, and the King recants:

Thou hast redeem'd thy lost opinion,
And show'd thou mak'st some tender of my life,
In this fair rescue thou hast brought to me.

At this, Hal cries, in reference to the same detractors,

O God! they did me too much injury
That ever said I heark'ned for your death.
If it were so, I might have let alone
The insulting hand of Douglas over you,
Which would have been as speedy in your end

As all the poisonous potions in the world,
And sav'd the treacherous labour of your son.

[V.iv.48–57]

These lines show the depths of the King's insult which—being the man he is—he does not deliver without having planned its effect. Its continuation, that he thinks it probable Hal will join Percy's forces and fight against his father, in fear of Percy's frowns, carries on the implication that thereby Hal will ascend the throne over his father's body, as a vassal of Hotspur. It is this implication, that he has planned to murder his father in the past and may take the opportunity to do so in the present, that fires Hal as much as the insult that he will join Percy's party through fear.

Henry's tactics succeed. Hal flares up:

Do not think so. You shall not find it so.

. . . .

I will redeem all this on Percy's head
And, in the closing of some glorious day,
Be bold to tell you that I am your son,
When I will wear a garment all of blood,
And stain my favours in a bloody mask,
Which, wash'd away, shall scour my shame with it.

. . . .

This in the name of God I promise here.

[III.ii.129–53]

Small wonder that the King, in satisfaction at the success of his stratagem, replies, "A hundred thousand rebels die in this! / Thou shalt have charge and sovereign trust herein" (III.ii.160–61).

Is it possible to reconcile this real flareup on Hal's part, marking the success of his father's plan, with the fact that the King did not need to provoke him since the night before the interview Hal had announced he was joining the wars? Is it possible to make a climax out of this false or nonclimax? I think it is. Let us grant that insofar as the decision to join his father was concerned, Henry's provocation was unnecessary. He may think that he has succeeded in firing his son to come over to his party, but the audience knows otherwise. That the audience has heard Hal's previous decision prevents it from thinking that Hal was so reluctant to leave his wastrel life in the taverns, so little his own man that he had to yield to outside forces and be shaped by them in this crucial decision, instead of moving into his new role of his own volition. Such a feeling would be fatal to Shakespeare's concept of Hal as the future Henry V who rises superior to each way of life that is offered him and in the end combines the best of them all to form a new concept of royalty, far superior to what any one of the pressures put upon him could have conceived.

But since Hal is to join the King and thereafter take his place as the protagonist, as Hotspur's main opponent, between whom the real issue is drawn, the light-hearted and almost casual decision at the end of the tavern scene makes clear his intellectual acceptance but leaves unclear his emotional commitment. The Elizabethans believed that Plato's white and black horses of reason and of passion had to pull the chariot of the soul in tandem. Passion, or emotion, was bad only if it rose to an excess, overpowered reason, and caused the chariot to swerve. Hal's "I know you all" soliloquy has been an eminently rational document. The question in the minds of the audience about the corroborating strength of his passion, or emotion, has not been answered by the tavern action preceding this interview, however, even though some clue has been given in the Francis scene. If Hal is deficient in passion—if he is what we would call overintellectualized or, at worst, the sort of schemer whom Traversi pictures—he is not a truly rounded man. He is not the future Henry V if the strength of his personal conviction does not equal his general intention.

The interview with his father, then, furnishes the dramatic spark missing from the previous action to demonstrate to the audience that Hal's emotional commitment equals his intellectual or rational commitment. What Spenser exhibits in the person of Guyon in *The*

Faerie Queene, following the lead of Aristotle's *Nichomachean Ethics,* now inspires Hal. Previously he has shown a satirical skepticism about the legendary deeds of the Douglas and a contempt for the mindless code of honor built on the number of Scots Hotspur can slaughter before breakfast. But what Henry succeeds in doing, thereby justifying the dramatic climax of the interview, is to arouse Hal to what Spenser would have called "honest anger" at the threat of the rebellion to his country. This we have seen only in the partial glimpse offered in his impatience during the jest with Francis the drawer and in the emotional bitterness of his soliloquy before the entrance of Falstaff slides him back into the play acting of his idle tavern nights. Useful as the Francis episode had been to show that Hal is not all intellect and that he balances wit with human emotion under control of his reason, it is not enough to motivate the conviction of his opposition to Hotspur on personal as well as on intellectual grounds. The interview, then, is not a formality but a dramatic and indeed an ideological, or psychological, necessity. But its rationale must not be perverted by the easy belief that somehow the King has "converted" his erring son during its course. Simply, an emotional force has been added to a decision rationally undertaken long before.

This emotional fire so necessary to action having been provided, Hal is now ready to move on to the third test posed by this play —the pressure on him to adopt the code of honor represented by Percy, the universally admired soldier, the man who, in King Henry's words, is "the theme of honour's tongue"; the man who Henry wishes might prove to be a changeling, his own son, replaced by Hal in the cradle.

Shakespeare's art, not just in comprehensive characterization but in understanding the issues which alone give character meaning, is magnificently demonstrated in the mixed nature of Hotspur. A man of action, the greatest soldier of the kingdom, he is yet such a mass of contradictions that his very strengths turn to weaknesses because the ideal that moves his conduct is as outmoded as is a knight's armor against the anachronistic cannon introduced into the account of Holmedon. Shakespeare brings the play to rest on the theme of honor. This touchstone for action has been much in Falstaff's mouth, and is the subject of his famous soliloquy, "Honour pricks me on," with its pragmatic conclusion, "What is that word honour? Air. . . . Who hath it? He that died a Wednesday. Doth he feel it? No. Doth he hear it? No. 'Tis insensible then? Yea, to the dead. . . . Therefore I'll none of it" (V.i.136–42). This theme is supported by his later conclusion, "Give me life; which if I can save, so; if not, honour comes unlook'd for, and there's an end" (V.iii.63–65). Henry has tacitly taken up the subject in his account to Hal of how he secured and maintained his throne. Hal has satirically applied the word to the Gadshill action and to his drinking bout with the drawers.

Hotspur's code is simply stated. It associates honor exclusively with courage, with reaction to danger regardless of the cause that is involved. A distinct link exists here with the artificial code of the duello well understood by the Elizabethans. That is, as it was stated, a man who inherited natural honor as the son of an honorable father and mother had to maintain, in addition, his acquired, or artificial, honor. Acquired honor was gained and kept only by means of constant wariness against its being impugned. If a single act of cowardice was observed, the whole fabric of acquired honor collapsed and could not be restored. This concept had no relation to the ethical source of action. The Elizabethans debated whether, if a man declined to fight because he was in the wrong, he could be called honorable. The answer was mixed. One side maintained that it was the higher honor to decline combat if one's cause was not just, since if one killed one's opponent defending the wrong, one's soul was inevitably damned. The other, and more powerful because more popular, side maintained that the code of honor required a man who was challenged to fight without regard for his cause, for otherwise who would know he was not a coward and therefore without honor? This is the code to which, in essence, Hotspur subscribed. At its heart was the concept that any one seemingly dishonorable action, no matter how motivated, could destroy the structure of honor painfully built up over years of effort. And once destroyed, acquired honor could never be restored. The Elizabethans noted this concept as pre-eminent among military men. Every action, therefore, must have as its central motive the defense of one's honor against any imputation that a temporizing action was taken from motives of cowardice.[11]

It is this code, as much as his natural choler, that makes Hotspur so touchy in Wales about the course of the river Trent as the boundary of his lands to-be. It moves him to abuse the lord who failed to join the conspiracy as a frosty-spirited coward: "O, I could divide myself and go to buffets for moving such a dish of skim milk with so honourable an action!" (II.iii.36–38). The lord had only pointed out, quite reasonably, that the "friends you have named [are] uncertain [as indeed they turn out to be], the time itself unsorted, and your whole plot too light for the counterpoise of so great an opposition" (II.iii.13–15). This is an accurate estimate of the conspiracy, but Hotspur's sole reaction is to accuse the lord of cowardice because he was unwilling to test himself against a danger.

The code of danger for its own sake as the sole test of courage, and thus of honor, is concentrated in Percy's reaction to Worcester's calculated warning that the conspiracy is

> As full of peril and adventurous spirit
> As to o'erwalk a current roaring loud
> On the unsteadfast footing of a spear.
>
> [I.iii.191–93]

To this Hotspur cries out, "If he fall in, good night, or sink or swim!" (I.iii.194). That is, the danger justifies the attempt without regard for the outcome so long, he continues, as honor opposes danger. The well-known speech then follows, beginning,

> By heaven, methinks it were an easy leap
> To pluck bright honour from the pale-fac'd moon,
> Or dive into the bottom of the deep,

with its conclusion,

> And pluck up drowned honour by the locks,
> So he that doth redeem her thence might wear
> Without corrival all her dignities.

[I.iii.201–7]

The only means known to Hotspur to maintain his honor is for him to endure no rival. This supremely selfish and personal code exhibits itself in various ways and throughout is carefully motivated as the conduct of a man governed chiefly by his passions. It leads him to a towering pride, for which Worcester reproves him. It also leads to various ungenerous actions, the most significant being his harsh refusal to listen to Vernon's praise of Hal and his bloodcurdling resolve to kill the Prince, just prophesied as his country's hope. Hotspur's narrow code denies his acceptance of any rival, whereas, in contrast, the Prince in the battle scenes is truly chivalric in his praise of Percy, except for one point.

Here we come to the heart of the problem. Hotspur's association of honor exclusively with warfare and danger denies all ethical and humane grounds for action in its exaltation of the single factor of risk. His honor, then, leads him to become a traitor to his country and to its proposed dismemberment as a nation. Self has been placed over country, not for Worcester's venal motives but in the pursuit of a private and artificial code divorced from all question of right and wrong. We cannot even say that his actions are basically motivated by self-aggrandizement, for the prize in the form that he seeks it has been accurately described in Falstaff's word as "air."

In contrast, Hal's concept of honor is firmly rooted in cause. He is not smirched by the apparent dishonor of his low-life activities, because his mind is not placed there. His actions are just when he enters the battle since he has dedicated himself, in honest anger, to the preservation of his country. He praises his great opponent for all chivalric actions but one—his treachery to his country. His re-

sponse to Percy's challenge, narrows the issue: "Why, then I see /
A very valiant rebel of the name." He continues:

> I am the Prince of Wales; and think not, Percy,
> To share with me in glory any more.
> Two stars keep not their motion in one sphere,
> Nor can one England brook a double reign
> Of Harry Percy and the Prince of Wales.
>
> [V.iv.63–67]

These words differ from Hotspur's ungenerous refusal to acknowledge a personal rival: that is, in part, they deny a sharing of true
glory with his rebellious leadership that has split the kingdom,
spilled English blood, brought in the Scotch enemies, and endangered the country's external security. The reign that is in dispute,
and that will be resolved by the single combat, is that of war and
chaos and civil disorder as reflected in the passion-ruled Hotspur
as against the order and law and national unity and glory as represented by the rationally-motivated Prince. Above all, however, it
is an ideological statement about England's destiny and the new
concepts that must rule the country. It is the contrast between
patriotism and feudalism, between a new code of honor based on
right and a discredited, outmoded code based on pride and personal
glory.

Thus the honor that Hal wins from this combat cannot be called
"air," because he serves a greater master than himself in the cause
of justice. The patriotic fervor of the play *Henry V* is fully anticipated here. Its association of personal and of national honor in
Hal as against their destructive opposition in Hotspur leads to the
ultimate definition, transcending Falstaff's materialism, Henry's
expediency, and Hotspur's fatal distortion. The education of the
future hero king, Henry V, is complete.

Iago's "if": An Essay on the Syntax of *Othello*

MADELEINE DORAN

Very soon after the opening of what is often called the temptation scene in *Othello,* Cassio, who has been talking with Desdemona, walks away as Othello and Iago enter, and this interchange takes place:

> *Iago.* Ha! I like not that.
> *Oth.*   What dost thou say?
> *Iago.* Nothing, my lord; or if—I know not what.
> *Oth.* Was not that Cassio parted from my wife?
> *Iago.* Cassio, my lord? No, sure, I cannot think it.
>
> [III.iii.35–38][1]

Iago's "if" is the great central *if* in the play. It is vague and in-complete, with neither condition nor conclusion stated. It is the small hole in the dike which, persistently widened by Iago, will let in the destroying flood. If Cassio's stealing away from Desde-mona means something sinister, if Desdemona is not a faithful wife, if Cassio is not a true friend, if certainties are not certainties, chaos is come again. For Othello cannot entertain *if*s. He cannot live as Hamlet does, weighing possibilities, holding hypotheses, thinking of consequences. To be once in doubt is once to be re-solved. This casual but calculated "if" has been prepared for by others in the play, and will be followed by others. Indeed, if we look closely, as I propose we do, we see that conditional sentences (by no means all Iago's) mark the stages of the action. When they express doubt they are disruptive of the assurance expressed in Othello's unqualified declarative sentences. Under Iago's *if*s, Othello's verse turns to prose and even his syntax goes momentarily to pieces. The conditionals of possibility are verticals coming up from below, first touching, then penetrating, the horizontal movement, distorting and disrupting it. They are like molten rock which, thrusting itself up from below into old sedimentary beds, heaves up, twists, cracks, and dislimns their level planes.

I propose to look at the syntax of *Othello,* for it is in the interplay of assertion and negation that the bare bones of a fable are given dramatic life and sensibility. Syntax is the most intimate way to show movement of mind; it is the dramatist's most refined tool in shaping monologue or dialogue. Revelation of character may or may not be in question; always important is the dramatic structure which the syntax helps to shape. In *Othello,* as in every one of his plays, Shakespeare uses syntax to create special effects appropriate to particular situations—as, for instance, in the dominant syntax of exclamation, command, and question in the three scenes of public disturbance begun by Iago (I.i and ii; II.iii; V.i). But in this play (as in *Lear* and perhaps others), Shakespeare does something more: he uses syntax, I believe, to inform in a subtle way his larger dramatic structure. It is with this second use that I shall be principally concerned.

There are two large syntactical patterns, I would say, which operate in the drama as a whole. These are chiefly sentences expressive of possibility in varying degrees (that is, conditional sentences of varying structure and mood) and operative within a framework of sentences expressive of certainty (mainly declarative sentences, not greatly complicated, in the indicative mood). The conditional sentences function in the way they do because they are intimately allied with the way in which action in the play is motivated and understood. The nonconditional declarative pattern must be looked at first, because it is the ground which the conditional pattern partly supports, partly disturbs.

The dominant voices in the play are Othello's and Iago's. If one takes Othello's love of Desdemona as the primary theme of the play in a major key, one may perhaps call Othello's directness and simplicity the tonic chord. His normal sentences are declarative, in the indicative mood, often simple in construction; if compound or complex, they are not greatly extended or involved. This is the way he is introduced to us when Iago rushes to him to warn him that Brabantio and his kin are coming to arrest him: "'Tis better as it is"; "I fetch my life and being from men of royal siege"; "Not I. I must be found" (I.ii.6, 21–22, 30). The assertions which help establish Othello's ethos[2] are not hedged with concessions and doubts. They are candid but brief, not emphatic because they need not be; they imply a natural confidence in himself, a confidence born of an innate self-respect and based on experience in the tented field: "The world is thus and so; I am thus and thus; I shall do what I need to do." He moves with quiet authority into the military man's imperatives when necessary: "Keep up your bright swords, for the dew will rust them. . . . Hold your hands, / Both you of my inclining and the rest" (I.ii.59, 81–82). Or, more sharply when disorder is threatened, as in the tumult on Cyprus: "Hold for your lives!"; "Silence that dreadful bell! . . . What's the matter?"; "Give me answer to't" (II.iii.165, 175–76, 196).

At the beginning, Othello has the same confidence in his love for Desdemona and in hers for him as in his profession; and his affirmations are as simple and frank:

> That I have ta'en away this old man's daughter,
> It is most true; true I have married her.
>
> [I.iii.78–79]
>
> She lov'd me for the dangers I had pass'd,
> And I lov'd her that she did pity them.
>
> [I.iii.167–68]

It is a confidence truly placed. Desdemona's declarations of love are as direct and as unqualified as his.

> I am hitherto your daughter. But here's my husband.
>
> [I.iii.185]

> My heart's subdu'd
> Even to the very quality of my lord.
> I saw Othello's visage in his mind,
> And to his honours and his valiant parts
> Did I my soul and fortunes consecrate.
>
> [I.iii.251–55]

There are, of course, normal variations of sentence pattern in Othello's speech, which is always sensitively responsive to any immediate situation. But we may take the uncomplicated sentences in the indicative mode, sometimes re-enforced by the imperative of wish or command, as the warp of his speech. To change the figure, it is in these that we hear the characteristic and distinctive notes of his speech.

His style is not always what one would call plain. But even when it is marked, as it often is, by courtly diction, richness of imagery, and beauty of rhythm, it rests on a base of directness of apprehension and simplicity of structure. The images are uncomplicated, given in similes or metaphors not greatly extended, certainly always lucid, rarely in mixed or knotted tropes.

The counterstatement to Othello's love, Iago's malicious hatred of Othello, also opens in a major key and is also simply declarative in form. The hatred is stated at the outset in plain terms, first in Iago's racy circumstantial narrative to Roderigo about Othello's promotion of Cassio to the lieutenancy—

> *Rod.* Thou told'st me thou didst hold him in thy hate.
> *Iago.* Despise me if I do not. . . .
>
> [I.i. 7–8]

and then in his promise to get even: "I follow him to serve my turn upon him" (I.i.42). The assertion of hate made to Roderigo is insisted upon ("I have told thee often, and I retell thee again and again, I hate the Moor" [I.iii.372–73]) and it is repeated in soliloquy (I.iii.392). Iago's mind seen straight into, when he is talking to himself (hence to us) or to Roderigo, is always vulgar and obscene. His plainness, therefore, quite as direct in assertion as Othello's, is in a wholly different key. Plain also is the mask of blunt soldier he wears to meet the world. The interesting thing is that the mask is remarkably like his own face. There are only shadings of difference in the language (to Othello it is cleaned up a little), or none at all (as in his obscenities to Brabantio about the Barbary horse and the old black ram). The essential difference is in the intent. His opening statement to Roderigo, true as we find it to be, is yet less candid than it seems, since he uses it to manipulate this stupid cat's-paw. His natural cynicism (the ethos Shakespeare invents for him) need hardly change its tone; or if it does, only enough to seem, in the context of its directed use, a healthy realism. Iago often assumes the style of the homely moralist. He states general moral truths (or seeming truths) in aphorisms or sentences ("Poor and content is rich . . ." [III.iii.172]), gives examples and analogies, draws plausible but subtly false conclusions, or misapplies the lesson, as in his homily to Roderigo on the hoary text that our bodies are our gardens to cultivate as we will (I.iii.322 ff). The differences in style, whether in prose or verse, are governed by the decorum of the person or of the scene as a whole; the verse to Othello is as plain, if not as vulgar, as the prose to Roderigo. The rhetoric of simplicity is a subtle mask, and he wears it with pleasure.

Iago's pattern of declarative sentences, therefore, differs from Othello's in two fundamental ways—in quality and in relation to the truth. Iago's prosy, if lively, vulgarity is counterpointed against Othello's poetic grace. Othello's assertions match the truth of himself and the truth he sees; up to the point of his deception they mirror reality. Iago's do not. His "honest" statements—sometimes true, sometimes false, sometimes partly one, partly the other, always devious in intent—do not reflect the world as it is. In fact, the truth of love Desdemona and Othello know Iago does not even recognize. To him love would appear to be, as he defines it to Roderigo, "merely a lust of the blood and a permission of the will" (I.iii.339–40).

Iago's method of operation is to introduce doubt into Othello's confidence. The conditional sentence expressing a condition assumed to be possible is the subtlest of his grammatical and logical tools.

We might consider the conditional sentence itself for a moment. It expresses relations in the world of contingent possibilities. Take the form in which the relation between condition and conclusion is assumed to be necessary: If *this* is true, then *that* is; if *this* should happen, then *that* would. The question in such a sentence is not about the conclusion, but about the condition on which the conclusion or consequence is, or seems to be, contingent. (In the alternative "seems" there is a trap, for even if *this* is true, *that* only may be. It is a trap Iago knows very well how to set.) The probability of the condition's existing or occurring has to be assessed on a scale of degrees. Probability amounting to certainty is at one end—what may be and is; improbability, also amounting to certainty, is at the other—what might conceivably be, but is not. Uncertainty lies in an indeterminate middle zone between. When the condition is assumed to be only possible, it has obviously less predictive force than when it is assumed to be fact. There is room, however, in nice distinctions of mood and tense, to suggest variations of relation (or rather, feeling about the relation) between condition and conclusion. Shakespeare uses such distinctions with more subtlety than we are accustomed to in modern English, in which the indicative mood so often usurps the prerogative of the subjunctive in conditional sentences of possibility. The condition contrary to fact has many uses. Suppose we say that if *this* were true (believing it not to be), *that* would happen; this carries us by implication to an assertion in the indicative. But *this* is not true; therefore *that* will not happen. By using the conditional form, however, we can do something we cannot in a simple assertion.

We may intend a relieved "Thank goodness it is not true!" or a wistful "If only it were!" Condition contrary to fact offers subtle possibilities of variation (which we shall find illustrated in *Othello*). It is a form capable of the most delicate nuances in expressing our responses to the contingencies among which we live. For excluded possibilities may affect us as much as open ones. They remind us of limits beyond which we cannot go, but sometimes, too, of our incredible escapes. And only to imagine the exclusion of the possibilities we live by may make either our worst fears or our strongest certainties. Possibilities still unrealized hold the door open to the future, hopefully or fearfully. But we do not put contemplation of them aside because they are over—when they have lived in act, died forever, or never come into being. These make our thankful deliverances, our regrets, or our frustrations. What if it had not happened! If only it had not! If only it had!

One way in which Shakespeare establishes Othello's ethos is to make him rarely speak in *if*s. He quickly creates for us an illusion of a full and adventurous past for Othello, a past in which the possibilities appear to have been always successfully dealt with or successfully escaped from. Here he is now, assured and serene, taking what comes, asking few questions, not worrying about contingencies, not thinking too precisely on the event. He uses few conditional sentences in the first two acts—that is to say, before Iago disturbs him. Most are in forms nearest improbability; they imply his confidence that the world will not be upset. One sort is the condition contrary to fact in the subjunctive: "Were it my cue to fight, I should have known it / Without a prompter" (I.ii.83–84). The other form has the condition in the indicative or subjunctive and the consequence in the imperative or optative subjunctive:

> when light-wing'd toys
> Of feather'd Cupid seel with wanton dullness
> My speculative and offic'd instruments,
> That my disports corrupt and taint my business,

> Let housewives make a skillet of my helm,
> And all indign and base adversities
> Make head against my estimation!
>
> [I.iii.269–75]

This is a strong form of asseveration, having almost the force of an oath. It calls for an unwished consequence to follow upon an incredible condition: If I am not what I am, then let this shame fall on my head. Conditions contrary to fact, subtly varied in form, often asseverative, recur in Othello's speech to the end of the play. How they are placed at strategic points in the action, usually as forewarnings, we shall see as we go along.

Iago, on the other hand, is continually holding the door open to hitherto unthought-of possibilities. To Roderigo it is the door to the enjoyment of Desdemona; to Othello it is the door to the unbounded darkness of nightmare. He keeps it open by a dexterous game of rhetoric that includes a game of false logic. He manipulates events so that his conclusions seem to follow on the conditions he has pointed to. The "seem" is important, because there is never a necessary relation between Iago's arranged and predicted condition, and the conclusion supplied. He works by false enthymemes, arguing from a sign that seems a true one but is not.[3] He traps Othello by the fallacy of multiple cause and can do it because, having suggested the cause he wants believed, he can then bring off the effect he has foreseen. Interestingly enough, Iago does not think too precisely on the event either. The conditional possibilities he phrases for himself are simply the confident opportunist's, with only an immediate consequence seen: If I can do this, so much will be done; then we'll see what next. He moves easily up the stairs, one at a time, in a *gradatio* of achieved possibilities: "If this poor trash of Venice . . . stand the putting on"; "If I can fasten but one cup upon him"; "If consequence do but approve my dream" (II.i.312–13; iii.50, 64). It always does—or almost.

The two fundamental conditions of the story, the given ones with which we start, are Iago's revengeful hatred of Othello, and

Othello's and Desdemona's love of each other. The drama is to be built out of the drive of the hatred to destroy the love, beginning with the antagonist's cry of "poison his delight" (I.i.68), and ending with the agonist's destruction of his wife and of himself.[4] Two other conditions are also given in the story, and it is with the leverage they give the villain that he operates against the hero. The first of these complicating conditions is the disparity between Othello and Desdemona—in race, nation, age, social background, and experience: between Othello the black Moor, in middle years, a soldier of fortune with an adventurous, far-traveled past, an "extravagant and wheeling stranger," and Desdemona the fair Venetian, "a maiden never bold," young, homekeeping, and innocent. The second complicating condition is the position and character of Cassio, the handsome and gracious young Florentine whom Othello trusts, whom he has promoted over Iago to the vacant lieutenancy, and who, we later learn, was an intermediary between him and Desdemona in his wooing. Iago's game begins by opening up the possibilities of doubt which would seem to lie in the disparity between Othello and Desdemona—doubt, that is, of the quality and permanence of their love. His first move against Othello, by slander and through Desdemona's father, does not work. But then, by bringing in the second condition, the attractiveness and familiar manners of the youthful Cassio, and by linking it with the doubts already raised about the strangeness of the marriage, he wakens a destructive jealousy in Othello and successfully makes him the agent of his own ruin.

Conditional sentences in asseverative form, set as they are in the frame of unqualified declarative sentences, mark with strong emphasis at the beginning of the play the given conditions of love and hate. Then, in varying forms, conditional sentences mark the entry and manipulation throughout the play of the complicating conditions. We shall examine the most crucial ones to observe how they operate with the movement of the action[5]—with Iago's undermining thrusts at Othello's peace and with the movement of Othello's mind from certainty to doubt of Desdemona's love, next, to certainty of her disloyalty (the false certainty which leads to murder), then back quickly through doubt of his cause to the final certainty of her love and of his irretrievable mistake. Every move to the catastrophe is marked by a conditional—an *if,* a *when,* a *but that.*

The play falls into three major movements, to which we may give the old grammarians' terms of *protasis, epitasis,* and *catastrophe.*[6] The protasis, or presentation, comprising the first act, lays down the initial circumstances of the story, introduces the principal characters, emphasizes the opposition of Iago to Othello out of which the drama will grow, and prepares the ground for Iago's future operations. The epitasis, or intensifying of the action, comprising the second, third, and fourth acts, ties the knot of complication, with Iago breaking Cassio and moving Othello to the point of murder. The catastrophe, or overturn, comprising the last act, brings the tragic consequence in the murder of Desdemona, the recognition by Othello of what he has done, and his suicide.

You will recall how boldly the play opens, not with the hero, but with the villain—the hatred before the love, the Serpent before Adam and Eve. Shakespeare starts the run toward tragedy swiftly and at once. All in the first scene, Iago makes the necessary exposition of circumstances (the promotion of Cassio, the marriage of Othello); states his feeling (hatred), his motive (disappointed ambition), his intent (revenge); adumbrates his future methods of operation (his use of Roderigo as a tool, his initiation of a public disturbance to cause fear and confusion, his rhetoric of innuendo, slander, and affected honesty); and makes his first move against Othello's peace. The two conditional sentences of Iago's which we must not miss are the two in his speech of self-declaration, defining him for us unequivocally:

> It is as sure as you are Roderigo,
> Were I the Moor, I would not be Iago.
> In following him, I follow but myself;
> Heaven is my judge, not I for love and duty,
> But seeming so, for my peculiar end;

For when my outward action doth demonstrate
The native act and figure of my heart
In compliment extern, 'tis not long after
But I will wear my heart upon my sleeve
For daws to peck at. I am not what I am.

                                                    [I.i. 56–65]

Taken together, the obvious condition contrary to fact ("Were I
the Moor") and the imagined condition ("when my outward action . . .") with its preposterous conclusion serve to announce his role
as antagonist, emphasize his absolute difference from the agonist,
and declare in essence what his mode of operation against him
will be. The conditionals are two forms of excluding possibilities;
hence they work to establish certainties. They are emphatic ways
of telling us, the audience, to keep our eyes open to Iago's covert
operations.

In the second scene, when Othello first appears, he also is given
a speech of self-declaration, which may be set against Iago's. Before
we see Othello, Iago has blackened his name in gross obscenities
to Brabantio and has roused a hue and cry after him for his elope-
ment with Desdemona. Before we have witnessed for ourselves
the quality of the love, Iago has obscured it in a murky cloud of
ugliness and doubt. When the outcry moves to Othello's door, it is
quieted by his calm and assured authority: "Keep up your bright
swords, for the dew will rust them"; "Hold your hands, / Both you
of my inclining and the rest" (I.ii.59, 81–82). In the magic of a few
brief sentences Shakespeare creates a figure which, in its simplicity
and dignity, expunges the memory of the leering preface. The sun
shines all the brighter for the clouds which have stained it. In the
same way as his character, the love appears for the first time in
its true and proper light. Iago's speech of self-declaration, for the
audience's sake, is now matched by Othello's:

                              'Tis yet to know—
Which, when I know that boasting is an honour,

> I shall promulgate—I fetch my life and being
> From men of royal siege; and my demerits
> May speak (unbonneted) to as proud a fortune
> As this that I have reach'd. For know, Iago,
> But that I love the gentle Desdemona,
> I would not my unhoused free condition
> Put into circumscription and confine
> For the sea's worth.
>
> [I.ii.19–28]

Othello's parenthesis, ironic in its condition contrary to fact, sets the decent reticence of the man conscious of his own worth against the practical concealment of the double-tongued. Iago, in his busy duplicity, says, "I am not what I am." Othello says that he is what he is.

In the second conditional sentence, the love is affirmed *simpliciter*, without need of description, but in a form which leaves no doubt of its worth. Here is the love and the cost, the choice and the consequence. The expected form of such a condition contrary to fact would be: "If I did not love Desdemona, I would not . . ." But putting the conditional verb in the positive rather than in the negative quite alters the emphasis, places it on the true condition, not the untrue one, marks its acceptance with no undertone of regret, makes the statement imply: "This is the only condition for which I would have paid such a price." The value of both the love and the free life is enhanced. Yet Othello's first words spoken of his love sound, unknown to him, with the dark undertone of prophecy. The cost will be more than anything Othello can imagine.

In this speech, Shakespeare has put for us in other terms than Iago's the unusualness of the marriage. Iago's way of looking at it —as lust on Othello's part, unnaturalness on Desdemona's—is the only one, however, which Desdemona's father can credit. Since his gentle daughter's voluntary part in such a union is unimaginable to him, Brabantio has found a way out in the only condition he

can understand: the use of charms or drugs. He enters soon after
Othello's speech to confront him and order his arrest:

> O thou foul thief, where hast thou stow'd my daughter?
> Damn'd as thou art, thou hast enchanted her!
> For I'll refer me to all things of sense,
> If she in chains of magic were not bound,
> Whether a maid so tender, fair, and happy,
> So opposite to marriage . . .
>
> . . . .
> Would ever have (t' incur a general mock)
> Run from her guardage to the sooty bosom
> Of such a thing as thou—to fear, not to delight.
> Judge me the world if 'tis not gross in sense
> That thou hast practis'd on her with foul charms,
> Abus'd her delicate youth with drugs or minerals
> That weaken motion.
>
> [I.ii.62–75]

Othello is willing to answer, at the proper time.

Brabantio makes his charge formally in an *ad hoc* trial of Othello
before the Duke and Senate of Venice. The episode has, in brief
form, most of the features of a trial: charge, questioning of the
defendant, defendant's reply (including a narrative of his past),
questioning of a witness, dismissal of charges. The syntax is partly
interrogative, but mainly assertive on both sides.

At one point, Othello, requesting that Desdemona be called to
speak for him, solemnly sets his condition against Brabantio's:

> If you do find me foul in her report,
> The trust, the office, I do hold of you
> Not only take away, but let your sentence
> Even fall upon my life.
>
> [I.iii.117–20]

Desdemona's testimony, as candid and unqualified as Othello's in his account of his wooing, settles the matter, and Brabantio must perforce dismiss his charge.

> Come hither, Moor.
> I here do give thee that with all my heart
> Which, but thou hast already, with all my heart
> I would keep from thee.
>
> [I.iii.192–95]

Do we hear an echo of Othello's acceptance of the same condition: "But that I love the gentle Desdemona, I would not . . ."? The same phrasing, but in another key. The same unalterable condition, but with all the difference of meaning, to father and husband, between separation and union. Brabantio's last word also carries a condition: "Look to her, Moor, if thou hast eyes to see. / She has deceiv'd her father, and may thee" (I.iii.293–94). Othello sees the truth now with unaided vision; but Iago will help him readily enough to false glasses. Again, there lies in the condition, unperceived of the speaker, a prodigious irony which time will bring to birth. Othello rightly replies, "My life upon her faith!" (I.iii.295).

This forensic episode is of great importance. Othello has been tried for a supposed crime, and the case has been dismissed for want of evidence. Before the self-evident truth of the love, the charge of unnaturalness has melted like snow in June. The very strangeness between the conditions of Othello and Desdemona which has called the love in question is, given the transparent honesty of the two, the best guarantee of its truth, as, later on, Othello's first, unprompted response to Iago's doubts is to tell him: "She had eyes, and chose me" (III.iii.189).

It does not matter to Iago that he has failed in his first attempt to bring Othello into disrepute. He promises Roderigo to find a way to succeed another time: "If sanctimony and a frail vow betwixt an erring barbarian and a supersubtle Venetian be not too hard for my wits and all the tribe of hell, thou shalt enjoy her"

(I.iii.363–65). These are the terms of the marriage he has seen, or chosen to see, from the beginning. In the soliloquy which ends the act he hits on a hopeful way to break the union apart, by making something of Cassio's charming person and "smooth dispose." The act ends as it began, in an affirmation of Iago's hate, but now with a promise as well: "Hell and night / Must bring this monstrous birth to the world's light" (I.iii.409–10).

Bringing the monstrous birth to light is the business of the epitasis, or second movement of the play, in which Iago moves Othello to a jealous and murderous rage. This long movement is broken into smaller movements, each marking a stage of Iago's maneuverings or of Othello's passion or of both together. But first there is a prelude to the whole. The "high-wrought" tempest which we hear of as the second act opens serves double duty, for it is both a fortunate dismissal of the Turkish threat and an omen of a more dreadful tempest to come in the mind and life of Othello. It is disorder of a huge kind, like the storm in Lear. Yet, the elements "As having sense of beauty, do omit / Their mortal natures, letting go safely by / The divine Desdemona" (II.i.71–73). That we should not miss the portent, Shakespeare makes Othello say, on his finding Desdemona safely landed ahead of him:

> O my soul's joy!
> If after every tempest come such calms,
> May the winds blow till they have waken'd death!
> And let the labouring bark climb hills of seas
> Olympus-high, and duck again as low
> As hell's from heaven!
>
> [II.i.186–91]

For Othello, who knows that after tempests such calms do not always come, the wish is a way of emphasizing the relief of this escape, this happy reunion, the feeling that any hardship or fear would be worth this conclusion. The condition might almost be true. For us, who see Iago standing by, weaving his spider's web for Cassio out of the young man's courtesies to Desdemona, the contrariness to fact is absolute, the wish for another tempest like a defiance of the omens. Another prophetic conditional comes immediately:

> If it were now to die,
> 'Twere now to be most happy; for I fear
> My soul hath her content so absolute
> That not another comfort like to this
> Succeeds in unknown fate.
>
> [II.i.191–95]

This clearly improbable condition with its conclusion in the superlative is a way of acknowledging the joy, the perfection of such a moment—and its rarity, too, for *happy* also means "fortunate." The joy and the fear are complementary. We must take the speech as something like the classical tragic hero's fear of too much good fortune and meant primarily as a warning to us. It is not, as the interchange between him and Desdemona makes clear (II.i.195–201), a pessimistic expectation on his part. It is only Iago and we who must perceive the full truth of the conclusion. As Othello kisses his wife, with the prayer, "And this, and this, the greatest discords be / That e'er our hearts shall make!" Iago promises,

> O, you are well tun'd now!
> But I'll set down the pegs that make this music,
> As honest as I am.
>
> [II.i.201–3]

The first discord Iago creates is another tumult—the drunken fight in the court of guard on the night of their arrival in Cyprus (II.iii). This oblique move, against Cassio, is of course preparatory to the direct move against Othello yet to be made. As Iago considers how to use to his advantage the evening of celebration Othello has allowed the garrison, he states the condition on which he will operate, Cassio's weak head for liquor:

> If I can fasten but one cup upon him
> With that which he hath drunk to-night already,
> He'll be as full of quarrel and offence
> As my young mistress' dog.
>
> [II.iii.50–53]

He can and does, and the consequences follow: Cassio enmeshed in a brawl, Montano the Cypriot governor seriously wounded, Othello scandalized and angry, Cassio dismissed in disgrace from his lieutenancy. In this maneuver Iago has also satisfied a second and larger condition he had mused upon: "If consequence do but approve my dream, / My boat sails freely, both with wind and stream" (II.iii.64–65). Consequences have approved his dream, and Iago's boat is well launched, on course for the larger prize.

Before the scene ends, Iago has arranged, out of the young officer's desperate need to be reinstated, a new condition, that Cassio will ask Desdemona to intercede with Othello for him. Iago's game is to work the condition two ways. To Cassio the argument that if Desdemona speaks for him he will have a better chance with Othello, must be made to seem compelling, and under Iago's persuasion it does. In point of fact, intercession would not have been necessary, for Othello has said, according to Emilia, that he "needs no other suitor but his likings" to reinstate Cassio when he can expediently do so (III.i.50–53). Still, Desdemona's word would have done no harm—far from it. "Let him come when he will!" Othello replies to her first importunings, "I will deny thee nothing" (III.iii.75–76). But of course Iago intends it to do great harm. To Othello the condition "If Desdemona speaks for Cassio" must be made to seem to require the conclusion "she is false to me." The spurious enthymeme must not seem so. Iago's method will be to predict the possibility he knows will happen and at the same time prepare Othello's response to it by supplying ahead of time a false interpretation. Unlike the brawl, the outcome of which had to depend on a certain amount of luck, the new condition he has arranged he can take wholly into his own hands.

The temptation scene opens with Desdemona's promise to help

Cassio, a promise assured by the conditions of her integrity: "If I do vow a friendship, I'll perform it / To the last article" (III.iii.21–22). Iago, entering with Othello in time to see Cassio leave, can now bring out his most cunning tools to work an upheaval in Othello's mind. Recall once again the exchange between the two:

> *Iago.* Ha! I like not that.
> *Oth.*   What dost thou say?
> *Iago.* Nothing, my lord; or if—I know not what.
> *Oth.* Was not that Cassio parted from my wife?
> *Iago.* Cassio, my lord? No, sure, I cannot think it.

The exclamation of surprise, the strong assertion of disapproval, the tentative "if" begin a long and intense dialogue between himself and Othello, a dialogue which occupies more than one scene and which does not end for 672 lines (III.iii.35–IV.i.227). The dialogue is broken by short episodes in which Desdemona's insistent suit for Cassio is renewed and in which the business of the handkerchief is introduced and continued. Each of these episodes supplies Iago with new "evidence" to work with, so that after each interruption the dialogue is resumed with a bolder line and with increased suffering and disorder in the mind of Othello. The whole has three parts: the movement to doubt, the movement to conviction, the movement to proof.

How this whole long movement toward "proof" will end is foretold in Othello's lines of unconscious prophecy, spoken, soon after Iago's "if," as Desdemona leaves with her husband's consent to see Cassio:

> Perdition catch my soul
> But I do love thee! and when I love thee not,
> Chaos is come again.
>
> [III.iii.90–92]

His love of Desdemona, the condition of his life, is twice affirmed in the imagined consequences of its unimaginable negation. Trem-

bling with the burden of our superior awareness, we watch Iago
make his nothing into a seeming something, shape his formless *if*
into a credible phantasm, flesh it out with seeming substance. The
first stage is to awaken an uncertainty Othello cannot stand, to
hint at something monstrous without saying what it is, yet to
prepare for the revelation by little cautionary lectures on reputation
and jealousy. Othello's rising impatience, expressed in a series of
conditionals truer than he knows—"By heaven, he echoes me, /
As if there were some monster in his thought / Too hideous to be
shown" (III.iii.106-8) ; "As if thou then hadst shut up in thy brain /
Some horrible conceit" (III.iii.114-15)—comes to a climax as he tries
to break out of the maddening phantasmagoria:

> Why, why is this?
> Think'st thou I'ld make a life of jealousy,
> To follow still the changes of the moon
> With fresh suspicions? No! To be once in doubt
> Is once to be resolv'd. . . .
>
> . . . .
>
> . . . No, Iago;
> I'll see before I doubt; when I doubt, prove;
> And on the proof there is no more but this—
> Away at once with love or jealousy!
> [III.iii.176-80, 189-92]

But Iago's reminders of the differences between him and his wife
and of Brabantio's warning dash his spirits. This is Iago's moment
to bring out his prediction with its false conclusion:

> Yet, if you please to hold him [Cassio] off awhile,
> You shall by that perceive him and his means.
> Note if your lady strain his entertainment
> With any strong or vehement importunity.
> Much will be seen in that.
> [III.iii.248-52]

The condition of Desdemona's love, the very thing that confirmed it, is being made to seem the negation of it; her innocence and her earlier reluctance to marry are being turned into Venetian subtlety. Othello, feeling himself a stranger in such a world, is at the mercy of Iago's evidently superior knowledge. He promises his own condition of future action:

> If I do prove her haggard,
> Though that her jesses were my dear heartstrings,
> I'ld whistle her off and let her down the wind
> To prey at fortune.
>
> [III.iii.260–63]

With the "If" at the beginning of the dialogue, Iago's muddy stream entered Othello's clear one. The two currents at first ran side by side, not mingling. But now the discoloring has begun and will not end until pollution is complete. Desdemona is later to say, with true observation of the state if not the cause of her husband's troubled mind: "Something sure of state . . . Hath puddled his clear spirit" (III.iv.140–43). Iago puts it differently: "The Moor already changes with my poison" (III.iii.325).

The first half of the temptation scene has brought Othello to doubt. The next brings him to certainty and decision. At the first interruption of the dialogue the sight of Desdemona as she enters clears his mind, and his right impulse makes him say: "If she be false, O, then heaven mocks itself! / I'll not believe't" (III.iii. 278–79). For a breathing space things are stood upright again. But it is the last time they will be. For now Desdemona drops her handkerchief; and Emilia, who finds it, gives it to Iago, with an upside-down condition of fearful import to us:

> *Emil.* What will you do with't, that you have been so earnest
>   To have me filch it?
> *Iago.*   Why, what's that to you?

Emil. If it be not for some purpose of import,
    Give't me again.

[III.iii.314–17]

Now Iago, with the handkerchief in his pocket, begins to shape his obscene phantasm with free and bold invention.

This second half of the scene, the movement to certainty, is different in tone from the first. It is prefaced by Iago's great cue lines for Othello's re-entrance:

Look where he comes! Not poppy nor mandragora,
Nor all the drowsy syrups of the world,
Shall ever medicine thee to that sweet sleep
Which thou ow'dst yesterday.

[III.iii.330–33]

Othello has crossed a bridge into another country. He has begun to inhabit the realm of perdition he spoke of so innocently at the beginning of the scene, and he now looks back to the place he knows forever beyond recovery:

                    O, now for ever
Farewell the tranquil mind! farewell content!
Farewell the plumed troop, and the big wars
That make ambition virtue! . . .

. . . .
Farewell! Othello's occupation's gone!

[III.iii.347–50, 357]

The price of his marriage, once so gladly accepted, is being exacted. While Iago's busy brain continues to invent more ingenious traps and more refined tortures, Othello's moves out into great imaginative reaches of perception and feeling. At one point of intense dramatic irony, he turns on Iago with a possibility that is a true description of Iago's *modus operandi:*

> If thou dost slander her and torture me,
> Never pray more; abandon all remorse;
> On horror's head horrors accumulate;
> Do deeds to make heaven weep, all earth amaz'd;
> For nothing canst thou to damnation add
> Greater than that.
>
> [III.iii.368–73]

But it is a truth he must not be allowed to recognize. With Iago's offended protest that "To be direct and honest is not safe" (III.iii. 378), the moment of insight has passed, and Othello, tortured by a divided mind, calls for proof:

> I think my wife be honest, and think she is not;
> I think that thou art just, and think thou art not.
> I'll have some proof. . . .
> . . . .
>   . . . If there be cords, or knives,
> Poison, or fire, or suffocating streams,
> I'll not endure it. Would I were satisfied!
>
> [III.iii.384–86, 388–90]

The time has come for another of Iago's false enthymemes. He prepares the way for its psychological reception:

> If imputation and strong circumstances
> Which lead directly to the door of truth
> Will give you satisfaction, you may have't.
>
> [III.iii.406–8]

The imputation and strong circumstances he supplies at once in the form of two lies, one the vivid and lewd narrative of Cassio's dream, the other a statement that he has today seen Cassio wipe his beard with the handkerchief Othello had given his wife. "If 't be that—," Othello begins. Iago widens the condition and supplies the plausible but false conclusion: "If it be that, or any that was hers, / It speaks against her, with the other proofs" (III.iii.440–41). Convinced by emotion and false logic, Othello cannot even wait on the possibility: "O, blood, blood, blood!" (III.iii.451). Othello's current must run, if not to love, then to vengeance:

> Like to the Pontic Sea,
> Whose icy current and compulsive course
> Ne'er feels retiring ebb, but keeps due on
> To the Propontic and the Hellespont;
> Even so my bloody thoughts, with violent pace,
> Shall ne'er look back, ne'er ebb to humble love,
> Till that a capable and wide revenge
> Swallow them up.
>
> [III.iii.453–60]

He kneels to make a solemn vow of revenge. This is the moment of decision, from which there is no turning back.

The third stage in this long dialogue is the movement to visible "proof"—that is, to the exhibition of the handkerchief in Cassio's hand. In Othello's mind it is the final movement to chaos. It is preceded by another interlude, this time a discordant antiphony between Desdemona's insistence to Othello that he keep his promise to hear Cassio's appeal and Othello's to her that she fetch the handkerchief. Othello's demand is accompanied by his story of the handkerchief and the grave conditions which possession of it imposes on the owner. The Egyptian who gave it to his mother had told her:

> while she kept it,
> 'Twould make her amiable and subdue my father
> Entirely to her love; but if she lost it

> Or made a gift of it, my father's eye
> Should hold her loathly. . . .
>
> . . . .
>
> To lose't or give't away were such perdition
> As nothing else could match.
>
> [III.iv.58–68]

What wonder that the frightened Desdemona lies, "It is not lost. But what an if it were?" (III.iv.83). What indeed! The rest of the interlude keeps us aware of Iago's legerdemain with the handkerchief, for we see Cassio, who has found it in his room, giving it to Bianca to have the pattern copied.

The dialogue between tormentor and tormented is resumed in a new scene, which is chaos enacted. Under the pressure of Iago's indecent suggestions and perverse *ifs*—"So they do nothing, 'tis a venial slip. / But if I give my wife a handkerchief—"; "What / If I had said I had seen him do you wrong?"—Othello's sentences break down and he falls in a fit: "Lie with her? lie on her? . . . It is not words that shakes me thus.—Pish! Noses, ears, and lips? Is't possible?—Confess?—handkerchief?—O devil!" (IV.i.9–10, 23–24, 35–44). A successful period is put to Iago's manipulation when his condition "If't be that . . ." is fulfilled and he can point out the handkerchief passing between Bianca and Cassio (IV.i.150–67). Othello is torn almost to incoherence with the conflict between what his own experience of Desdemona tells him and what Iago has led him to see.

> Ay, let her rot, and perish, and be damn'd tonight; for she shall not live. . . . O, the world hath not a sweeter creature! She might lie by an emperor's side and command him tasks.
> *Iago*. Nay, that's not your way.
> *Oth*. Hang her! I do but say what she is. . . . But yet the pity of it, Iago! O Iago, the pity of it, Iago!
>
> [IV.i.191–207]

Iago proposes strangling in the bed she has contaminated, he offers to be "undertaker" for Cassio, and the long dialogue is over. A trumpet announces the emissary from Venice, come to call Othello home.

This epilogue to the scene provides Iago with his moment of triumph. After the shocked Lodovico has seen Othello strike Desdemona, Iago hints at Othello's ruin in the fine duplicity of a pious wish:

> He's that he is. I may not breathe my censure.
> What he might be—if what he might he is not—
> I would to heaven he were!
>
> [IV.i.281–83]

This is surely the masterpiece of all conditional sentences.

Although the stage leading to proof has ended, one more scene rounds it out. It is the "gate of hell" scene in which Othello, having viewed with his own eyes the evidence of guilt, interrogates the supposed criminal. It is forensic, like the scene which ended the protasis, although more loosely so. This time the legal procedure of question and answer, statement and denial, is distorted in purpose and operation, for the prosecuting attorney is also the plaintiff and he has no ears to hear the truth. The defendant rests her oath of denial on the condition of a true definition:

> No, as I am a Christian!
> If to preserve this vessel for my lord
> From any other foul unlawful touch
> Be not to be a strumpet, I am none.
>
> [IV.ii.82–85]

In the midst of this cruel process, Othello expresses another of his great poetic insights into experience, yet one dreadfully ironic in the untruth on which it is founded:

> Had it pleas'd heaven
> To try me with affliction, had they rain'd
> All kinds of sores and shames on my bare head,
>
> . . . .
> I should have found in some place of my soul
> A drop of patience. . . .
>
> . . . .
> But there where I have garner'd up my heart,
> Where either I must live or bear no life,
> The fountain from the which my current runs
> Or else dries up—to be discarded thence. . . .
>
> [IV.ii.47–60]

He weighs excluded possibilities against the one which seems to have come into being: If only it had been that, not this!

Emilia has "the office opposite to Saint Peter" and keeps the gate of hell. Part of the dramatic irony with which the scene is saturated comes from her clear-eyed perception and downright statement of the true relations between conditions and conclusions. This logical sequence, spoken in answer to Othello's questioning before the interview with Desdemona, has everything which Iago's *ifs* do not:

> I durst, my lord, to wager she is honest,
> Lay down my soul at stake. If you think other,
> Remove your thought; it doth abuse your bosom.
> If any wretch have put this in your head,
> Let heaven requite it with the serpent's curse!
> For if she be not honest, chaste, and true,
> There's no man happy; the purest of their wives
> Is foul as slander.
>
> [IV.ii.12–19]

And when Othello has left and Iago himself is present, Emilia in a strong asseverative conditional hits the truth precisely:

> I will be hang'd if some eternal villain,
> Some busy and insinuating rogue,
> Some cogging, cozening slave, to get some office,
> Have not devis'd this slander. I'll be hang'd else.
> *Iago.* Fie, there is no such man! It is impossible.
> *Des.* If any such there be, heaven pardon him!
>
> [IV.ii.130–35]

Desdemona's optative subjunctive is counterpointed by Emilia's: "A halter pardon him! and hell gnaw his bones!" Desdemona's own solemn asseveration, in a pitiful appeal to the author of her ruin, follows:

> Here I kneel.
> If e'er my will did trespass 'gainst his love,
> Either in discourse of thought or actual deed,
> . . . .
> Or that I do not yet, and ever did,
> And ever will ...
> ... love him dearly,
> Comfort forswear me!
>
> [IV.ii.151–53, 156–59]

The catastrophe occupies the last long scene of the play. It is foreshadowed poetically by the bedchamber scene: "If I do die before thee," Desdemona says to Emilia, "prithee shroud me / In one of those same sheets" (IV.iii.24–25). Emilia has laid the wedding sheets on the bed, Desdemona sings her forlorn Willow Song, and they talk of the conditions under which women betray their husbands. Emilia would do it if the world were the price; Desdemona, not for the world.

The ground for the catastrophe is cleared by Iago's last maneuverings: his scheming to get Cassio and Roderigo killed (IV. ii.172 ff.)—his last promise to Roderigo ("If thou the next night following enjoy not Desdemona ..." [IV.ii.219–20])—his last con-

ditions of operation ("If you will watch his going thence . . ."
[IV.ii.241–42])—his assessment of alternative possibilities ("Now
whether he kill Cassio, / Or Cassio him, or each do kill the other,
/ Every way makes my game" [V.i.12–14])—his recognition that
his own fate hangs on the success of this last act of violence
("If Cassio do remain, / He hath a daily beauty in his life / That
makes me ugly; and besides, the Moor / May unfold me to him;
there stand I in much peril. / . . . This is the night / That either
makes me or fordoes me quite" [V.i.18–21, 128–29]). The scene
is another one of tumult, of swords clashing in the dark, of
outcries and arrests, like those beginning the protasis and epitasis;
but this time it is a huggermugger. Cassio, though seriously
wounded, escapes with the "daily beauty" of his loyalty unimpaired
to make Iago ugly.

The long last scene falls into three parts: the deed of violence,
the discovery or recognition, and the suicide. The first part opens
with Othello's illumined awareness of the finality of his act of
execution on Desdemona:

> Put out the light, and then put out the light.
> If I quench thee, thou flaming minister,
> I can again thy former light restore,
> Should I repent me; but once put out thy light,
> Thou cunning'st pattern of excelling nature,
> I know not where is that Promethean heat
> That can thy light relume.
>
> [V.ii.7–13]

This is awareness only in idea, clothed in the beauty of metaphor.
When the deed is done—not as it was meant to be, sternly and in
justice, but in rage and violence—it is followed by an anticlimax
of bewilderment about the merely practical question of what to do
next. At this moment, with Emilia's cry, the immediate world is
at the door; reality strikes in the homeliest of ways and is inex-

pressible: "If she come in, she'll sure speak to my wife. / My wife! my wife! what wife? I have no wife" (V.ii.96–97).

Recognition, or discovery, begins with Emilia's insistence on Desdemona's fidelity (V.ii.125 ff.). The recognition Othello has to make is that the monster Iago has shown him, the monster at whose prompting he has killed his wife, has never been anything but a monstrous fantasy, housed in his own mind. The recognition is so bewildering and so damning that he must resist it:

> O, I were damn'd beneath all depth in hell
> But that I did proceed upon just grounds
> To this extremity.
>
> [V.ii.137–39]

This is one of his old forms of asseveration, based on a condition he believes contrary to fact; only now the affirmation is not a promise for the future but a justification of the past. Another follows:

> Nay, had she been true,
> If heaven would make me such another world
> Of one entire and perfect chrysolite,
> I'ld not have sold her for it.
>
> [V.ii.143–46]

The lines are heavy with the nearly unbearable irony that the condition is most true. Do we hear Desdemona's voice saying, as she prepared to lie down on her wedding sheets, "Beshrew me if I would do such a wrong / For the whole world" (IV.iii.80–81)?

But when, with Emilia's testimony about the handkerchief, Othello's awakening is complete, the recognition of the truth is so dreadful that he can imagine only damnation:

> Now, how dost thou look now? O ill-starr'd wench!
> Pale as thy smock! When we shall meet at compt,

> This look of thine will hurl my soul from heaven,
> And fiends will snatch at it.
>
> [V.ii.272–75]

The conjunction is temporal, not an *if* but a *when*. An *if* follows as he makes a wounding, but not fatal, thrust at Iago: "If that thou be'st a devil, I cannot kill thee." The consequence seems to approve the condition.

The *ifs* are over. We are again in a world of fact, monstrous but true. At last a crime has been committed, and it is Othello's. Were he tried, he must this time be found guilty. In place of a trial, we have his last formal speech. It is cast fittingly in the hortatory imperative to express a plea in the strongest possible way: "I pray you, . . . Speak of me as I am. . . . Set you down this; . . . say besides that in Aleppo once, . . ." (V.ii.340–52). Notice that the form of his plea, though imperative, implies a condition: if you tell the truth impartially, without a bias either extenuating or malicious, you will be bound to say these things about me. His hearers must then speak:

> Of one that lov'd not wisely, but too well;
> Of one not easily jealous, but, being wrought,
> Perplex'd in the extreme; of one whose hand
> (Like the base Indian) threw a pearl away
> Richer than all his tribe; of one whose subdu'd eyes,
> . . . .
> Drop tears as fast as the Arabian trees
> Their med'cinable gum.
>
> [V.ii.344–51]

The obligation is placed on us to understand the speech precisely. The relation of the condition to its conclusion is necessary. The truth is this and no other. To read the speech otherwise, with reservations about Othello's motives or the psychology of jealousy, is not to have attended to the syntax of the play in its dramatic functioning. From beginning to end there has been a precise discrimination between the true and false relations of a condition to its conclusion. Iago's monster was created from the false relation. The imperative form of this last speech is an adjuration to Othello's hearers (and to us) to speak of him truly and justly.

But notice that Othello is also declaring something. What his hearers are bound to report are his final affirmations—of his love, his jealousy, his folly, and his remorse. They are the only declarations he can make; the old simple truth cannot be had again. The final declaration in the speech—a report of the act of justice he did on a turbaned Turk—is, with the utmost economy, caught up in the final adjuration that they report the act of justice he does at this instant on himself.

Othello's last sentence is nevertheless simply declarative:

> I kiss'd thee ere I kill'd thee. No way but this—
> Killing myself, to die upon a kiss.
>
> [V.ii.358–59]

Simple as it is, it goes beyond the kiss before the murder and ties the end to the beginning. The tragedy lies all between.

Tragedy in the Spanish Golden Age

C. A. JONES

Not for the first time in the history of criticism of Spanish Golden Age drama, a number of arguments have recently appeared in favor of the claim that the seventeenth century produced examples of the tragic genre among plays which are not actually described as *tragedias,* and notably among plays by Calderón, who did not in fact use the term *tragedia* to describe any of his known works. Of these arguments we may make mention of two in particular, both put forward by British Hispanists.

Professor A. A. Parker in an article published in the *Bulletin of Hispanic Studies* of 1962 under the title "Towards a Definition of Calderonian Tragedy" concluded a study of three plays in particular—*La devoción de la cruz, Las tres justicias en una,* and *El pintor de su deshonra*—with an assertion that Calderón had contrived a new and profound kind of tragedy which linked together the guilt of a central character with a common fund of guilt which was an inevitable part of the human makeup. One long paragraph from the article might serve by way of summary of the most striking part of Professor Parker's argument:

> This linking of dramatic causality with some degree of moral guilt in all the major characters of the play constitutes the centre of Calderón's conception of tragedy. The individual human being must base his judgement and actions on "I and my circumstances"; yet an individual's circumstances are never his own: they are the tangled net of human relationships cast wide in time, a net in which all men are caught up by the inescapable fact that, though individuals, they are cast in a collective mould. The dramatic originality that flows from this sense of human solidarity is to have extended the traditional

conception of tragedy as a catastrophe resulting from a flaw in the character of the individual hero or from an error in his judgement. The flaw is not his alone, there is a flaw in each and every character; each single error trickles down and combines with all the others to form the river that floods the tragic stage of life. No single man has the right to protest in indignation against the unjust suffering that is the lot of humanity, since all men in solidarity together make life what it is. In the Calderonian drama individuals are caught in the net of collective circumstances, in which they cannot know all the facts because they cannot see beyond their individually restricted range of vision. The fact that every single human action is a stone cast into the water of social life, producing ripples that eddy out into unforeseeable consequences, makes it the inescapable duty of each man to look outwards towards other men, and not inwards towards himself. Self-centredness, the self-assertive construction of a private world of one's own, is, for Calderón, the root of moral evil. In his drama, the individual cannot see beyond his restricted range of vision; yet with the confidence born of self-centredness he deludes himself into the belief that his vision is complete and aims at what seems a clear goal, only to blunder into something unforeseen. [P.233]

In 1963, also in the *Bulletin of Hispanic Studies,* Dr. A. I. Watson published an article under the title *"El pintor de su deshonra* and the Neo-Aristotelian Theory of Tragedy." Dr. Watson examined the Calderonian honor play alongside the rehashings of Aristotelian dramatic theory contained in three key works of literary criticism written between 1596 and 1633. These works were the *Philosophia antigua poética* of Alonso López (el Pinciano) of 1596, the *Tablas poéticas* of Francisco Cascales (1617), and the *Nueva idea de la tragedia antigua* by González de Salas (1633). Dr. Watson drew particular attention to el Pinciano's distinction between the *tragedia patética* and the *tragedia morata,* and studied *El pintor de su deshonra* alongside the definition of the former type, attempting to show that Don Juan Roca, the protagonist of the play, was "a tragic hero in the neo-Aristotelian mould" (p. 33), who through some fault (*error* is the word used by López Pinciano as the equivalent of Aristotle's *hamartia*) fell into misfortune.

In 1967, again in the *Bulletin of Hispanic Studies,* appeared Mr. Gwynne Edwards' "Calderón's *La hija del aire* and the Classical Type of Tragedy." He indicates that modern critics, although they have rectified Menéndez Pelayo's omission of the play from the list of Calderonian tragedies, "have also, possibly because they have not gone very deeply into the question, unreservedly presented the work as a classical-type tragedy." Mr. Edwards goes on: "This view is partly true but it is not the whole truth. In this paper, therefore, I propose to examine the traditional tragic elements in the two plays in order, firstly, to suggest how much there is which does not conform to this pattern, and, secondly, to consider, if the first point is established, what significance there is in the juxtaposition of the tragic and the non-tragic" (p. 161). As a result of his close study of the play, Mr. Edwards concludes: "If the broad framework of the play is a Christian one—the virtues of reason are extolled— Calderón places his classical-type tragedy within this framework, suggesting that in the modern, Christian world, man's predicament can be as tragic as it was in the ancient, pagan one. . . . *La hija del aire* is possibly Calderón's most moving expression of man's tragic predicament" (p. 194).

It is with some trepidation that one plunges into the deep waters of genre study in the Spanish Golden Age, knowing that one is about to swim against a strong prevailing current. Nevertheless, Mr. Edwards, in his suggestion that Calderón places his classical-type tragedy within a Christian framework, gives me courage to put my proposition that the concern to trace signs of classical tragedy, or indeed of tragedy at all, may lead us to lose sight of what seem to me the much broader concerns of the Spanish dramatists of the Golden Age (or at least of the seventeenth century) and in particular of Calderón. The articles which I have mentioned are extremely helpful and enlightening studies of Calderón's drama, but it seems to me that they might have been even more helpful if they had not linked their arguments so closely to the term *tragedy*.

It is very likely, as Dr. Watson pointed out in the article from which I have quoted, and as other critics have presumed, that Calderón was acquainted with the work of theorists like Alonso López, Cascales, and González de Salas. It is also undeniable that these theorists were much concerned with the question of tragedy in the Aristotelian sense. It is however true, too, that Calderón stood as the latest in a line of dramatists who consistently rebelled against classical precept, at least in theory, and that Calderón never used the term *tragedia* to describe any of his plays but preferred to use the title *comedia,* even for his most serious works.

To claim that Calderón followed a tradition of rebellion against classical precept is not to say that Lope and his followers owed no debt to the classics, either in precept or in practice. Mr. Duncan Moir, in his essay "The Classical Tradition in Spanish Dramatic Theory and Practice in the Seventeenth Century," has amply proved the extensive survival of classical elements in Spanish Golden Age drama.[1] The important point is that Lope and his followers refused to be bound by classical rules and traditions in their creation of a drama which catered mainly to the audience; and they refused to look over their shoulders at the authorities. Lope's controversial *Arte nuevo de hacer comedias en este tiempo* of 1609 asserts this principle beyond doubt, mentioning among the components of his *comedia nueva* the mixture of "lo trágico y lo cómico," which he praises as being true to nature.

Although Lope's peculiar creation was the *comedia,* he also wrote plays of other types, including at least eleven known works which bear the name *tragedia.* But *tragedia* for Lope was something much looser than what is implied in most of the definitions of the theorists. Edwin Morby has pointed out that "the essentials of tragedy were, for Lope, a serious, non-fictional plot, exalted characters, an elevated style and an unhappy ending."[2] In *El castigo sin venganza,* one of his latest plays, and the last to bear the name *tragedia,* Lope asserted that this tragedy was written "in the Spanish manner, and not in the manner of Greek antiquity and Latin severity, avoiding Shades, Messengers and Choruses."[3] Mr. Victor Dixon, in his review of my edition of *El castigo,* comments that this "truculent *advertencia* . . . suggests . . . that he meant it to be compared, favourably, with the best classical models; perhaps, even, that in writing this least unclassical of his plays he was consciously challenging the ancients on their own ground (rather as in half-a-dozen comedies he shows that he can very well employ the Unities when he pleases)" (p. 190). It is true that Lope may have been hitting at the Valencian tragedians and at other traditionalists like Cervantes (as far as drama was concerned) rather than at the ancients; but his "Spanish style" could hardly be said to diverge from that of his predecessors and contemporaries in the direction of neo-Aristotelianism. If Lope was moving toward a new style of tragedy and not merely moving away from tragedy or an out-worn conception of it, it is somewhat surprising to find that his followers chose to ignore the term *tragedia,* even if they continued something like the serious tone of *El castigo sin venganza.* If, as Mr. Dixon suggests, we have in this play "a foreshadowing of what was to be, consciously in Calderón—as Professor Parker has argued —a profound conception of the nature of human tragedy" (p. 191), then it is strange that Calderón did not use the term *tragedia,* any more than Tirso did in serious plays like *El burlador de Sevilla* or *El condenado por desconfiado,* for which the all-embracing term *comedia* suffices.

The *comedia nueva* of Lope, as we have said, envisaged a mixture of both comic and tragic elements. An earlier definition of the *comedia,* indeed possibly the first, was that of Torres Naharro who, in the *Proemio* to his collection of plays called the *Propalladia,* of 1517, wrote of the *comedia* as a series of notable events, ending happily.[4] It may well be that Lope, having the implications of this definition in mind, felt it necessary to distinguish plays which ended unhappily from the *comedias* and that he simply found *tragedia* to be the most convenient term, although one which might

lead to misunderstandings, since it had been used much more deliberately by the Valencians and by playwrights like Cervantes and
Juan de la Cueva, and had become associated with the "Shades,
Messengers and Choruses" referred to in the Prologue to *El castigo
sin venganza*.[5]

It is certainly interesting that Calderón chose to ignore the term
and that among his contemporaries and followers, Rojas Zorrilla,
whom Professor Raymond R. MacCurdy considered to be the only
true writer of tragedy of his age,[6] used it to refer to what is certainly a very different kind of play from most of Calderón's serious
works. For these more serious works Calderón found the term
comedia still sufficient; and it is surprising that if, as has been
claimed, he was preoccupied with the problems which exercised
the neo-Aristotelian theorists who wrote about tragedy or with a
new conception of tragedy, he should not have wanted to use the
term *tragedia* and should instead have been content with the older
broad and indeed loose term.

For me there is only one explanation, namely, that as a dramatist at least, Calderón followed the tradition associated with Lope de
Vega, a tradition which looked to the audience rather than to the
rule book. *Tragedia,* which Lope had used occasionally, was a
term too closely associated with a classical formula; and Lope himself had tried to dissociate his own use of the term from its classical
implications. The neoclassical theorists, however different from
the sixteenth-century tragedians, were still concerned with formulae, and therefore of little interest to a working dramatist like
Calderón, who preferred the term which was now accepted for the
audience-oriented theater.

To claim that Calderón was more concerned with his audience's
reaction than with the rules of drama is not to minimize the seriousness of his intention. Indifferent rather than hostile to formulae,
like most of the dramatists from Lope on, Calderón was nevertheless vitally concerned with the manner of presentation in all its
aspects, as well as with the matter of his plays. A serious Christian,

he called all the arts of stagecraft as well as of rhetoric to his aid in the writing of plays which were intended to instruct as well as entertain, indeed to instruct by entertaining.

Aristotle wrote of the "tragic pleasure," and the strange term *deleite* appears in the writings of the principal theorists of the Spanish Golden Age. Pinciano explains that the *deleite* comes to the tragedy from the pity of the audience and that it cannot have it unless the actor appears to be very passionate.[7] I have suggested elsewhere that Calderón, like the modern German dramatist Brecht, although starting from a very different standpoint, was equally unwilling to accept a kind of drama where the feelings of the audience were so engaged by the action that thought was suspended and subsequent action inhibited.[8] Brecht's opposition to the "Aristotelian" drama led him to adopt the *Verfremdung,* or "alienation technique," which is one of the most obvious characteristics of his theater. Calderón did not in the nature of things have to contrive such elaborate devices as Brecht to break the illusion of reality which could absorb the emotions and dull the will; but one suspects that he would not have been satisfied to have his audience feel *deleite* and leave it at that. For this, if for no other reason, it seems to me that Calderón would not have found attractive the theories about tragedy propounded by the neoclassicists.

Professor Parker is much nearer to the truth when he writes in "Towards a Definition of Calderonian Tragedy" that "the human world, as Calderón presents it, is not one to arouse in us any exaltation; his view of the human predicament is not a heroic but a sad one" (p. 236). But I should go further and say that not only do we not experience the sense of exaltation often associated with tragedy, but that we do not experience the *deleite,* or involvement of emotion which Aristotle and his followers have consistently associated with tragedy. The "sadness" is not an emotion so much as a reaction of the reason to the events and characters presented on the stage. We do not feel "sorry for" the protagonists of Calderón's honor plays, any more than we feel exalted by their fate. We may reflect on their character, their fate, and the beliefs and circumstances which brought such men and women to such a fate; but if we merely praise or blame them, if we feel glad or sorry at their fate, if we praise or condemn their beliefs, or rejoice in or deplore their circumstances, we are being satisfied with something less than the dramatic whole which the playwright offers for our entertainment, but ultimately for our instruction.

Professor Morby, in "Some Observations on *Tragedia* and *Tragicomedia* in Lope*,*" quotes Aldous Huxley's remark in *Music at Night:* "Tragedy is chemically pure. . . . To make a tragedy the artist must isolate a single element out of the totality of human experience and use that exclusively as his material." Morby comments: "The tragic artist is not interested in the whole truth. A small portion only concerns him" (p. 204). The accuracy of these observations seems to have been borne out by Mr. Edwards' examination of Calderón's *La hija del aire,* which leads him to the conclusion that "if the broad framework of the play is a Christian one—the virtues of reason are extolled—Calderón places his classical-type tragedy within this framework, suggesting that in the modern Christian world man's predicament can be as tragic as it was in the ancient, pagan one" (p. 194). This is surely the right emphasis, to see tragic elements in a kind of drama which is broader than tragedy, a genre which, for all the dignity conferred upon it by Aristotle and his followers, is less than the "whole truth," in Huxley's terms. It is surely no slight upon Golden Age Spanish drama to claim that its creators were more interested in the "whole truth" than they were in the creation of tragedy.

Shakespeare's Dark Vocabulary

PAUL A. JORGENSEN

One of the most quietly dramatic beginnings of any scholarly article was that of Alfred Hart, writing in *The Review of English Studies* in 1943: "When I decided to count the words in each play and long poem of Shakespeare . . ." As was Mr. Hart, I am grateful for the concordances, old, recent, and forthcoming; but for my purpose, the sketching out of a prevalent kind of vocabulary, it seemed best to count, mainly because only counting while reading could make me fully aware of the dramatic weight and meaning of each word. However, the latest concordances will certainly make possible a statistical reliability not claimed for this tentative essay. One needs to know, for example, percentages and fuller lexical contexts. It is to be hoped that scholars better trained than I in statistics will pursue this subject with the full resources of the computerized concordances. I suspect, however, that subjectivity in vocabulary studies, as in textual editing, will always be partially necessary.

My concern in this essay has been to ascertain the quantity, the kind, and the variety of what, for me, constitute the "dark words" in three of Shakespeare's tragedies: *Titus Andronicus, Hamlet,* and *Macbeth.* There are many possible notions of dark words and how they may help to create and define the quality of tragedy in a play. It may even be contended that apparently pleasant words, words of brightness, contribute to darkness of effect. I have rather arbitrarily chosen words that fit into the following categories: words of dread atmosphere, of torment of body, of torment of mind, of death, and of opprobrium. Several years ago I had studied single key words in several plays. Now it seemed inviting to investigate larger segments of the tragic vocabulary, in order to correct the inevitable oversimplification that resulted from my earlier study. But only a fuller investigation than the present one will bear out my conviction that it is the vocabulary, even more than the imagery, that tells us what a play is about. In most cases, I find, the nature of the vocabulary reinforces our preconception of the play, though in so doing it tells us something new about how Shakespeare achieved the effect that we have accepted.

My method of presentation, involving much listing of words, will not make for good reading, but I trust that it will be conducive to reflection by others who share my devotion to Shakespeare's words. Nor, I would re-emphasize, can I claim the strictest of statistical accuracy. With so many words, there will be numerical errors, differences of opinion and text, and even some important words ignored. To avoid endless lists, I have simplified most of the variants of a word to one form, usually the most common. Thus, *blood, bloody, bloodier, bloodiest,* and *bleed* all become *blood.* This is similar to the method used by Josephine Miles in her numerical studies of the vocabulary of poetry. There are also problems of classification. Words are, at heart, images and are perhaps even more difficult to categorize without doing harm to their subtlety, range, and ambiguity. I have had to lump together all uses of *blood,* even though it may mean gore in *Macbeth* and may have more frequently a figurative meaning in *Hamlet.* I am also limited by the plays I have chosen. These are meant to be illustrative only, though they do represent early, early-middle, and mature Shakespearean tragedy, and being Senecan, are comparable. One final note about method: after each word I have put in parentheses its frequency in the play being discussed. The prominent words tend of course to be those most frequently used. On the other hand —and this is one service that cannot be obtained from concordances —an important idea or feeling may be achieved almost as effectively from a large number of near synonyms as from the repeated insistence upon one word. Furthermore, it is the range and precision of the vocabulary rather than the monotonous, though strong, single word that attest Shakespeare's development in the vocabulary of tragedy.

If one can trust vocabulary, the atmosphere of *Titus Andronicus* is one of singular gloom, an ominous, fatal cheerlessness. Characteristic words creating the mood are *baleful* (2), *chilling* (1), *dire* (3), *dismal* (5), *dread* (7), *dreary* (1), *fatal* (5), *forlorn* (3), *gloomy* (1), *joyless* (1), *pale* (4), and *sad* (9). *Dismal* is particularly suggestive, since it not only had its modern sense of "dreary," but more strongly connoted, in its etymological sense of *dies mali*, something fatal or ill-boding. *Blood* (38) is a much more prominent word and doubtless contributes to the atmosphere, but I do not feel that it can alone outweigh the widely dispersed vocabulary of a more abstract dismalness.

Suffering, as Bradley noted, is an indispensable part of Shakespearean tragedy. There is a danger of oversimplification but also an essential usefulness in dividing the suffering into physical and mental. As would be expected, *Titus Andronicus* is strong in torment of the body; indeed, I doubt whether the range of its vocabulary of physical affliction is matched elsewhere in Shakespeare. What is more, it is remarkably specific for Shakespeare's first tragedy. There are words of general force, such as *afflict* (3), *hurt* (3), *torment* (2), *torture* (1), and *wound* (10); and there are words of a more specific violence like *beat* (5), *bind* (6), *blind* (3), *break* (7), *burn* (8), *pluck* (4), *scar* (3), and *strike* (9). But the words of physical torment are generally expressive of the two important themes in the play, mutilation and rape. Mutilative words are so specific as almost to recall to the student the context in which they occur: *carve* (1), *chop* (3), *cut* (11), *grind* (2), *hew* (3), *lop* (2), *mangle* (1), *mash* (1), *rend off* (1), *tear* (2), and, one of the most gruesomely apt, *trim* (3). There are only two words for rape: *rape* itself (14) and *ravish* (8), but their incidence is sufficient to verify that the play is insistently concerned with this form of bodily outrage, ironically suggestive of fertility in a loveless, barren world of dismemberment.

There is not, predictably, so rich a vocabulary of mental suffering in this early play, even though Shakespeare seemingly tried to depict it. The trouble is surely that the physical suffering is overwhelming. Many of the words of mental suffering are prompted by the physical. These are generally not words that depict a highly cerebral or philosophical reaction. Typical are *grief* (15), *groan* (3), *heavy* (6), *lament* (6), *misery* (9), *mourn* (3), *rue* (2), *sad* (9), *sigh* (15), *sorrow* (29), *tears* (42), *weep* (15), *woe* (18), and *wretched* (6). The prominence in dramatic action of tears and weeping is clearly indicated, as well as a monotony, dangerous to the play, of woe and sorrow. But there are two somewhat more specific kinds of affliction. From the dismal atmosphere we should expect fear, and we get it: *fear* (18) and *terror* (2). The other specific affliction is madness, in large part a result of intolerable physical torment. The vocabulary of madness, as elsewhere in Shakespeare, is limited: *frantic* (3), *frenzy* (2), *mad* (13), and *lunacy* (1).

For the subject of death, obviously secondary to suffering in this play but still important even for a Shakespearean tragedy, there is a limited vocabulary; but the few words are abundantly used. Since the subject of burial is initially important, one expects and finds *bury* (17), *funeral* (20), and *grave* (3). The rest of the death vocabulary is, surprisingly, just about as strong for death itself as for killing. This is not, like *Hamlet,* a play philosophically interested in death, yet one finds the following incidences: *dead* (23), *death* (27), and *die* (21). The vocabulary for killing is more varied, but not rich: *butcher* (1), *execution* (3), *hang* (9), *kill* (19), *murder* (25), *sacrifice* (4), *slay* (4), and *slaughter* (4). One word, *broach* (1), stands out with the grim humor of *trim.* There are not generally, however, the kinds of violent words that Shakespeare might have been expected to seek to match the vocabulary of physical torment. But the dramatist never quite got away from his heavy reliance on *murder.*

The language of opprobrium is more important in assessing the meaning of a tragedy than criticism has so far recognized. This is particularly true of a play in which evil is so overwhelming as to need vivid description and rebuke; and it is even more so in a villain-play. What is repeatedly labeled as badness is likely to be the evil in the play. But one must always be aware in a Shakespeare villain-play that the opprobrious words are often violent rather than specific. Despite his enormous vocabulary, Shakespeare sometimes wasted character and audience indignation by using excessive, general words. *Villain* is a good example.

Titus Andronicus, in which the quality of evil is almost unsurpassed, taxes the early Shakespeare's vocabulary. There is a moderate range of words of sheer loathing: *abhorred* (1), *abominable* (2), *detest* (5), *hateful* (4), and *loathsome* (4). These words suit a world in which there is almost unrelieved hate. There is also a vocabulary, less unified, describing general wickedness: *accursed* (6), *curse* (5), *foul* (10), *heinous* (5), *villain* (24), and *wicked* (3). One cannot, either here or elsewhere in Shakespeare, take *villain* to be a reliably specific label. Even the context seldom makes the word sufficiently meaningful to justify Shakespeare's using it as his most frequent noun of opprobrium. But there are, in *Titus Andronicus,* words that more helpfully define the evil. One group of these, interestingly similar to some he was to use in *King Lear,* is that of words suggesting the inhuman, the beastly: *barbarous* (7), *beastly* (3), *fiend* (2), *inhuman* (2), *monstrous* (3), *ruthless* (2), and *unnatural* (1). Perhaps *abominable* should be included in this category; Shakespeare and his age are sometimes inclined to the false etymology suggested by *abhominable. Black* (11) also may belong. It has of course mainly a color significance in this play and commonly denotes the barbarous. An unexpected group of specific opprobrious words is *traitor* (10), *treacherous* (1), and *treason* (4). These are explainable, as they would be in *Richard III,* only as coming from the villain as ruler.

Even though *Titus Andronicus* is a short play and does not have a large vocabulary, it does demonstrate, especially for its major ideas and actions, a fair number of dark words. Doubtless a study of its other kinds of vocabulary would show a corresponding paucity. But, I suspect, this paucity was not due mainly to any lack of words within Shakespeare's control. Rather, the vocabulary is ideally suited to the monotonously dismal and brutal atmosphere of the play.

Hamlet is at once Shakespeare's longest play and the largest in vocabulary. And though it is a tragedy, it has not the uniformly tragic temper of *Titus Andronicus,* and hence a study of its dark words cannot do justice to Shakespeare's increased articulateness. Still, however, amidst a brilliant diversity of other words, there will be found a reluctance to abandon many of the favorite stereotypes of tragic vocabulary: *mad, murder, tears, villain,* and *weep.*

Under the subject of atmosphere, it would be natural to take up the words of disease, since these, like the images classified by Caroline Spurgeon, are a major ingredient in the tragic overcast; but it has seemed more accurate to consider disease under the subject of bodily suffering. This procedure serves to make more emphatic the quality which the vocabulary of the play indicates, contrary to most interpretations of imagery and theme, to be dominant. This quality can best be expressed by one of the frequent words, *danger* (8). But so various is the vocabulary of *Hamlet* that no single word, with one possible exception, is employed to express iteratively the idea of danger. Rather, it is more emphatically and disturbingly forced upon our emotions by words that suggest the different guises of the subject, words of impetuosity, passion, haste, violence, and lack of control: *accident* (5), *amiss* (2), *burn* (7), *dare* (7), *desperate* (6), *excitements* (1), *fiery* (3), *fire* (3), *flash* (2), *haste* (14), *impetuous* (1), *mutine* (2), *ominous* (1), *outbreak* (1), *passion* (12), *perilous* (1), *rage* (4), *rash* (5), *savageness* (1), *splenitive* (1), *threaten* (3), *turbulent* (1), *unbated* (1), *violence* (7), and *wild* (6). None of these words, except the predictable *passion,* is used a sizable number of times, but the total effect is unmistakable, and reflection will quickly show that danger (not of course the murky foreboding of *Macbeth*) is a dominant part of the play's emotional atmosphere. The danger is concentrated, if we accept the point of view of almost every one of the dramatis personae, in the person of Hamlet. Though he is more frequently referred to as "mad," the court sees him above all as dangerous, and it is as such that Claudius repeatedly refers to him. But in a larger sense the entire play is tense with danger, from the anxious, frightening air of the first scene, through the menace of Hamlet, with his combination of rashness and intelligence, through the suave menace of Claudius, and through the fiery activity of Laertes. The sense of danger is heightened by the theme of revenge and its vocabulary, with thirteen uses of *revenge* and two of *vengeance.*

The atmosphere of danger results in, and is enhanced by, a mood of fear. There is not so much fear as in *Macbeth,* but the vocabulary of *Hamlet* suggests that fear is thematically more important than we have heretofore recognized—probably in performances as well as in criticism. Typical words are *afeard* (1), *affrighted* (1), *afraid* (1), *amaze* (1), *astonish* (1), *cold* (6), *dread* (8), *fear* (25), *frighted* (1), *quake* (1), *start* (5), and *wonder* (3). Here again the vocabulary is various rather than concentrated. There is not an overstatement of the emotion, with strong words like *horror* which we shall find in *Macbeth.*

The vocabulary of physical suffering is understandably not so violent or so interestingly specific as in *Titus Andronicus.* There is, however, a minimum of general terms: *afflict* (3), *pain* (1), and *torment* (1). More specific are words suggesting incision in the body: *bite* (1), *blister* (1), *blow* (2, excluding *blowing*), *cut* (2), *mince* (1), *nip* (1), *prick* (2), *sting* (2), and *tent* (1). These are not, I think, thematically significant, though they do underline the minor harassments of life that Hamlet feels. A more agitative kind of torment, suited better to the world of *King Lear* than to *Hamlet,* is expressed by words of larger, brutal violence: *grunt* (1), *lash* (1), *pluck* (3), *shock* (1), *smite* (1), *tear* (2), *whip* (4), and *wring* (2). These are mainly Hamlet's words and perhaps are a good clue to his sense of outrageous life.

But the body in *Hamlet* is tormented more by sickness than by bites or blows. *Disease,* however, is used only three times, and *sick* (7) is not much more prominent. It is in the more specific symptoms that the play is impressive. Many of the words of disease bear out Miss Spurgeon's conclusions about corruption in the body, the concealed cancer. But there are almost equally important disease words denoting external rottenness, principally of an infection which suggests the plague. Through his vocabulary of disease,

Shakespeare was picturing, even more precisely than in his imagery, a sick and infectious society. Some of the typical disease words are *apoplex'd* (1), *canker* (2), *contagion* (2), *corrupt* (4), *eruption* (1), *imposthume* (1), *infect* (3), *leperous* (1), *mole* (1), *pestilent* (3), *plague* (1), *rot* (4), *ulcerous* (1), and *unwholesome* (1). None of these is iterative, but there is an impressive array of synonyms for *contagion*.

The vocabulary of mental torment in *Hamlet* is surprisingly not so large as that for bodily affliction, but it has done its work well. Much of this vocabulary is rather general: *dismay* (1), which is appropriately Claudius' word; *distress* (1), with equal appropriateness applied to Ophelia; *groan* (3); *grunt* (1); *harrow* (2); *heartache* (1); *heavy* (4); *moan* (1); *mope* (1); *oppress* (3); *pangs* (1); *thought-sick* (1); *tristful* (1); *trouble* (4); *woe* (6); and *wretched* (4). It is a vocabulary of suffering, descriptive of passion rather than action. This tendency is extended by the vocabulary of grief, the passion which according to Lily B. Campbell dominates the play: *grief* (16), *lament* (1), *tears* (9), and *weep* (4). I do not find that the vocabulary of grief in *Hamlet* is demonstrably larger or richer than that in *Titus Andronicus*. Rather than grief, the mental state which the vocabulary shows to be most prominent is madness, even though, as with *Titus Andronicus,* the vocabulary is concentrated rather than diversified: *distemper* (4), *ecstasy* (3), *lunacy* (2), and *mad* (40). *Mad* is perhaps the most prominent word (except for Hamlet's own name) in the entire play, and its repeated use should give pause to critics who would disparage psychology in interpreting the play. On the other hand, of course, Shakespeare's age had, except for the humors, a relatively limited vocabulary for mental pathology.

As one reads through *Hamlet* looking for repeated words, the complex of *dead* (25), *death* (39), and *die* (13), to take only one example, is persistent and instructive. Probably the subject of death is more important in this play than in any other. But here, as elsewhere in this essay, iteration is not in itself a full index to idea, since too often a usage is wasted upon such a phrase as "dead body" or is subordinated in the gravedigger disquisition. What is significant for our present purpose is that, unlike *Titus Andronicus* and *Macbeth,* the vocabulary indicates that this is a play about death rather than murder, not that the latter is, initially at least, unimportant. One finds the following: *kill* (13), *murder* (18), *slaughter* (3), and *slay* (7). These, however, make a total of forty-one as opposed to eighty-two for the words of death and dying.

The opprobrious words in *Hamlet* are a fair clue to the nature of the evil. Although they come mostly from Hamlet, they are in accord with our other means of insight into the play. One should remember, however, that other characters use words appropriate to them. Claudius, for example, is the principal user of *offense.* Words of general wickedness include the relatively weak *bad* (6), *vice* (2), *vile* (6), *wicked* (6), *wretched* (3), as well as the ubiquitous *villain* (26). A stronger word of abuse, but lacking the literal significance it had in *Titus Andronicus,* is *black* (8). *Damn* (14) is an important word because it so often carries a theological implication. More clearly specific, and easily identifiable with the ideas of the play, are *adulterate* (1), *guilt* (8), *incestuous* (5), *lecherous* (1), *shame* (3), and *treacherous* (3). There are also, though fewer than in *Titus Andronicus,* words that point directly to the inhuman and that are in *Hamlet* expressive of the important antithesis between man and beast: *bestial* (1), *hell* (9), *monster* (3), and *unnatural* (4). The limited number of such words would suggest that there is less emphasis than in *Othello,* for example, upon the fiendish. There are really no monsters in *Hamlet,* and if there is a devil, it is the urbane devil of *Doctor Faustus.* The most important group of specific words for opprobrium turn out to be not those of aggressive wickedness but rather those reinforcing the disease motif. Corruption is the principal evil in *Hamlet,* and this evil is labeled unmistakably and variously by such condemnatory words as *corrupt* (4), *foul* (11), *rank* (7), *soil* (3), *stain* (1), *sullies* (1, excluding *sallies* and the possibility of *sullied flesh*), and *taint* (2). Probably the vocabulary of sex should be added to this list, with words like *nasty sty* and Hamlet's words

of revulsion from woman; but this vocabulary is unusually difficult
to classify. Indeed, it cannot be overstressed that the vocabulary of
Hamlet is not amenable to the extraction of dark words, and that
only a study of the total vocabulary of this play, a play so much
concerned with the full range of life, could do it justice.

Macbeth is a play of complex gloom, and a study of its dark
vocabulary such as the present one will inevitably be only less im-
perfect than that of *Hamlet*. But at least such a study is no more
subjective than those of the image hunters, and may serve to temper
recent assertions based upon imagery. It is true that the imagery, as
has been pointed out by L. C. Knights and F. R. Leavis, is occasionally bright and suggestive of fertility. But even a study of the
play's total vocabulary would not support allowing such imagery,
as Leavis in particular recommends, to contradict what is obviously
the starkly tragic and dark tone of the play and the play's ideas
and actions.

From Dowden to Kenneth Muir, critics have noted that the atmosphere of *Macbeth* is dominated by blood. Muir, in his Arden
edition, goes so far as to cite, without skepticism, the assertion of
Kolbe that the word *blood* is used over a hundred times. This frequency would make it easily the most prominent word, and any
study of the play's meaning based upon vocabulary would have to
utilize this fact in seeking the tragic center of the play. My own
count, however, even if I include *bleed* (6) and *gore* (2), would
give *blood* a frequency of only fifty, making it second to the
vocabulary expressing fear. (Bartlett's count shows a frequency of
only forty-five, and the omission of the Hecate scenes accounts for
but three of the concordance shortages.) Even so, however, blood
is extremely important, for it is not the controlled, metaphorical
blood of *Hamlet,* but a blood that smears, sticks, and smells—what
Leo Kirschbaum has called "stage blood." It is also animated by
words like *reek* (1) and *smoke* (2).

What is more, it is made more hideously prominent, as Bradley
noted, by being set against a dark background, so that it provides
the only illumination in the play. As in *Titus Andronicus,* the

darkness of the atmosphere can best be epitomized in the word *dismal* (3), for this is the word best expressive of the air of joyless foreboding. But there are also *dark* (6), *dunnest* (1), *fog* (1), *hell* (11), and *murky* (1). Probably with *dismal* should be grouped the vocabulary of fatal horror, unusually strong in this play: *deadly* (1), *fatal* (3), *hideous* (1), *horrible* (3), *horrid* (3), *horror* (6), and *terrible* (4). Another powerfully sinister word is *strange* (18), often related in meaning to *strangers* (2). It is a word of alienation, of *strange* in its etymological sense of *"extraneus."* But *strange* also had its modern meaning, and Shakespeare in employing it so prominently, even thematically, perhaps knew that it was a word used in the titles of many of the sinister and sensational books of the time. For example, there was Thomas Day's *Wonderfull Straunge Sightes Seen in the Element* (1583) and an anonymous work, *The Most Strange and Admirable Discoverie of the Three Witches of Warboys . . .* (1593). Within the complex of *strange* in the play should be included such words as *wild* (3) and *wither'd* (2). *Weird* (5), though applied always to the Witches and not having its modern meaning, nonetheless contributes to the effect of something unusual and sinister.

There is also in *Macbeth* an almost uniquely effective use of sound in creating atmosphere. It is a sound which superbly underscores the other effects we have noted. Typical words of sound are *alarum* (3), *bell* (3), *clamor* (2), *cry* (16), *groan* (1), *howl* (3), *knock* (16), *lamenting* (1), *scream* (2), *shriek* (3), *thunder* (3), *uproar* (1), *wail* (2), and *yell* (1). None of these is a pleasant kind of sound. All have in common a disturbing quality, snapping the taut nerves of Macbeth and his lady, and making the audience participate (often by the accompanying stage sound) in a world audible with portent, lamentation, and fright. Probably nowhere else did Shakespeare, with the full resources of language, create so palpably and audibly dark an atmosphere.

There is likewise an impressive vocabulary of physical torment. Only a few of the words are wasted upon general sensation: *affliction* (1), *harm* (7), *suffer* (4), and *wound* (4). Of the more definitive kinds of affliction there is a moderate segment of words denoting blows and beating: *beat* (2), *blow* (2), *break* (5), *buffets* (1), *dash* (1), *pluck* (4), *strike* (8), and *thrust* (1). But these are not thematically significant, except in so far as they contribute to the occasional violence of metaphor in a world almost as agitated as that of *King Lear*. A more predictable kind of vocabulary of agitation is that suggestive of shaking, wrenching, or straining the body: *fever* (2), *fit* (4), *fling* (1), *seize* (2), *shake* (10), *tug* (1), and *wrench* (1). The most numerous and important of these are the words of shaking, mainly from fear but with an added suggestion of fever, and usually with an internal agent of agitation. In the oppressive murk of the world of *Macbeth,* it is understandable that words of suppression and restraint should be used: *choke* (1), *heavy* (6), *smother* (1), and *strangle* (1). But this aspect of the vocabulary will be found more importantly in words of mental rather than physical torment. Probably the most frequently iterated quality of bodily affliction in the play is represented by words of violent incision: *butcher* (1), *carve* (1), *cut* (4), *gash* (5), *hack* (1), *prick* (3), *rend* (1), *rip* (1), *scotch* or *scorch* (1), and *tear* (2). These help to contribute to the play's bloodiness, and are as appropriate as similar words in *Titus Andronicus* in a play writhing with a more sophisticated kind of torture.

The mental torment of *Macbeth* is expressed with a violence probably exceeded only by that of *King Lear* and probably even more impressive if we compare the lengths of the two plays. Its variety shows an immeasurable advance over *Titus Andronicus.* There are many of Shakespeare's favorite words of woe and grief: *care* (2), *distress* (1), *dolor* (1), *grief* (7), *groan* (1), *pine* (2), *sad* (1), *sorrow* (9), *tears* (2), *trouble* (10), *wail* (2), *weep* (3), and *woe* (3). But these are almost lost sight of in relation to the total dark vocabulary.

The more precise words of mental suffering are much more appropriate to the play, and particularly to its protagonist. These words are given an emphasis partly through a group of them that accord with an already noticed quality of bodily torment: they express a sense, almost claustrophobic, of binding, bowing, confining: *bound* (1), *bow'd* (1), *cabin'd* (1), *charg'd* (2), *confin'd* (1), *constrained* (1), *cribb'd* (1), *curb* (1), *entomb* (1), *o'erfraught* (1), *overcharg'd* (1), *trammel* (1), and *weigh* (1). These words apply partly to the oppression of a state under a tyrant, but mostly they are spoken by the tyrant himself. It is he who becomes increasingly "bound in / To saucy doubts and fears." And thus bound in, the forces of agitation become more intolerably vehement. The major kind of agitation is the passion of fear. Word counts suggest that *fear* is even more important to *Macbeth* than *mad* or *grief* is to *Hamlet*. The fear words include *afeard* (3), *afraid* (5), *amaze* (4), *appall* (2), *blanch* (1), *dread* (3), *fear* (44), *fright* (1), *shake* (10), *start* (6), and *tremble* (2). To these may well be added *rapt* (3), with its stronger Elizabethan meaning of *extra se raptus*. There is thus not only the massive iteration of the word *fear* but considerable stress upon the physical (and dramatic) symptoms of the emotion. Other words of agitation are mainly, though not exclusively, expressive of madness or at least a distraught and weary mood: *agitation* (1), *despair* (2), *dismay* (1), *distemper* (1), *distract* (1), *ecstasy* (2), *enrage* (2), *insane* (1), *mad* (4), *mated* (1), *rage* (1), *rancors* (1), *scorpions* (1), *torture* (1), and *weary* (3). It is a good vocabulary of mental suffering; and if we weigh *fear* as it should be, we can with some confidence state that this is the first play we have studied in which such a vocabulary is more impressive than that of bodily suffering.

Word counts bear out our a priori impression that death as a subject is much less important in *Macbeth* than in *Hamlet*. There is a respectable number of the common words *dead* (15), *death* (21), and *die* (12). And there are a few graveyard words like *bury* (1), *charnel house* (1), and *grave* (5). But these are not generally used thematically. Much more interesting, and one of the highest verbal achievements of *Macbeth,* is the vocabulary of murder. These words vary from open violence to sinister or fearful understatement. The words which, usually in Macbeth's mind, honestly confront the horror of murder, are *assassination* (1), *destroy* (5), *execution*

(2), *hang* (9), *kill* (8), *murder* (22), *parricide* (1), *quell* (1), *strike* (7), and *tear to pieces* (1). *Murder* itself is, numerically at least, an influential word. But it is first used prominently by Macduff. The protagonists themselves initially try not to let the eye behold the hand, and their horrified reticence accounts for many of the following, usually euphemistic, locutions for murder: *absence* (1), *business* (5), *cancel* (1), *deed* (12), *enterprise* (1), *exploit* (1), *feat* (10), *surcease* (1), *taking-off* (1), and *work* (1). The bleeding sergeant's ironic "unseam'd" reflects the manly, stolid manner of a soldier and does not belong to the horror-motivated circumlocution of Macbeth.

The vocabulary of opprobrium in *Macbeth* is more various than massively definitive. There is not the emphasis upon *villain* (2) or *villainies* (1), to make this obviously a villain-play. Most of the language both general and specific suggests a wide dispersal of evil throughout a wicked world, by no means limited to Macbeth and his lady. The general words of evil are *abhorred* (1), *accursed* (4), *bad* (1), *black* (7), *deadly* (1), *dire* (5), *disjoint* (1), *disorder* (1), *evil* (3), *fell* (3), *hate* (3), *hideous* (1), *malice* (4), *pernicious* (2), *shame* (4), *sin* (3), *vile* (1), and *wicked* (2). These are not especially definitive for the play or for Macbeth. Words denoting unnaturalness are not varied, but are obviously intended by iteration to be strong: *devil* (10), *fiend* (4), *hell* (11), *monster* (2), *savage* (2), *serpent* (1), and *unnatural* (2). These are words usually applied to Macbeth himself, but one must be wary of overweighting them. Every reader knows that although Macbeth becomes an agent of the instruments of darkness, he often appears to be a not inhuman character who is ensnared by the fiendish actions. Other characters call him *fiend,* but name-calling in this play notoriously fails to satisfy the sympathies of the audience.

This is true to an extent even of the more temperately specific words: *avaricious* (2), *cruel* (6), *damn* (8), *deceitful* (1), *dishonors* (1), *false* (8), *filthy* (3), *foul* (6), *luxurious* (1), *merciless* (1), *rebel* (4), *sudden* (1), *traitor* (6), *treachery* (3), *treason* (6), *tyrant* (15), and *voluptuousness* (1). Of these, only *cruel, damn,* and especially *tyrant* satisfyingly express our more intuitive feeling about Macbeth's sinfulness. Many of the other words, like *merciless,* are of course not applied to the evil of Macbeth. But just as the total imagery of a play is important, so can we learn something from the total dark vocabulary.

However, as has been already proposed, there is a peculiarly sophisticated feature about the vocabulary of *Macbeth*. Evil and torment and murder are well enough named. But even more remarkable in this unusually atmospheric play is what is not said, or what is said only slantingly, with averted eye. By comparison, the manner of Hamlet's "bloody, bawdy villain" seems almost melodramatic. True, Hamlet himself has a taste for "a passionate speech." But there is a quality in the darkness of *Macbeth* that defies a vocabulary study, even as it has made impossible any agreement about the imagery (compare, for example, the sharply divergent views of Caroline Spurgeon and R. A. Foakes, and the wise silence of Wolfgang Clemen). Even so, the dark vocabulary does—more so than discussions of sleep, clothes, and procreation—make us more nearly adequate to appreciating fully Shakespeare's skill with his most important tools: words.

The Comedies of Calderón

KENNETH MUIR

Many recent critics have written on Calderón's tragedies and tragi-comedies; but to his comedies, which constitute a third of his work, comparatively little attention has been paid.[1] Yet Calderón is one of the few dramatists who could be used to support Socrates' opinion, expressed in *The Symposium,* that the poet who excels in tragedy should be equally successful in comedy. No one would pretend that *Les Plaideurs* is worthy to stand beside *Phèdre,* admirable as it is, or that *The Mourning Bride* is a tragic masterpiece. But Calderón's comedies, though poetically inferior to the best of the tragedies, are dramatically very effective, and they were used as a quarry by English and French playwrights in the seventeenth century. Even today, one would expect them to be more acceptable to an English-speaking audience than those tragedies which depend on the code of marital honor prevalent in Calderón's day.

In the present essay I shall discuss a representative selection of the comedies, using my own versions.[2] The comedies lose less in translation than the tragedies inevitably do, if only because in them the intrigue is more important than the poetry.

It is useless to expect from Calderón's comedies the same power of characterization displayed in the best Elizabethan comedies or in those of Molière or Congreve. There are no characters in his plays comparable in stature to Rosalind, Shylock, Malvolio, Volpone, Tartuffe, Alceste, or Millamant. His characters have just enough life to satisfy the demands of his plots, and characters could often be transferred from one play to another without loss in transit. Calderón, indeed, is so careless or so indifferent to this aspect of the art of the dramatist that he uses the same names in play after play. It would be difficult, and pointless, to attempt to distinguish between the dozen characters who are christened Beatriz or Laura or Leonor or Fabio, and the still larger number who are named Don Juan or Ines.

Nor can it be said that Calderón attempts to correct the manners or morals of his age. He does not, like Jonson, satirize avarice; nor, like Shakespeare, self-love or pride; nor, like Molière, hypocrisy or affectation; nor, like Congreve, the coxcombs and the fops. He does not even appear to criticize his jealous heroes and heroines: jealousy is the natural and inevitable result of suspicious circumstances.

Whether Calderón means to criticize the conventions of the age with regard to love and marriage is more debatable. We certainly sympathize with the heroines who manage to evade the vigilance of fathers or brothers, but there is little evidence that Calderón regarded such vigilance as unreasonable. Its function in the plays is generally to prevent the path of true love from being smooth. Yet in *The Phantom Lady (La dama duende),* the libertinism of Don Luis is criticized, at least by implication; and there are some plays in which the code of honor appears to be treated with some irony and others in which he is more outspoken. In *The Worst Doesn't Always Happen (No siempre lo peor es cierto),* for example, Don Pedro seems to be the poet's mouthpiece when he exclaims, in the second scene of the second act:

> Woe to the first who made so harsh a law,
> A contract so unjust, a tie so impious,
> Which deals unequally to man and woman,
> And links our honor to another's whim.

It must be admitted that the "cloak and sword" comedies (*capa y espada*) are all very much alike. Whereas the five comedies Shakespeare wrote between 1595 and 1601 differ widely one from the other, Calderón's formula remains remarkably consistent. He presents us always with the love affairs of two or three couples. There is always a father or a guardian to be outwitted—never a mother—and the lovers are aided by their servants of both sexes. When a male visitor arrives at the house of the heroine, she is compelled to retire to her own apartments. When she goes out, she conceals her face and is often taken for another. Fathers, guardians, and brothers live in perpetual fear that their daughters, wards, and sisters will be compromised. The heroes frequently become jealous when they are driven to believe—usually mistakenly—that they have a rival.

One other limitation of Calderón's comedies remains to be mentioned. It would seem that the verse, though perfectly adequate for its purpose, is seldom poetically distinguished, and it is certainly inferior to the poetry of the tragedies. But this is a matter on which an English reader must hesitate to express an opinion. In any case, this is not a serious limitation, any more than it is with Molière. No one reads *Le Misanthrope* or *Tartuffe* for the poetry.

The supreme quality displayed by Calderón in his comedies is his power to exploit a dramatic situation so as to extract from it the maximum of entertainment. His initial assumptions are often simple enough but they suffice for his comic purposes; the causes of misunderstanding—a sliding panel between adjacent rooms, a veiled lady, the borrowing of a friend's house for an assignation —are less important than the variations he plays on them and the complications which result.

The initial situation in *A House with Two Doors is Difficult to Guard (Una casa con dos puertas mala es de guardar)* is caused by Felix's fear that his sister will be compromised if people learn that his friend, Lisardo, is staying in their house and meeting his sister. He therefore shuts off part of the house and does not allow Marcela to meet his guest. Not unnaturally, Marcela is consumed with curiosity, and she goes for a walk along a road she knows he will take. They meet and fall in love. Anxious to see him again in order to swear him to secrecy, she arranges a meeting in the house of her brother's fiancée, Laura, pretending it is hers. Lisardo imagines he has fallen in love not with Marcela but with Laura, and he is torn between love and the duties of friendship. Felix, finding that a stranger is visiting Laura's house, becomes violently jealous, and Laura is jealous of his former mistress. After numerous additional complications, Laura's father returns unexpectedly, and he assumes that her honor has been compromised.

The characters are all bewildered, but the audience is fully aware of the truth. In this Calderón's method resembles Shakespeare's, who, as Professor Bertrand Evans has demonstrated, never leaves the audience in the dark.[3] We know, but Bassanio does not, that Portia is confronting Shylock; we know, but Orlando does not, that Ganymede is Rosalind; and we know, but Olivia and Orsino do not, that Cesario is a girl. So in *The House with Two Doors* the audience is aware that Lisardo is in love with Marcela and not with Laura; and when he describes to Felix his meeting with the mysterious lady, the audience knows it is the sister that Felix has tried to prevent him from meeting.

Another comedy, *From Bad to Worse (Peor esta que estaba)*, also depends on conventions of honor and propriety. The governor's daughter, Lisarda, knowing that everything she does arouses the comment of her neighbors, goes for walks with her face covered, accompanied only by her maid. She meets a man who calls himself Fabio. His real name is Cesar. Having killed a man in a duel, believing him to be the lover of his mistress, Flerida, he has fled. Flerida, anxious to prove her innocence, searches for him in vain and under the name of Laura takes service with Lisarda. The governor arrests Cesar and sends the veiled lady who is with him at the time of his arrest to his own house, with instructions that his daughter look after her. He thinks that the lady is Flerida, but she is in fact his own daughter, and Lisarda thinks he has recognized her. This is the situation at the end of the first act. Before the end of the play, after many misunderstandings, Cesar marries Flerida, and Lisarda, not without reluctance, agrees to marry Juan, to whom she had been betrothed. Once again, the audience is let into the secret of the various disguises, and the laughter comes from the fact that all the characters on the stage are deluded. Cesar does not know that Flerida is living in the house of Lisarda, nor that she is guiltless. Lisarda and Flerida do not know that Fabio is Cesar. Juan does not know that the woman to whom he is betrothed is in love with his friend, Cesar. The governor does not know that he has arrested his own daughter, and Lisarda does not realize that he does not know.

The best-known of Calderón's comedies is probably *The Phantom Lady*. The heroine is a young widow, Angela, who is confined to the house by her brothers. She slips out with her maid to see the entertainments in the grounds of the palace. There she is seen but not recognized by one of her brothers, Don Luis, who pursues her. She appeals for help to the first gentleman she encounters, Don Manuel, and the two men fight a duel which is interrupted by Angela's other brother, Don Juan. It turns out that Manuel is an old friend of Juan's and that he is to be his guest. Angela's apartment is separated from that of Manuel by a movable panel, unknown to him. Grateful and attracted, she uses the secret entrance to find out more about him. She and her maid rummage through his luggage, purloin a portrait of a lady, presumably someone he loves, and substitute charcoal for coins in his servant's bag. Angela leaves a note by Manuel's pillow. Cosme, the servant, assumes the room is haunted, while Manuel assumes that the veiled lady is Luis's mistress and that there is a secret entrance to his room. This is the situation at the end of the first act.

In the remainder of the play Calderón exploits the situation for all it is worth. Angela's maid blows out Cosme's candle and leaves Manuel holding a laundry basket, thereby giving him the impression that there has been supernatural intervention. Later on, Manuel, returning to fetch some papers, finds Angela in his room. She pretends to be a ghost, but is forced to confess she is a woman when he offers to run his sword through her. She makes an assignation with him in her own room, which he is tricked into believing is far away, as Tony Lumpkin tricks Mrs. Hardcastle in *She Stoops to Conquer*. In the end Manuel has to fight another duel with Luis, and Angela confesses her identity and her love to Manuel. He agrees to marry her, and Juan marries her cousin Beatriz, whom Luis has been pestering with his attentions behind his brother's back.

Mr. Honig is doubtless right in thinking that the play is a criticism of the code of honor and that Angela's stratagem is designed to convert the rule of honor into the rule of love. Her brothers, like Ferdinand and the Cardinal in *The Duchess of Malfi,* want her to remain a widow, wish to confine her to the house, and object when—in the privacy of her own room—she doffs her mourning.[4]

The Phantom Lady is sometimes regarded as Calderón's best comedy and it certainly contains some of his most effective scenes. But the play as a whole is spoiled, as others are not, by a number of loose ends and improbabilities. It is difficult to believe that Manuel, who deduces that his room has a secret entrance, would have no suspicion of the movable mirror. Angela finds a portrait of a lady in his luggage and asks her maid to purloin it, but in a later scene she goes back to Manuel's room to have another look at the portrait, and it is never explained whom the picture represents nor to what extent Manuel's affections are free. At the end of the play he appears to marry Angela to protect her honor rather than because he loves her, and this is somewhat disturbing after we have heard Angela's very beautiful confession of love. Beatriz has quarreled with her father, but we are not told how she becomes reconciled with him, nor how she can marry, apparently without his permission. In the final duel, Manuel disarms Luis, and instead of handing him his sword, allows him to go off to find another—a clumsy device to get him off the stage.[5] Lastly, Luis behaves badly or foolishly throughout the play, but his brother seems quite unaware of his character, while Manuel speaks of him in the most flattering terms. It would seem that Calderón, who wrote an enormous number of plays, was here guilty of some carelessness.

Another comedy, *The Secret Spoken Aloud (El secreto a voces),* depends on the use of an ingenious code by which two people can convey a message without those not in the secret being aware of it. The first words of each line of verse convey the secret message, while the meaning of the whole lines is quite innocent. This suggests that the delivery of the verse, here unrhymed, must have been somewhat formal, the line divisions being distinctly marked.

One of the best plays, *The Advantages and Disadvantages of a*

Name (Dicha y desdicha del nombre), violates the unity of place, the first two scenes being set in Parma and the remainder of the play in Milan. Felix offers to take the place of his friend Cesar in carrying an official letter to the Prince of Urbino at Milan, so that Cesar can keep a rendezvous with the woman he loves, Violante. Felix takes Cesar's name, delivers the letter, rescues a woman, Seraphina, from abduction during the carnival, and is given hospitality by her father, Lidoro, who knew Cesar's father. Felix does not know that the daughter of the house is the woman he rescued. Nor does he know that the would-be abductor, Lisardo, is determined to kill Cesar, who had killed his brother in a duel. Cesar arrives in Milan and is arrested under the name of Felix, and by the end of the second act Seraphina also arrives, searching for Cesar, who thinks wrongly that she has betrayed him to an ambush. Everything turns out right in the end. The various misunderstandings are cleared up, the fathers agree with some reluctance, to the marriage of their daughters, and only the unpleasant Lisardo is deprived both of his vengeance and of his love.

A last example of Calderón's plotting, *The Worst Doesn't Always Happen,* is concerned with the theme of deceptive appearances. Carlos, finding a man hiding at night in Leonor's room, naturally assumes the worst; his friend, Juan, seeing a man leaving his house in the darkness, assumes that his sister Beatriz has a secret lover. The plots are linked by the fact that Carlos, still loving Leonor, has arranged for her to take service with Beatriz and by the fact that Leonor's supposed seducer, Diego, is in love with Beatriz. After many misunderstandings and complications—the arrival of Diego and of Leonor's father, the hiding of Carlos in Juan's house, and what appears to be proof of Leonor's continued guilt—Beatriz and Carlos are persuaded by Leonor's obvious dislike of Diego and by their refusal to marry that appearances were deceptive, that the worst is not always certain.

It is fairly easy to illustrate the ingenuity of Calderón's plotting, though one would have to examine a play scene by scene to demonstrate fully his skill as a playwright; but it is less easy to suggest in translation the liveliness and variety of the dialogue. The humor of his comic servants is a bit repetitive, but in the conversation between his nobly born characters he is remarkably successful. The main difficulty of translating his plays is that they are mostly written in octosyllabic verse, much of it unrhymed; and this is a form which is difficult to naturalize in English. The normal form used by English dramatists in Calderón's day was, of course, blank verse, and this seems the natural medium for a modern translation.

The first passage is taken from the first scene of *A House with Two Doors,* where Marcela encounters Lisardo and neatly mocks at his high-flown compliments by using the same similes:

> *Lisardo.*   Madam, the sun
>   Could hardly stop the heliotrope from turning
>   Toward its light; the polar star could hardly
>   Prevent the magnet from pursuing it,
>   Nor would it be less difficult for the magnet
>   To stop the steel from being attracted by it.
>   Then if your brightness equals that of the sun,
>   I'm like the heliotrope; if your indifference
>   Is like the polar star's, then my regret
>   Is like the magnet's; and if you are harsh
>   Even as the magnet, then my eagerness
>   Is like the steel's. Then how can I remain
>   Contented, when I see my sun depart,
>   My polar star, my magnet, I who am
>   The heliotrope, the magnet, and the steel.
> *Marcela.* But sir, the sun each evening disappears
>   And leaves the heliotrope; and every morning
>   The northern star departs and leaves the magnet;
>   Then if the sun and northern star may go,
>   You have no better reason to complain
>   At my departure. You should tell yourselves
>   For consolation, Sir Heliotrope or Sir Magnet,
>   That there is night for the sun, day for the star.

Another passage from the third scene of the first act of the same play is a good example of one of the frequent quarrels between lovers. Felix tries to explain to Laura that she has no reason to be jealous of Nise, with whom he had once been in love:

Felix.　　　By heaven above,
　　Whether you are annoyed or merely jealous,
　　You have to hear me now, before I say
　　Farewell for ever.
Laura.　　　　You'll go away at once
　　If I do listen?
Felix.　　　Yes, I will.
Laura.　　　　　　Well, speak
　　And then be off.
Felix.　　　　Should I attempt to deny
　　That I loved Nise . . .
Laura.　　　　　　Kindly stop at that.
　　If you have nothing else to say to me,
　　It's useless to proceed. I was expecting
　　A thousand courteous protestations, true
　　Or false—for sorrows are consoled by lies—
　　I thought you'd give a thousand more assurances
　　Of infinite fidelity, of an attachment
　　Absolute, exclusive and unalterable,
　　And then you throw the confession in my face
　　That you have loved her. Does it not strike you, sir,
　　That while you think to appease me, you are still
　　Insulting me?
Felix.　　　Why won't you let me finish?
Laura. What! Sir, you think you can excuse yourself?
Felix. Without a doubt.
Laura.　　　[*aside*] May love permit it!
Felix.　　　　　　　　Hear me!
Laura. And afterwards you'll go?
Felix.　　　　　　Yes.

Laura.   Very well. Speak
     And then be off.
Felix.   It would be foolish of me
     To say I did not love her once; more foolish
     For you to imagine that my love for her
     Had any likeness to my love for you.
     No, it was not a genuine love, but merely
     A kind of apprenticeship. I learned with her
     How to love you.
Laura.   But, sir, the science of love
     Cannot be learnt; and love does not require
     A course of study at the university.
     It gets enough instruction on its own,
     And of itself knows all it ought to know;
     And it can only lose by trying to make
     Itself more clever; and therefore, it is said,
     Those with the most experience of love
     Are always the least capable of loving.
Felix. I have expressed my meaning very badly ...
Laura. No, on the contrary, only too well.

The language of Calderón's gallants is often precious and absurd, but his heroines, like some of Shakespeare's, expose the absurdity. When, in the second scene of the first act, Cesar, going under the name of Fabio, compares Lisarda to a sun, whom the flowers worship, and at her sight burst into bloom, she replies:

                              I'ld like to think,
     Lord Fabio, for politeness, that the flowers
     Would tell me pretty things, if they should listen
     To you, my flatterer; for your gallantry
     Is so refined, that even the very flowers
     Would learn love's language from you.

The same couple, later in the same scene, discuss whether it is

possible for Cesar to love Lisarda before he has seen her unveiled.
Cesar argues that a blind man's love is loftier than she allows:

> The chief object
> Of a rational soul is the light of understanding.
> That's what I love in you, with that I love you.
> If I beheld your beauty's light, that instant
> My soul and eyes would have to share my love,
> Which therefore would be less, being so shared.
> I leave it you to judge if it would be
> Proper to rob the soul of half its love
> And give it to the eyes.

Lis. Even though the soul
> Should share with the eyes its love, which is its light,
> The soul would not love less, but there would be
> Merely more love.

Ces. I don't quite understand.

Lis. If when there is a light, another spark
> Is brought against it, it communicates
> Its flame, but does not thereby cease to burn.
> Love is a fire which burns within the soul;
> If it's communicated to the eyes,
> It does not cease to be as bright a fire
> As formerly. The very eyes, which once
> Were sad and dull, shine with a sudden radiance
> But yet, the fire has entered in the eyes
> Without departing from the soul.

Calderón is the least performed of all great dramatists outside his
own country. But the world's repertoire of first-rate comedies is not
so extensive that it can afford to dispense with the dozen or so
masterpieces to be found among his works. Whenever they have
been given a performance in recent years they have been remarkably successful.

La Venexiana in the Light of Recent Criticism

BODO L. O. RICHTER

Among the Italian comedies of the Renaissance, Machiavelli's *La Mandragola* stands out as a play that far transcends the period during which it was written. Attilio Momigliano, surely not a critic who was prone to take quick recourse to the categorical imperative, nevertheless wanted to eliminate any possible doubt concerning the primacy of Machiavelli's achievement as a dramatist: "*La Mandragola* is the most powerful play of our theater."[1] But it was Momigliano himself, ever aware of newly emerging esthetic values, who pointed out the discovery of a comedy that he did not hesitate to place alongside of Machiavelli's masterpiece: "A few years ago there came to light an anonymous comedy, *La Venexiana,*[2] the only impassioned comedy of the century, the only one—together with *La Mandragola*—which goes completely beyond the conventional schemes."[3] This was written in 1934 about a play that had first appeared in print in 1928.[4] Ever since its editor Emilio Lovarini introduced it as "the very beautiful comedy which we are publishing here,"[5] the critical acclaim has increased, although rather fitfully and with many repetitive statements shrouding the few really fresh looks at the play. An American edition with an English translation, published in 1950, did not draw much attention,[6] and it is doubtful that many readers, even in Italy, could have agreed, some twenty years ago, with Lovarini's understandably wishful remark that *La Venexiana* was "by now well-known and famous."[7] It is symptomatic that the play has not yet found its way into the fourth edition of Renda and Operti's *Dizionario storico della letteratura italiana* (1957) and, less surprisingly, into the third edition of *The Oxford Companion to the Theatre* (1967).

The long burial of the Venetian comedy par excellence[8] among the three thousand or so manuscripts in the Biblioteca Marciana cannot be ascribed altogether to the indifference of a long parade of viewers. The Italian manuscript (MS IX 288) is replete with problems that require exceptional expertise in paleography and dialectology. The very fact that the play is written in Venetian dialect, with a strong sprinkling of Bergamask, has kept it from becoming widely known. Other things being equal, Machiavelli and Aretino would always have an easier time of it than, for instance, Angelo Beolco (il Ruzzante) and Andrea Calmo, the Florentine hypocrite or courtesan being more readily intelligible than the Paduan peasant or the Bergamask porter. A recent work dealing with Italian Renaissance comedy points up again the prejudicial treatment, as it were, of comedies written in dialect. Achille Magno's vast bibliographical investigation *La Commedia in lingua nel Cinquecento: Bibliografia critica*[9] is prefaced by a long introduction by Vito Pandolfi in which Beolco's work occupies a large place and *La Venexiana* a very creditable one. However, in the much briefer foreword with which Magno ushers in the bibliography itself, we are taken aback by the following statement: "On the other hand, I felt that I should exclude from my survey a comedy like *La Venexiana* since it seemed better to me to link it, although it is written in a literary dialect, with the other type of dramaturgy—the popular one—which in my opinion can be characterized only at the linguistic level."[10] Perhaps Pandolfi had not originally written his introductory essay for this particular volume, since he says, quite differently (and, I think, correctly): *"La Venexiana* is the first literary composition written solely in Venetian dialect, but its contents and its characters are popular to only a very small degree."[11] In time, the anonymous author of our comedy and his confreres Beolco, Calmo, and Giancarli (among many others in other dialects) should get their separate bibliography where they can be at home without feeling downgraded because they did not write in *the* language.[12]

This is not to say that the play itself would be of difficult access for those who want to read it. Quite to the contrary. The two Lovarini editions of the text (see n. 4 above) have been out of print for some time but other editors and publishers have filled the breach and, one might add, with increasing eagerness. Silvio d'Amico, with Mario Apollonio and Vito Pandolfi one of the great authorities of the Italian drama as a whole, gave to our anonymous author equal billing with Beolco in the first volume of his long anthology of plays, urging us, however, not to view *La Venexiana* with unbridled enthusiasm.[13] Aldo Borlenghi included the play in the second volume of his *Commedie del Cinquecento,* published in 1959.[14] Just one year later it was included, as it had to be, in the comprehensive anthology *Teatro veneto* prepared by G. A. Cibotto, whose pretentious and garbled introduction does not contribute much to an understanding of the plays, and whose comments on *La Venexiana* are, by his own admission, on loan from Diego Valeri.[15] On the other hand, the reader who is not turned away by the classification of our anonymous author as an early *verista,* "who anticipated by more than three centuries the *tranche de vie* poetics," will benefit greatly from the "Scheda per *La Venexiana*" and the notes which Lodovico Zorzi has appended to his text of the comedy with facing translation.[16] Close upon the heels of Zorzi followed Riccardo Scrivano, who made room for the play in his anthology *Cinquecento minore.*[17] There is a familiar ring to Scrivano's introductory note: "Even in the very abundant production of the Italian comic theater of the sixteenth century, there are not many comedies which, like *La Venexiana,* can be placed securely alongside of *La Mandragola.* Having flowered in two profoundly different cultural situations, the subject of the *Mandragola* is the bitter denunciation of the corruption of the various members of society, whereas in the *Venexiana* it is the spectacle of the passions that dominate the mind of man, passions which should not be repressed but satisfied."[18] In order to make sure that there will always be a good supply of the text of our comedy, we have a publisher's promise for yet another anthology, "Il Teatro veneziano del Cinquecento," which is being prepared by G. Gambarin.[19]

Five short acts in prose, six characters still in search of their
author, a prologue written in humanistic Italian, sparse stage directions in Latin and identification of the personae in the same language, a complete unconcern for the unities of time and place and
other bench marks of the *commedia erudita* (entangled plots,
disguises, etc.), the use of various idioms, a realistic and psycho-
logically astute view of human nature—these are some of the characteristics that immediately strike the reader. It seems as if the
classicizing elements in the framework were purposely brought
into contrast with the immediacy of the action and the spontaneity
of the characters.

The Prologue, brief and to the point, introduces Cupid with considerable decorum: "The Ancients ingeniously depicted Cupid, the
son of Venus, as a blind, naked boy, with wings and quiver."[20]
The workings of Love are put forth unequivocally and, no doubt,
as Giorgio Padoan has pointed out, "with implied anti-Bembistic
polemics."[21] "L'incentivo amoroso," we are told, is motivated by
sensual passion, which obfuscates the mind and forces it to gratify
the body. This happens to all of us but in particular to women,
because of the smallness of their intellect. After this theoretical
preamble of about a dozen lines, the author proceeds quickly to
the situation at hand: "You will see this clearly today, ladies and
gentlemen of the audience, when you hear how the boundless love
of a noble fellow-citizen of yours was entrusted to a young stranger;
. . . similarly, the love of another, given to this very same youth.
. . . From this, through understanding the joy of the one and the
grief of the other, you will see how powerful love is in woman.
. . ."[22] The audience is then asked not to be shocked by what
"will be declaimed in public today without shame by our co-
medians," since love cannot be fully understood without knowing all
of its effects.[23] The author finishes with a didactic flourish, en-
joining the audience to let the intellect understand love and be
careful not to come under the sway of the senses.

It is evening in Venice. Iulio, a "young stranger" ("iuvenis for-
[esterius]"),[24] has arrived recently, "with little money" ("con pu-

ochi danari"), determined to fill his heart and his purse. Valeria, a young woman of good family whom he has already ardently admired at a distance, seems to be the one he would like to take back to Milan as his bride (provided she has a dowry). Beauty, nobility, and riches, that would be the perfect combination. The comely young man, whose rosy face and velvety dress should help him greatly to make his sweet nothings ("parolette" and "paro-luzze") convincing, obviously represents a threat to the ladies. That much is clear from the start.[25]

Along comes Oria, Valeria's maid, whom Iulio asks please to tell her mistress that a stranger in town is completely devoted to her. Oria seems a bit afraid, and she refuses to run the errand but naturally hurries home just the same to deliver the message. Through the use of innuendoes she creates a nervous curiosity which readily betrays Valeria's feelings for Iulio. Oria's description of the dandy with the black curly hair and the plumed beret makes Valeria realize quickly that he is indeed the one she has been pining for.

In scene iv of Act I, another part of the multiple stage setting introduces the other woman to whom the author alluded in his Prologue—will she be the happy one or the one who had to suffer so much grief? As we meet Angela, we find her in a sorry state. She has also seen the lady-killer, and he is "an angel face with a precious little snout who has come down here from Paradise."[26] But while the married Valeria, despite her obvious infatuation, showed no more than a smouldering impatience, Angela, widowed not long ago, is raging with passion. She is exasperated—and a sad note creeps in here—because Iulio doesn't even look at her, perhaps thinking that under the mourning veil he might find an old face. Nena, her maid, is in bed, but she cannot find any rest as she is continually beset by her mistress. Angela wants Iulio desperately, at any cost—money, gifts, whatever it may take. A fire is consuming her, her flesh is burning, she is bathed in sweat. When Nena asks her what she intends to do, Angela throws her arms around her and acts out the illusion with such ardor that the servant finally has to call a halt, "Stop it, you are choking me! . . . You are forgetting that I am a woman. . . . Why are you doing these crazy things?"[27] But that does not deter the desperate woman. Instead, she goes to new extremes (and here one can really get worried about *bienséance*): she asks Nena to swear like a man (no mention of Iulio at this point), to curse the body of Christ, to utter foul words such as men say in brothels; "Dear Nena, be just a little shameless for my sake," she begs.[28] After this daring scene, we hope that help will not be slow in coming. Nena has a difficult assignment on her hands although she does know that the man she must find is staying at the Osteria del Pavone ("Peacock Inn").

At the beginning of the second act, Nena is looking for Iulio, but she considers it best to engage the help of Bernardo, the porter from Bergamo, a man who is trustworthy and personally appreciated by Angela; he is always ready to drop his heavy loads for lighter assignments, as long as the price is right.[29] Bernardo, who says proudly that he wouldn't be afraid to talk to the doge, should not find it difficult to make Iulio partake of "la dolce vita" ("vita dulcedo"), especially since he already knows who the wanted man is. The ten ducats offered by Angela will do very nicely, but since Nena does not have the money with her, she gives a ring from her finger in pledge.

Meanwhile Oria has spotted Iulio and she returns the greetings that he had sent to her mistress. This encourages Iulio to ask for a rendezvous with Valeria, but, "Do you want her to be killed by her husband?" Oria asks, explaining that Valeria is a newlywed.[30] Still, just fifteen minutes, just enough for a few solemn declarations, could perhaps be arranged. In fact, after having received some outlandish promises, the maidservant suddenly becomes plenipotentiary and, calling him "Vostra Magnificenzia," offers him a meeting with the lady of the house at nine o'clock. The elated suitor naturally promises to be on time.

This plan is thwarted by Bernardo. He has prowled around the Osteria del Pavone, San Marco, and the Rialto, but finally, near Valeria's house, he gets sight of Iulio, the one with the curly hair "and effeminate looks" ("e quel'ari da fomnèla"). When our

Adonis, rather impatient with the porter's initial *double-entendre* about benefices, states plainly that the kind of benefice he is after is some nice place where he can put his youthful forces into action and enjoy himself, the go-between promises him "*gloria in esel-cis.*"[31] A gondola is in readiness. Will it take Iulio to Valeria's house? Perhaps his ladylove, not being sure enough of the diffident Oria, interposed the crafty porter. Regardless, this invitation seems more promising than the other one, and furthermore, "The first lady, if she is not the second one, knowing nothing about it, will excuse me."[32] Bernardo, in reporting to Angela the success of his mission, does not change his direct discourse: "I didn't tell him anything, save that I wanted to bring him to sleep at a certain place tonight."[33] But then, when Bernardo urges Angela to "give a good show" ("boni spesi") to Iulio, who "looks every bit like an angel" ("A l'è lu tal com u angiol"), the widow, elated as she is, seems to realize for an instant that she is past the first flowering of beauty and that the adventure before her will be a passing one, followed by sadness and disappointment: "He is too beautiful for me."[34]

"Tertius actus." While Oria and Valeria are waiting in vain (Valeria: "Do you know what? Some woman in love wants to sleep with him"[35]), Bernardo moves his gondola with the prized passenger toward Angela's elegant *palazzo*. After a few strategically placed *ritardandi* that involve Bernardo and Iulio on the one hand and Angela and Nena on the other, we reach the central scene of the play, scene iii, "ANGELA, IULIUS *amantes.*" This must be one of the most explicit, yet also one of the most tender and touching love scenes of the theater. Angela, her head in a Pirandellian shroud so as to conceal, at least for the moment, her identity and perhaps also her age,[36] has barely the patience to go through with a ceremonious greeting: almost immediately she takes Iulio's hands and confesses, "Dearest, how much I have desired you!"[37], although she does apologize for having asked him to come so "crudely and shamelessly" ("grossamente e liçenziosamente"). When Iulio seizes her around the waist, the disintegration is rapid. But Angela has made the mistake of interpreting this gesture as meaning that from now on the initiative can be all hers: when she wants to help Iulio with the removal of his clothing, he politely pushes her back, "This I don't permit. Your ladyship should disrobe, so that I may help her."[38] And a few seconds later, as if she had caught Iulio searching too inquisitively for her face, she begs him not to look at her.

This scene, like the entire play, is full of psychological insights of this kind. It is especially interesting to transfer words and gestures which Angela used toward Nena (I.iv.) to her intimate encounter with Iulio, where these attitudes have found their true object. In the presence of her lover, who uses a florid language that is dripping with gallantry, Angela raises the level of her own speech accordingly, moving from the maid's bedroom to her own boudoir.[39] But some of the images, and even some of the details, remain fundamentally the same. Thus Angela had complained to Nena that Iulio wouldn't look under her veil because he thought she was old, but now she feels that he is looking too intently. Or, again in Act I, "My flesh is on fire! The pain is killing me."[40] And now, after the consummation, which the author has separated from the amorous exchanges that follow by means of the notation "Somewhat later" ("Alquantulum postea"): "Sweet soul of mine, I believed that you had brought water to quench the fire in my breast, but you have brought wood and coal to make it burn more."[41] As part of the early mirage, Angela was kissing Iulio "la lenguina in boca," and here, with the reality in her grasp, she uses the expression "dàme la lenguina" when asking for the same kind of kiss.[42] Such comparisons hardly help us recreate the charged atmosphere of this scene—actually, the conflagration is spread over three scenes—but they *do* allow us to preserve something for the imagination.

A bell in a nearby campanile has struck two o'clock long ago. Bernardo and Nena continue their vigil in the kitchen on the upper floor. The porter has food and drink, he thinks about the money he is making and laments that he is no longer able to do what is being done within painful hearing range. It strikes seven o'clock, time to leave. Angela removes a fine golden chain set with an emerald and places it around Iulio's neck: the chain to signify that the two are eternally linked together, the precious stone to remind her lover that he should touch no other living woman. We would hardly expect Iulio to be at a loss for words on this solemn occasion, and indeed he does not let us down: "There is no need of mentioning my love to you, since, in life and in death, Iulio is yours."[43] As the gondola glides away, the contented gallant wants to pry loose the lady's name, but Bernardo puts him off.

A new act and a new day show us Oria looking for the Prince Charming who has broken his appointment, declaring that she wants to speak clearly, so he will understand. The renewed invitation takes place off stage. In scene ii, Iulio reviews his conquest, puzzled by Angela's secretiveness but grateful to her, "for she is a most noble woman, whether widowed or married"[44] (but surely not single). Fortune, always so capricious, is already offering him another adventure. He doesn't know which way to turn, toward fidelity or infidelity. It would be discourteous to disappoint Valeria again, "and if she were prettier, what then?" ("e se fosse piú bella, come farae?"); but she had been haughty, while the other one . . . Nevertheless, he could go there without getting involved and frustrate all her plans. The chain and the emerald would remind him not to break the oath he had taken.

Iulio, on his way to Valeria's house ("in itinere"), fully armed (as he was for the previous appointment), has some uneasy premonitions about this rendezvous, but he has no trouble in shaking them off: "Experiment is an excellent thing; it gives you the edge through what you learn."[45] Valeria, deeply resentful, comments upon the sword as a sign of distrust, enough for Iulio to motion his departure. Valeria quickly holds him back but continues her interrogation. The accused says that he was indisposed and therefore could not come. He remains distant and, with affected courtesy, insists that his absence does not mean that he is not her servant and that he does not love her more than himself. He recounts that he had first seen her in church and, naturally, like Petrarch, became a prisoner for life on the spot. He bows in reverence and Angela's chain slips out a moment from under his collar. Valeria wants to see it. She realizes quickly how the object has changed hands, and she raises her voice, "There is something rotten here. Enough! I understand perfectly."[46] Iulio, outwardly unruffled, still insists that he was indeed ill the night before and that he does not know Angela (putting one hand on his breast). This becomes too much for the woman scorned, and jealousy, pride, and resentment spill forth helter-skelter. She even threatens court action and deportation. With tears in her voice, she exclaims, "Enough! Angela and you have assassinated me!"[47] But some day she will get even with her rival, and she sends Iulio on his way, adding a sarcastic greeting for Angela.

Outside in the street again, Iulio is "all perturbed" ("tutto turbato"), although there is not much emotion in his soliloquy. Of course our hero must have been shaken a bit by the fact that Valeria recognized the chain so quickly and that the donor, so carefully concealed so far, was the widow Angela. But he continues to calculate coolly: "Since this one is suspicious, it would be a smart move for me to reveal her hatred for the other, who, when she perceives it, if she loves me, will become even more passionate."[48] We can readily see from this that a bleeding heart along the way will not induce Iulio to make a detour.

Act V. It is the following morning.[49] Oria is hurrying along a canal near Valeria's house. She must find Iulio in order to deliver a letter of apology from her mistress. During the night it was Oria who was not allowed to sleep, and this time it was Valeria who was tortured to the point that she exclaimed, "I am dead" ("sun morta") because her love might be lost forever.[50] When Oria asked (as she relates in her monologue) why she had chased him away, Valeria had the courage to give a straightforward answer: "Because I was too jealous."[51] The humiliation inflicted upon her no longer counts: let him hurry and get into bed to make peace.

Will Bernardo ruin this second attempt on Valeria's part? He appears on the scene and speaks of the pleasant tune of two days ago, adding an appropriate wink. But Oria gets her chance to speak to Iulio (the plot requires this) and she is quite effusive about the sufferings of her mistress. The most-wanted man can afford to remain casual and ironic: "I should not like, by coming, to increase her troubles. She is hot-tempered and does not believe me. Should she see me, she would get so angry that it could hurt her later on."[52] After having read the letter, Iulio has his triumph, and he radiantly accepts the renewed invitation.

However, the *embarras de richesses* (called by Iulio "la via de Croce" ["the Way of the Cross"]) is not completely solved. Iulio's stratagem is to insist on getting the family name of his benefactress, otherwise he won't come along. Since Bernardo is sworn to secrecy and we know that he won't betray the secret, he is in a predicament: "Things are going badly when roses stink."[53] But he guides his gondola in the direction of Angela's place in order to take Iulio's strange demands to the proper authorities.

Now Iulio can slip away. Valeria has left the door ajar. She is waiting downstairs with Oria. The maid is happy that the success of her mission will put her in the good graces of her mistress, but the latter is even happier: "You [Iulio] have gained a body and soul that were lost."[54] That quickly becomes the cue for Iulio to make one of his pretty speeches: "*Signora,* I only want to have won the good graces of your ladyship, who has been kind enough to take me as a servant."[55] It is time to go inside now, "because the winds have ears and eyes" ("perché i venti ha orece e oci"); and with Iulio behind her, Valeria approaches her chambers, murmuring endearments very like those Angela has spoken before her. But what about the husband? "Oria, my dear, close the door and go up to *Misser* Grando and make sure that he won't grumble. And if he asks about me, tell him that I am not feeling well and that for tonight I don't want to be bothered."[56]

Here the comedy ends, leaving a suggestion of incompleteness. We know that for Valeria the feeling of happiness will also be no better than transitory and that she and Angela will have to share in the same disenchantment. There are even darker overtones: will Valeria carry out her threat and avenge herself upon Angela? Since the play does not end with a pat solution, the projection of the action beyond the confines of the last act—in itself a proof of its vitality—has led to various speculations. They range from Croce's vision of blood and tragedy to Apollonio's view that the end is a fade-out, with Alfred Mortier and Zorzi holding intermediate positions.[57] My own feeling is that as the play progresses, one thinks less and less of it as a comedy, with Bernardo's humorous sallies having an increasingly contrapuntal effect. E. O. B. Bergerhoff's remarks on the denouement of Molière's *Le Misanthrope* are curiously applicable here: ". . . the play has to end of course. But precisely, there could be no satisfactory end, because there is no humanly satisfactory general solution to the problem of human behaviour."[58]

Problems of a very different and more immediate nature confront us as we return to the manuscript. I don't think anyone could say today that he has read successfully the entire play in the handwritten original without having the Lovarini transcription (or one of the later ones based on his) by his side.[59] We owe the same scholar further gratitude for his description of the entire manuscript, comprising four plays in all.[60] But once these physical problems, as it were, had been solved, there remained others which the first editor faced rather obliquely and with only partial success.

For the reader who wants to push beyond the esthetic values, the most pressing questions that remain concern the dating, the sources, and eventually also the authorship of the play. We are here in the terrain that attracts detectives: no direct information has been supplied but we have bits of evidence that can be used in order to solve the mystery. I have intentionally kept these data out of my summary and I have not mentioned the notations that precede and follow the play proper in the manuscript.

The date "Jesus 1521 adj. [unidentified month] 7" heads the 143 leaves that constitute this "libro de comedie de piu hautori" ("book of comedies by several authors"), as we read on leaf 6. The first play is the only one whose author is given: "and first a comedy in rustic style composed by Mr. Angelo Beolco of Padua—called *La Pastoral*" ("et prima comedia ala villana composta per misser anzolo biolcho da padoa—dita la pastoral").[61] Of the others, we have editions of *La Bulesca*[62] and our *Venexiana,* while the last one (in order of transcription), *Ardelia,* has not yet appeared in book form. As we reach our comedy, we are immediately tantalized by the omission of the name of the author of "La Veniex[na] comedia de" (fol. 70[v]) and by the fact that only the title is written in a hand different from the rest. It seems likely that the copyist knew the name of the author but considered it best not to reveal it. Why such scruples? As we examine the pages that follow the *finis* of the play (fol. 96[r]), we find a group of love lyrics that occupy five pages, and on the last page of this appendix (fol. 99[v]) two Latin distichs which summarize the subject of the comedy by distilling the prologue into four lines:

Qua resculptus Amor quorum mihi nomina tantum
    qualis amant unum nupta simul vidua
flectitur in juvenem mulier turbatur et ardet
    utraque dic queso.—Tu lege disce sile.[63]

[How love between two persons whose names only are known to me is refashioned; how a bride and a widow love the same youth at the same time; how each woman becomes perturbed and kindled; tell, I pray.—Read, thou, learn, and be silent.]

Finally, in the middle of the last page, and arranged in such a way as to give it prominence, we find the epigraph, "Non Fabula non Comedia, ma vera Historia." This is followed, at the very end, by two more lines that arrest our attention, "fidelis s[er]vus v[ester] hieronymus zarellus sc[rips]i" ("written by your faithful servant, Hieronymus Zarellus").

Lovarini was not one to overlook the significance of these addenda. Thus he was perfectly correct in assuming that the sorry state of the Latin on the last page would have to be charged to the ignorance of the copyist, although he did not exclude the possibility that the Latin distichs were "born deformed" ("mal nati") through a bad delivery by the anonymous author himself (1928 ed., p. 21). The first editor also sensed correctly that there are enough verifiable references to persons and places in the play to make "vera Historia" into more than a generic allusion to Venetian customs and morals in the early sixteenth century. After having weighed also certain remarks by the personae, especially Bernardo, for their possible historical content, Lovarini felt prepared in the second edition of 1947 to place the play early in the century, within the span of 1509–17, that is, a period that corresponds to the duration of the hostilities against Venice from the formation of the League of Cambrai[64] to the Brussels agreement which allowed Venice to come out of the long series of conflicts relatively unscathed. Lovarini missed the target by some twenty years, but his conclusions could easily have gone unchallenged if Giorgio Padoan of the University of Padua had not re-examined every exhibit, attaining results which should give a fresh perspective to our understanding of *La Venexiana*.[65]

Which are the internal data that allow us to establish with some certainty the year during which the play was written? Here is one example of what we have to look at in a new light. In Act II, scene v, where Iulio still is not sure whether he can really trust Bernardo, the latter shows him a medal and protests: "Let's look a bit closely here. As you can see, this means Ghibelline allegiance, the same as yours, man from the duchy" ("Guardòn un po' fis quilò [Guardimo un po' fisso qui]. E, vedí la fed gubelina. E la to', duchesche").[66] Lovarini saw no reason to separate the two political references "gubelina" and "duchesche," since during the wars against Venice many Lombard cities, among them Mantua, Brescia, and Bernardo's home town, Bergamo, had cast their lot with the imperial forces (*Ghibelline* meaning "imperial," as it did during the Middle Ages). But Padoan probes deeper. Using a powerful battery of historical arguments, he moves the entire political scene to the next cycle of conflicts, which began in 1522. As he suggests, Lovarini had fallen into the not uncommon error of unhesitatingly pointing the finger at the most critical moment of the situation, forgetting that nothing was fundamentally changed for many years. When could a citizen of Bergamo really equate, with a basis in fact, the imperial and the ducal policy? Not before the last week of October 1535. The Congress of Bologna in 1530 had once again brought peace. Charles V was crowned emperor. The citizens of Brescia and Bergamo could return home and expect restitution of their belongings, a clemency which was hardly apt to assuage their anti-Venetian feelings. Francesco Sforza, subscribing to a pro-imperial policy, got back his duchy. But he died on 24 October 1535 without having an heir, and the territory was left by testament to Charles V, who was quick in asserting his rule over Lombardy. So, it was at this precise moment, in early November 1535, that the imperial rule comprised also Milan, thus giving meaning to Bernardo's reassuring remark to the effect that he and Iulio belong to the same political camp.

But is this enough? Padoan moves from politics to numismatics and comes up with a valuable piece of supporting evidence. At the end of the second act Angela promises Bernardo a most generous reward for his help: "I want to give you new Mocenigo ducats, fresh from the mint" ("Mozenighi gniovi te voio dar, de zeca"). Here the words to be emphasized are *mozenighi,* silver lires first struck in 1475, at the request of doge Pietro Mocenigo, and *de zeca,* "mint," that is, brand new. Padoan, after having consulted Aldobrandini's *Le monete di Venezia,* Lovarini's study of Ruzzante's *Betìa* and the play itself, and several volumes of that most minute record of matters Venetian, Marino Sanudo's *Diari,* reaches the verdict that the coins in question must have been the new issue struck during the dogate of Andrea Gritti (1523–38). Thus the time span to which we can ascribe the origin of the play has been narrowed down to the period that extends from late 1535 (the imperial take-over of the duchy of Milan) to the death of Gritti in 1538 (the new *mocenighi*).

There are other matters to be considered. In order to establish a clearer *terminus ante quem,* we should take into account that on 22 March 1537, the feared Council of Ten, alarmed by the many attacks and the frequent rioting in the city, decreed that anyone carrying arms, day or night, would be arrested immediately. Recent arrivals were not exempt. Hence, the gainly young Lombard could not have sported a sword dangling from his side without risking confiscation and arrest in short order. Staying right on Padoan's trail, we should also take into account that at seven in the morning Angela speaks of the beginning of daylight, which would put the action into the winter months. Finally, it is noteworthy that no reference to the play can be found in Sanudo's *Diari,* in which every fact and every whisper for the years from 1486 to 1533 seems to be mentioned. Anyone who has consulted some of these fifty-eight massive volumes must be convinced that Sanudo would have given some account of the comedy (if it had been performed) or the gossip that flew around it (if it had been forbidden), but the records on 1533 are closed without any such reference.[67] Adding up all the historical evidence that he has gathered and examined so scrupulously, Padoan concludes: "The facts narrated in the *Veniexiana* therefore must be placed in the winter of 1535–36 or the following one."[68]

The plausibility of these dates gains further strength from an investigation of the places and people in the play. Did the personae live not only in art but in life, did they have experiences similar to those put before us? Padoan helps us to answer this question in the affirmative. Building upon the foundation laid by Lovarini, Padoan revisits the Osteria del Pavone and the Gallipoli warehouse, checking in every nook and cranny. Men and women whose presence in Venice was more sensed than proven by the earlier searcher now arise in flesh and blood. "Misser Antonio," the doctor Nena wants to call in order to cure Angela's fever, was Antonio Secco who came to Venice in 1531 and died there in 1581. Both Anzola (Angela) and Valiera (Valeria)[69] were of noble birth; they were distantly related; they lived in the same neighborhood, in the San

Barnaba quarter; Anzola Valier lost her husband Marco Barbarigo in 1535; she was rich and lived in a splendid palace; Valiera Valier was between twenty and twenty-five years old and had a sister Laura (Laurina in the play). We also learn that in 1535 Valiera married a man in his forties, Giacomo Semitecolo, although even now we don't have a satisfactory explanation of *"Misser Grando,"* the appellative Valeria uses in her last speech of the play.[70] Enough proof that at least the two leading ladies were real and recognizable. "Tu lege disce *sile."*

Does this firm footing in reality mean that the play is without literary antecedents? Altogether without any, that seems unlikely. At the same time it is true that there is not much to glean for those who are not satisfied with the end product without knowing the raw materials. The source-conscious might, however, find solace in one of the first articles that followed upon the publication of the play, Ireneo Sanesi's *"La Venexiana."* [71] Sanesi, obviously annoyed with those who immediately praised the new find to the skies, did not look ahead to Goldoni and beyond, but rather turned backward, insisting that the play was a late fruit of humanistic comedy in Latin of the previous century—aided and abetted in this assumption by Lovarini's erroneous dating of the play. Through this comic theater of the fifteenth century, our anonymous author was linked with the Middle Ages and the tradition of the *novella.* He was a reactionary, a diehard, whereas the authors of the classicizing comedies à la Plautus and Terentius, bound by rules but devoted to the vernacular, heralded the new day.[72] But, regardless, when one reads Sanesi's own summaries of such humanistic comedies as the *Janus sacerdos,* Ugolino Pisani's *Philogenia* (ca. 1435–37), and Antonio Barzizza's *Cauteraria* ("The Branded"), all of which could be *novella* stories, one wonders what our author should owe to these patently farcical situations.[73] Of course the entire argument is undermined by Padoan's dating of *La Venexiana,* which proves that our comedy was written after the triumph of the *commedia erudita.*

We are on much safer ground if we stay closer to home and

look for a contribution from a Venetian poet of the fifteenth century, Leonardo Giustinian (1388–1446).[74] The second of his *Contrasti* (fairly long poems in dialogue form) is so close in tone and in some of the details to the mistress-servant relationship in *La Venexiana* that one is tempted to introduce Marta as Oria and Madonna as Valeria.[75] It is true that Marta first advises her mistress not to take a lover, out of consideration for the husband, but when this voice of moderation is interpreted as a sign of timidity, the servant leaps into action and contrives the visit of "that precious stone" ("sta pietra preziosa," as the lady calls the one she desires). The last stanza, where Madonna[76] advises that the visit should take place in the dark of night, at two o'clock, when her husband luckily will be very busy at his desk, is also so close to the conclusion of our play that it is hard to imagine that our anonymous author should not have seen this particular dramatic dialogue.[77]

It is much more difficult to ascertain what may stem from the vast stock of *novella* literature—and on this score it would be unwise to make short shrift of Sanesi. One of the short stories of Bandello, the twenty-fifth of Part IV, deals with a rich noblewoman who has been widowed for about a year and does not intend to remarry, but, being unable to contain herself any longer, astutely finds means to provide for her needs. Like Angela, she is anxious not to be recognized; the gentleman of the story is, like Iulio, Milanese; the *balio* ("preceptor," but in fact the go-between) has a certain affinity with Bernardo; there is a sumptuous palace, there is a vigil of the faithful helpers, all this enveloped in the same mysterious and sensual atmosphere which surrounds the first three acts of *La Venexiana*.[78] The chronological difficulties—first considered rather serious, since in the dedicatory letter there is a reference to an event that took place in 1537—must now be considered minor, especially if we take into account that Bandello's stories circulated in Venice well before their appearance in print.[79] Of course, even the elimination of Bandello would not preclude the existence of this story in an earlier form, in some *novellino* or *contafavola* to which must always be added the oral tradition.

It may some day come to light that our author's literary debts were heavier than we now know, but this could hardly alter the effect of freshness and spontaneity which impresses the reader.

There remains the search for the author. In 1928 Lovarini asked: "Was Girolamo Zarello—who knows him?—perhaps the author of this very original little work?"[80] In 1946, a few months before the publication of the second edition of the play, he had an answer: Girolamo Zarello was Girolamo Fracastoro.[81] Lovarini was led to Fracastoro along the following route: among the love lyrics which follow the play but which in fact can be considered a dedication to a distinguished lady, there are two compositions by H[ieronymo] Frac[astoro], other contributors being Navagero, Sannazaro, and Aretino (among lesser names). Lovarini, admitting that the family name Zarello must be fictitious, banked heavily on the identical first name, Hieronymo. Internally, the serious, compassionate handling of a licentious subject would suggest that the author of *Syphilis sive de morbo gallico* (Verona, 1530, but written in 1521) could well have composed *La Venexiana* early in his career. But our researcher was straining too hard. He thought that Fracastoro, the physician and philosopher, was ideally suited to understand the sickness of the two leading ladies. No one else could combine a deep understanding of human nature with sensitive expression to the same degree, so that Fracastoro should be considered the author of our play, at least "in all probability" ("con molta probabilità").

Manlio Dazzi relied on another aspect of *La Venexiana,* its licentious elements, when he associated it (and the *Contrasti* of Giustinian) with the poetry of the incredibly outspoken Maffìo Venier. Maffìo's mastery of the Venetian dialect, his poetic debate (*tenzone*) with Veronica Franco, which might have shocked even Angela, along with streaks of an almost incongruous sensitivity, are all elements that would have made an ascription to this poet a possibility. However, since Maffìo was born in 1550, this conjecture cannot survive.[82]

So the question remains, although one hopes that the riddle

won't persist as long as that of the last line of the *Chanson de Roland*.[83] The solution may be close at hand now: near the end of his study of *La Venexiana*, Professor Padoan announces a separate investigation dealing with his candidate for authorship, Girolamo Zanetti, a friend and emulator of Beolco. And since Padoan does not go into battle without all the scholarly accoutrements, we may anticipate that the elusive Zarello will be speared. But at that very moment we should again return to the play itself, read it, and judge for ourselves why it is indeed a small masterpiece.

Shakespeare the Ignoramus

S. SCHOENBAUM

The concept of Shakespeare the Ignoramus[1] has still not entirely relinquished its sway, although its adherents would certainly choose a more euphemistic phrase to describe it. A number of circumstances have nourished this tenacious concept: Shakespeare's formal education, restricted to the Stratford grammar school; the allusions, legends, and traditions that cling to his name (would a rustic, deer-poaching fugitive lead the life of the mind?); the representation of the poet that graces—if that is the word—the monument in Holy Trinity Church; the fact that he was an actor, an unexalted profession in his own time and one which, whether we like to admit it or not, many of us regard with condescension today. And, if we are candid with ourselves, we shall acknowledge that playwriting too is not always seen as the most intellectual of literary occupations. I should not wish to suggest that the image of Shakespeare that furnishes my title has not had rivals—sometimes antithetical rivals—through the ages; of course it has. But in its various manifestations this image, so repugnant to the academic mind, has received a remarkable degree of support. It appears even in contexts that would seem at first glance to deny its validity. Thus Carlyle glorifies Shakespeare as "the greatest intellect who, in our recorded world, has left record of himself in the way of Literature," and more than once in the same lecture, "The Hero as Poet," he speaks of the Bard's "superiority of Intellect."[2] But Carlyle means "unconscious Intellect"—his Shakespeare is "our poor Warwickshire Peasant" through whom the voice of Nature speaks.

I

We know that by the standards of his own age Shakespeare was not considered learned. Francis Beaumont seems to have been the first to comment on the poet's scholastic limitations, in a verse epistle written around 1615 and addressed to—who else?—Ben Jonson. "Heere I would let slippe," he diffidently enjoins himself,

> (If I had any in mee) schollershippe,
> And from all Learninge keepe these lines as ⟨cl⟩eere
> As Shakespeares best are. . . .[3]

Preachers in their sermons, Beaumont goes on to say, will seize on Shakespeare as an example of "how farr sometimes a mortall man may goe / by the dimme light of Nature."[4] Leonard Digges, the translator of *Gerardo,* in a tributary verse for the 1640 edition of the *Poems* cites Shakespeare as an example of a different sort: an instance of the truism that poets are born, not made. "Looke thorow / This whole Booke," Digges beseeches, in dubious commendation,

> thou shalt find he doth not borrow,
> One phrase from Greekes, nor Latines imitate,
> Nor once from vulgar Languages Translate. . . .[5]

But the definitive statement for the age is of course Jonson's celebrated remark in his offering to the memory of his beloved: "thou hadst small *Latine,* and lesse *Greeke.*" Because the assertion appeared in a poem included in the preliminary matter to the First Folio, and because Jonson knew Shakespeare personally and was universally respected for his learning, his judgment carried immense authority. If we can trust Rowe's report, Jonson repeated his point with greater vehemence when not under eulogistic obligations: a Mr. Hales of Eton in conversation heard *"Ben* frequently reproaching him [Shakespeare] with the want of learning, and Ignorance of the Antients."[6]

The idea stuck. John Ward, who was vicar of Stratford in the latter part of the seventeenth century, recorded in his diary that "Mr. Shakespeare was a natural wit, without any art at all"; that this astute verdict is based entirely on hearsay, and not to the slightest degree on familiarity with his subject's writings, is affirmed by a further entry: "Remember to peruse Shakespears plays, and bee versd in *them,* that I may not bee ignorant in that matter. . . ." [7] Thomas Fuller, who combed the countryside diligently gathering material for his *Worthies* but was unable in his memoir of Shakespeare to provide more than a blank space for the date of the dramatist's death (although it is inscribed on the monument in Holy Trinity Church), can yet declare, "He was an eminent instance of the truth of that Rule, *Poeta non fit, sed nascitur,* one is not *made* but *born* a Poet. Indeed his Learning was very little, so that as *Cornish diamonds* are not polished by any Lapidary, but are pointed and smoothed even as they are taken out of the Earth, so *nature* it self was all the *art* which was used upon him." [8] The simile of the Cornish diamonds made a great impression, and Fuller became a source for subsequent accounts of Shakespeare in Winstanley's *Lives of the Most Famous English Poets* (1687), Langbaine's *Account of the English Dramatick Poets* (1691), Blount's *Remarks on Poetry* (1694), and Collier's *Great Historical, Geographical, Genealogical and Poetical Dictionary* (1701). Although his account is not directly indebted to Fuller, Edward Phillips in *Theatrum Poetarum* (1675) also expresses wonder at the phenomenon that a writer with no extraordinary learning could please with "a certain wild and native Elegance" and command "an unvulgar style."

Serious biographical investigation of Shakespeare got under way in the eighteenth century, and Rowe deserves his place of honor in the annals of scholarship for being the first to attempt a connected life. In his behalf, Betterton, heavy with years and in any event more accomplished as an actor than as a scholar, consulted for the first time the Stratford parish registers and came back with the misinformation that William was the eldest of ten children born to John Shakespeare. The presumed existence of a large family suggested to Rowe that the father was unable because of "the narrowness of his circumstances" to provide for these numerous mouths; and so William was untimely ripped from the Stratford free school, in order to help at home, before he had acquired much proficiency in Latin—or, for that matter, any education at all to speak of. Malone would later sneer that of the eleven biographical facts which Rowe purports to offer in his *Account* eight are demonstrably false and one dubious. Yet for almost a century Rowe's life was accepted as standard and reprinted, with an accretion of notes, in successive editions of Shakespeare. Thus was promulgated the gospel of Shakespeare the Ignoramus.

Some dissidents held another view. As far back as 1681 Aubrey noted down that "Though as Ben: Johnson sayes of him, that he had but little Latine and lesse Greek, He understood Latine pretty well: for he had been in his younger yeares a Schoolmaster in the Countrey." [9] But Aubrey's jottings lay untapped in the Ashmolean Museum until Warton printed extracts from them in a footnote to his *Life and Literary Remains of Ralph Bathurst* in 1761. By then a swelling tide of bardolatry had given rise to a different concept of Shakespeare, based not on contemporary allusions or biographical information and misinformation but on the writings themselves. This rival image offered the Bard as Sage. In the earliest monograph on the subject of the poet's learning, Peter Whalley in 1748 argued that *"Shakespeare* was more indebted to the Ancients than is commonly imagined"; he not only knew Greek and Latin, but also "arrived to a Taste and Elegance of Judgment, particularly in the latter." [10] John Upton in his *Critical Observations* (1746) and Zachary Grey in his *Critical, Historical, and Explanatory Notes* (1754) went further. "As to his ignorance in the *Greek* and *Latin tongues,"* Grey declared, "though that point has been more than once discussed, and much said on both sides of the question; I cannot but think from his exact imitation of many of the antient *poets* and *historians,* (of which there were no tolerable translations in his time,) that his knowledge in that respect cannot reasonably be call'd in question." [11] The showpiece of evidence is *Hamlet,* "in many places . . . an exact translation of *Saxo Grammaticus,"* but Grey bolsters his case with numerous parallels, some of them curious, from other plays: the First Murderer's fairly nondescript line in *Macbeth,* "We are men, my liege," is traced to Terence's *Heau-*

tontimorumenos ("Homo sum; humani nihil a me alienum puto").[12]

Upton, Grey, and others persuaded of the Bard's profound learning were sitting ducks for Richard Farmer, who had the incalculable advantage over his predecessors of a wide and intimate familiarity with the literature of Shakespeare's day. In the publication with which he made his reputation, his *Essay on the Learning of Shakespeare* of 1767, Farmer demonstrates with ease that Shakespeare read Plutarch not in the Greek but in North's translation and that elsewhere too he trusted to English sources: Sidney's *Arcadia,* Painter's *Palace of Pleasure,* Golding's *Ovid.* When he cannot account for a passage in this way, Farmer postulates interpolations by other hands after Shakespeare had quitted the stage: in such a way did the "French ribaldry" find its way into *Henry V.* Disintegration has many uses. In his summing up Farmer adopts an extreme position: "He [Shakespeare] remembered perhaps enough of his *school-boy* learning to put the *Hig, hag, hog,* into the mouth of Sir Hugh Evans; and might pick up in the Writers of the time, or the course of his conversation, a familiar phrase or two of French or Italian; but his *Studies* were most demonstrably confined to *Nature* and *his own Language.*"[13] Farmer's *Essay* was the most decisive treatment of the subject that the age produced. "Dr. Farmer," Johnson congratulated him, ". . . you have done that which never was done before; that is, you have completely finished a controversy beyond all further doubt."[14] Editors reprinted the *Essay* in their collected editions of Shakespeare on into the nineteenth century. Thus was the gospel of Shakespeare the Ignoramus vindicated.

Inevitably, of course, there would be a reaction. Scholarly inquiry, especially as enshrined in T. W. Baldwin's overpowering volumes, would yield a more accurate understanding of the training provided by an excellent provincial grammar school in Shakespeare's day. It would be realized that if sometimes the dramatist relied on translations rather than originals, this fact does not necessarily prove that he was unequipped to consult the originals or that he did not on occasion do so. For some sources—Ser Giovanni's *Il Pecorone,* for example, or Cinthio's *Epitia* and *Hecatommithi*—translations were unavailable to him. But the doctrine of Shakespeare the Ignoramus would be nourished by other springs besides assumptions about his education.

II

There is the likeness of the poet carved from soft bluish Cotswold limestone by Gheerart Janssen and set into the north chancel wall of Stratford church. Frozen in the stereotyped attitude of the writer, Shakespeare stands with a quill pen in his right hand, a sheet of paper under his left, both hands resting on the cushion before him. Like Yeats's Magi in the presence of the Christ child, we stare at this ikon with eyes fixed and remain unsatisfied. It is the image of an affluent burgher of Stratford, redolent of sleek, well-fed, middle-aged prosperity. The eyes—set too close together beneath eyebrows that are situated too high—stare vacantly ahead above a nose, too small for the face, placed between plump, sensual cheeks. The mouth gapes open; the poet is in the throes of composition—or is it indigestion? More assurance is offered by the Droeshout engraving, however vacuous the expression, with its massive perpendicular forehead: a capacious receptacle for thought. To Dover Wilson, who yearns for the Bard to resemble Shelley, the Stratford bust presents the contemptible image of a "self-satisfied pork-butcher." [15] This aristocratic jibe has prompted Professor Harbage to doubt, pertinently and democratically, whether Professor Wilson has made any systematic study of the faces of pork butchers, who might not on inspection turn out to be so disagreeable-looking a lot. [16]

In any event, no intellectual peers out from the chancel wall of Holy Trinity. I should not wish to overemphasize the significance of a sculptor's conception, but the Stratford monument has influenced students formulating an idea of Shakespeare the man. I take as my examples the two most considerable nineteenth-century biographers of Shakespeare, Halliwell-Phillipps and Sidney Lee, both of whom visited Stratford and paused before the monument on numerous occasions. "There is, in truth, a convincing and a mental likeness in this monument," Halliwell-Phillipps asserts in the 1853 *Life of Shakespeare* that prefixes his elaborate illustrated edition of the *Works,* "one that grows upon us by contemplation, and makes us unwilling to accept any other resemblance. . . . [T]o those who can bring themselves to believe that, notwithstanding his unrivalled genius, Shakespeare was a realization of existence, and in his daily career, much as other men were, the bust at Stratford will convey very nearly all that it is desirable to know of his outward form." [17] He was "much as other men." Now, Halliwell-Phillipps, a factual scholar in the splendid tradition that extends from Malone to E. K. Chambers, was not so simple as to deny the Bard high intelligence; but to the extent that a characterization emerges from the documentary pages of his several biographies of Shakespeare, it is that of the prudent burgher of Stratford rather than of the thoughtful intellectual—or even, for that matter, of the conscious artist. "It is not probable that scholastic [i.e., schoolbook] learning was ever congenial to his tastes," Halliwell-Phillipps remarks in his *Outlines of the Life of Shakespeare,* and elsewhere he alludes to the poet's upbringing by "illiterate relatives in a bookless neighbourhood." His art is the outpouring of "unfettered instinct" serving pecuniary ends. "That he did not love money for its own sake, or for more than its relative advantages, may be gathered from his liberal expenditures in after life," Halliwell-Phillipps suggests; "but that he had the wisdom to make other tastes subservient to its acquisition, so long as that course was suggested by prudence, is a fact that cannot fairly be questioned." [18] However distasteful to "the flowery sentiments of the aesthetic critics," the views expressed by Pope have been verified by the researches of scholars:

Shakespeare, whom you and ev'ry playhouse bill
Style the divine, the matchless, what you will,
For gain not glory, wing'd his roving flight,
And grew immortal in his own despight.

The same passage from the *Imitations of Horace* is quoted by Sidney Lee in his biography, which was standard for his day, and went through numerous editions, revisions, and even an abridgement for students. Lee entitles one of his chapters "The Practical Affairs of Life" and in it demonstrates that Shakespeare brought to such affairs "a singularly sane and sober temperament." Lee's reflections on the dramatist's personal character follow, perhaps not entirely by chance, his account of the tomb in Stratford church. "His [Shakespeare's] extant work attests his 'copious' and continuous industry," Lee finds, "and with his literary power and sociability there clearly went the shrewd capacity of a man of business."[19] The "literary attainments and successes" of the creator of *A Midsummer Night's Dream* and *Romeo and Juliet* "were chiefly valued as serving the prosaic end of providing permanently for himself and his daughters. His highest ambition was to restore among his fellow townsmen the family repute which his father's misfortunes had imperilled." [20] Thus does the utilitarianism of the nineteenth-century economists serve to pluck out the heart of the poet's mystery.

III

Nowadays scholars who consult Halliwell-Phillipps' *Outlines* for its antiquarian riches, not yet superseded, are unlikely to concern themselves much with his analysis of Shakespeare as a man. The passage of the years has dealt less kindly with Lee's biography, which (as Chambers demonstrated without malice in his *William Shakespeare*) is vulnerable in points of factual detail; it has ceased to be influential. The twentieth century has brought new emphases. One modern approach dwells on Shakespeare as a man of the theater: his role as (to apply Stephen Spender's deliciously mixed metaphor) "one cog in a golden singing hive." I should say straightaway that I find much merit in this emphasis. Shakespeare, after all, was not only a playwright but also an actor. True, other writers also acted—Heywood, for example, or William Rowley— but, in addition, Shakespeare owned an interest in the playhouse and was a prime mover in his company's affairs. For over two decades he remained with the same troupe. No other dramatist of the period can be identified so comprehensively and so consistently with a theatrical milieu. Yet in the past, biographers have scandalously neglected Shakespeare's professional life. It is good to have the balance redressed. Thanks to Professor Bentley we can now appreciate the importance, in terms of Shakespeare's career, of the acquisition by the King's Men in August 1608 of the Blackfriars Theatre: an entirely enclosed, artificially illuminated playhouse which, being smaller than the Globe, charged higher admissions and consequently catered to a more select clientele.[21] Although we have little certain information regarding the theatrical provenance of Shakespeare's last plays, it is not unreasonable to suppose that—except for *Henry VIII*—he wrote with an eye to the special conditions at the Blackfriars. This factor may help to account for the new direction taken by his art in *Cymbeline, The Winter's Tale,* and *The Tempest.*

Now, the theatrical critic will pay special heed to such matters as the tastes of the audience, the physical characteristics of the playhouse, the size of the acting troupe and the particular skills of its members. These considerations are certainly extremely important. Let us take, for example, *Cymbeline,* on the Blackfriars context of which Granville-Barker has written so suggestively, if without absolute historical accuracy. In Act II, scene ii, Imogen dismisses her woman from the bedchamber and then falls asleep, Iachimo climbs out of the trunk, takes notes on the furnishings of the room, and examines minutely the body of the sleeping girl. It is an intimate scene that takes place in a darkened chamber lit only by tapers; the dialogue is conversational, much of it whispered. Would Shakespeare have conceived such a scene for the large, open-air Globe Theatre? Of *Cymbeline* as a whole, with its incongruities of design, Mr. J. M. Nosworthy has remarked that "it has the appearance of being the outcome of some peculiar, and perhaps decisive, turning point in Shakespeare's private or professional life, and if it were possible, by external reference, to ascertain more about his aim and methods in this play, much that remains obscure concerning his final years as a dramatist might be clarified."[22] Might not the leasing by Shakespeare's company of the Blackfriars provide just such an external reference? Seen in this light, *Cymbeline* is an experiment in which the dramatist is adjusting himself to new conditions.

If such speculations are well worth pursuing, the danger however exists that the pursuit will be carried too far. There is a deterministic aspect to such criticism which should, I feel, be resisted. The playwright is denied his full intellectual assertion; we may be tempted to regard him as merely a passive instrument entirely at the disposal of his company, playhouse, and audience. Some Elizabethan dramatists no doubt contentedly or restlessly remained just that as long as they earned their bread, but it is in the nature of a great artist to rise superior to the shackles of the immediate. In an illuminating recent paper Professor Clifford Leech has stressed the dramatist's independence.[23] John Webster, in his view, wrote *The White Devil* not merely to furnish a suitable vehicle for the Queen's Men at the Red Bull, with its boisterous and unappreciative auditors; the play, rather, satisfied the author's inner necessity to confront the challenge of tragedy. If such is the case with Webster, how much more so with Shakespeare, a greater artist and a greater intellectual than his contemporary. The point holds true (as Professor Leech observes) as early as the *Henry VI* trilogy, which appears to be the first set of popular plays to offer a total view of English society. It is indeed imperative that we recognize the playwright's independence, lest we be drawn to that most ghastly *reductio ad absurdum* of all, according to which *King Lear* is show biz.

Shakespeare was no intellectual, Dr. A. L. Rowse flatly states in his controversial biography.[24] On the face of it, this would appear to be a curious judgment to pass on the creator of *Hamlet* and *Troilus and Cressida*. Yet through the centuries a great many commentators have made it in one form or another in the long line that extends from Rowe to Rowse. A special and emphatic denial therefore seems warranted. In the theater of life Shakespeare played many parts: he was a husband and father, a provincial, a poet, a playwright, an actor, a shareholder in a theatrical company, a real-estate investor. Not least, he was also an intellectual, not an ignoramus. To the biographer falls the unenviable task of reconciling with one another the various personae adopted by this most extraordinary of men. Only when that is done—if it can be done—will we be able to tell the dancer from the dance.

The Comic View of Life in Shakespeare's Comedies

M. A. SHAABER

If current criticism of Shakespeare's comedies is something less than fully satisfactory, as it is to me, the main reason, I believe, is the failure to recognize their diversity and to readjust one's view from play to play accordingly. The search for the quiddity of Shakespearean comedy can blur one's ideas of the individual plays quite as much as the search for the quiddity of Shakespearean tragedy has impeded understanding of the tragedies. A frequent result is that the comic spirit which is very strong in some of them is lost sight of, since it is no part of the common denominator which criticism seeks.

Perhaps the trouble is partly semantic: we are intimidated by the label *romantic comedy* indiscriminately attached to all the plays that are not histories or tragedies. It seems to be generally assumed that the operative word in this phrase is the adjective. In most of Shakespeare's comedies this is true. Most of them evoke responses that are not properly comic. There is nothing essentially comic about romance. Romance excites the sense of wonder; it manipulates our sympathies through apprehension to triumph. It does not force upon our attention those disparities and incongruities in life which we regard as amusing. When we see a play like *The Two Gentlemen of Verona, The Merchant of Venice, All's Well that Ends Well,* or *The Winter's Tale,* we may exult over the success of the characters for whom our sympathy is solicited—we are certainly intended to do so—and we may laugh at the incidental comic turns with which all these plays are furnished, but we are not really amused; our pleasure depends upon an altogether different kind of response. Such plays are comedies only in the elementary sense that they end happily, that they are not tragic. I should prefer to call them romances, for indeed the triumphant happy ending itself, the general distribution of rewards—sometimes, especially in Shakespeare, including even reformation rather than punishment for the villains—is more distinctive of romance than of nonromantic comedy, which, while it may award success to some, is very likely to deal out a large measure of discomfiture and disillusion to others. Everybody knows this, but it has not checked the habit of generalizing about all Shakespeare's comedies as if they were plays of just the same kind or the affixing of a label which conceals the fact that in different plays the romantic and the comic are mixed in quite different ways and quite different proportions. Of Shakespeare's eighteen so-called comedies—setting aside the three farces, which are certainly comical but don't imply a view of life of significant depth or even of genuinely comic interest, and *Troilus and Cressida,* which is comic with a difference —there are just five plays which are truly comic: *Love's Labour's Lost, A Midsummer Night's Dream, Much Ado about Nothing, As You Like It,* and *Twelfth Night.* My point is that these plays are romantic comedies in a different sense of the term from that in which *The Two Gentlemen of Verona* and *All's Well that Ends Well* are romantic comedies, that *romantic comedy* is so far a misleading term for them that *anti-romantic comedy* would be no worse, that these plays embody a comic view of life.

Now, in all these plays, the main subject is the quest of love. Lovers struggle to overcome the obstacles that stand in their way and in the end succeed. This is a common formula of romance, and these plays afford us romantic satisfaction. But since they also embody a comic view of life, I should like to examine these components separately and to weigh their respective parts in the combination. For I think there has been a strong disposition to overstress the romantic component, to regard the plays as delightful affirmations of a rose-colored view of life and love which stirs us to a sentimental response. But as a matter of fact, in this combination the romantic component is slight, or at least it is not vigorously insisted upon. The background of these plays may strike us as romantic and it must have struck Shakespeare's contemporaries the same way, though probably less forcibly, not so much because they felt closer to Italy, Illyria, or the Forest of Arden as because they rarely saw plays with anything but romantic backgrounds. There is not much romantic derring-do in these comedies of Shakespeare's: in *Love's Labour's Lost* and *Much Ado about Nothing* none whatever; in *A Midsummer Night's Dream* next to none; in *As You Like It* and *Twelfth Night* just a little—Orlando's wrestling, his flight and then that of Rosalind and Celia, Orlando's off-stage slaughter of a lioness, the shipwreck of Viola and Sebastian. The most characteristically romantic motif in all these plays is the deception which overthrows the marriage of Hero and Claudio; this has nothing to do with romantic love, for if Claudio and Hero love each other romantically they never mention it—to tell the truth, have scarcely an opportunity to mention it, for we are never permitted to see them alone from the beginning to the end of the play. The romantic component of these plays, in fact, exists chiefly at the level of bare plot: each one of them is a love story in which a young man and a young woman, or several pairs of young men and young women, fall in love and overcome the obstacles that stand between them and the altar. Sometimes the obstacles themselves are not very romantic: nothing keeps Beatrice and Benedick apart but pride; nothing keeps Rosalind and Orlando apart but Rosalind's arbitrary maintenance of her disguise after it has served its purpose.

Indeed, even at the level of plot, the love story is not seen exclusively in the bright hues of romance. In *Love's Labour's Lost* the lovers are humiliated and are condemned to penance in the end, though their eventual reception into grace is forecast. In *A Midsummer Night's Dream* the lovers are confused, baffled, set at loggerheads until a moment before the end, when they are satisfactorily re-sorted in a fashion almost perfunctory. Love is inflicted on Titania as a punishment. In *Much Ado about Nothing,* there is just enough love between Claudio and Hero to make their marriage a little more than a commercial transaction and certainly nothing in Claudio's wounded pride or Hero's shame to convert a skeptic to the religion of love. As for Benedick and Beatrice, they do nothing to inflate the price of romance but agree with obstinate reluctance to marry in spite of everything. In *As You Like It* the love story of Rosalind and Orlando or Celia and Oliver answers all reasonable romantic requirements, though the presentation of it is cursory, but beside them are set the antiromantic triangle of Phebe, Silvius, and Ganymede and the utterly unromantic courtship of Audrey and Touchstone, which converts love into something ridiculous. In *Twelfth Night* Viola attains the bliss appointed for romantic lovers, but the duke, Olivia, and Sebastian merely blunder into marriages which our good nature agrees to call happy.

If these plays were thoroughly saturated with the romantic conception of love, one would expect them to reflect the religion of love as practiced by its Elizabethan votaries: the recitation of love's litany, the subtle analysis of love's force and of its effects on lovers. Actually there is very little of this kind of thing; indeed, there is comparatively little even in Shakespeare's romances. There are plenty of discussions of love and lovers, but they are rarely in the exquisite key of the poetry of courtly love. Where will you find a panegyric on love like some of Spenser's sonnets or a proud affirmation of its awful supremacy like some of Sidney's? Shakespeare's characters deliver themselves of this vein very rarely, chiefly when, like the king and his courtiers in *Love's Labour's Lost* or Orlando in the Forest of Arden, they write messages of love to their ladies. And in both instances these outpourings of sentiment are immediately covered with ridicule—in *Love's Labour's Lost* by their revelation of the young men's oath-breaking, in *As You Like It* by Touchstone's parody and Rosalind's caustic comments on Orlando's insufficiency as a poet. An instructive comparison may be made with Lodge's *Rosalynde,* obviously parallel in plot with *As You Like It.* But there is a world of difference in the dialogue. *Rosalynde* is largely composed of passions, discourses, meditations, and complaints in which the characters explore at great length their situation or their feelings by means of the conventional dialectic of love. There is nothing they do more readily or more volubly unless it is writing verses in the same strain, as Rosader did when, after overthrowing the wrestler and receiving a jewel from Rosalynde, he found himself "unfurnished" with a suitable reply and, stepping into a convenient tent, found there the pen and paper to write a sonnet. The explanation is not simply that *Rosalynde* is a euphuistic novel instead of a play; Shakespeare could have made his heroes and heroines analyze the sentiment of love and their own feelings equally well. The proof lies in the fact that, in *The Two Gentlemen of Verona,* he comes so much closer to doing so than in any other play. The truth is that Shakespeare's characters are Laodiceans in the religion of love. Not heretics: there is nothing in their conduct or their ideals which is clearly repugnant to its tenets, but they are perfunctory and indifferent worshippers at its altars, neglecting most of the more esoteric devotions upon which the typical devotee expends so much elegant language.

Indeed, it may be that even so we overestimate the romantic allure of these plays. We accept and approve romantic love: we automatically give it our sympathy; we assume that it is the proper basis of marriage. But when Shakespeare wrote these plays romantic love was still far from being universally sanctioned and approved. The literature of the time takes an ambiguous view of it. It is a common theme of fiction, and its exciting possibilities are often sensationally exploited, but half the time such stories are offered as examples of the folly and sin of love, and their authors more or less openly, and no doubt more or less sincerely, advise their readers not to follow the example of the lovers in the story. The most notorious instance, I suppose, is Arthur Brooke's version of the story of Romeo and Juliet. This he offers to his readers as a story of

> a coople of vnfortunate louers, thralling themselues to vnhonest desire, neglecting the authoritie and aduise of parents and frendes, conferring their principall counsels with dronken

gossyppes, and superstitious friers (the naturally fitte instru-
mentes of vnchastitie), attempting all aduentures of peryll, for
thattaynyng of their wished lust, vsyng auriculer confession
(the kay of whoredome, and treason) for furtheraunce of
theyr purpose, abusyng the honorable name of lawefull mar-
iage, to cloke the shame of stolne contractes, finallye, by all
meanes of vnhonest lyfe, hastyng to most vnhappye deathe.

Brooke is not unique. Many other writers offered cooling cards
to fond lovers to cure them of their infatuation. Robert Greene,
who published a long series of lucrative "love-pamphlets" of the
romantic allurements of which he could not possibly have been
unconscious, often admonishes his readers of the deplorable consequences of passionate love and still more often makes a distinction between ungoverned love, which leads to folly and sin, and
love governed by reason, which from the romantic point of view
is hardly love at all. The fiction which Greene called *Tullies Love*
is advertised on the title page as "setting out in liuely portratures
how young Gentlemen that ayme at honour should leuell the end
of their affections, holding the loue of countrie and friends in more
esteeme than those fading blossomes of beautie that onely feede
the curious suruey of the eye"; his *Gwydonius* purports to be a
story "wherein the folly of those Carpet Knights is decyphered,
which guyding their course by the compasse of Cupid, either dash
their ship against most daungerous Rocks, or els attaine the hauen
with paine and perill." Lodge's *Euphues Shadow* is offered as a tale
"Wherein youthfull folly is set downe in his right figure, and vaine
fancies are prooued to produce many offences."

   If writers like Greene who busily exploited romance were at the
same time suspicious of romantic love, perhaps even partly hostile
to it, the attitude of the right-thinking moralists of the day was
perfectly unambiguous. They could hardly say too much against it.
To them it was one of man's most sinful aberrations. Romantic
love in fact had been condemned by moralists and theologians for
many generations. They could hardly have done otherwise. A pas-

sion which so often overrode all other considerations, which paralyzed reason and put the unbridled individual will on the throne where reason should sit, could not have inspired them with anything but horror. The theologians of the middle ages even tried to differentiate between passionate love, which they utterly detested, and conjugal love, which they could not but tolerate. This experiment in hairsplitting led to such appalling pronouncements as that of the Spanish Dominican Peter de Ledesmo, quoted by Burton, that every kiss a man gives his wife after marriage is a mortal sin or the judgment of St. Jerome that any man who loves his wife ardently is an adulterer.[1] "Love of beauty is a forgetting of reason" (this is Jerome again[2]); it is therefore necessarily bad. The idea of choosing a wife or husband because of romantic attraction was especially repugnant to the best authorities. A spouse should be chosen for sobriety and wisdom, and consequently by one's parents, who are more likely to be sober and wise than their children; they that marry for love shall lead their life in sorrow is the regular burden of advice on this subject.

It would seem then that we may be overshooting the mark a bit in assuming that Shakespeare responded as warmly as we do to the romantic triumphs of his lovers. That he was unmoved by them I cannot believe for a moment, but it may be that in his mind they were figments of the idealizing imagination rather than viable modes of happiness for real people. In the sixteenth century, romantic love was still chiefly a literary convention, of which courtly-love poetry was a peculiarly exacting, unreal, and difficult form probably with no counterpart whatever in reality. When Bacon said that the stage is more beholding to love than the life of man, he was stating a fact, not simply coining an epigram. Perhaps, therefore, we ourselves supply much of the romantic magnetism of these plays out of our own prepossessions in favor of romantic love. Perhaps our enthusiastic response to the plays as love stories is self-generated. I sometimes think that a good part of it is due to the superlative desirability of the heroines, who, though no less susceptible to romantic love than other heroines, far excel them in wit and high spirits. Certainly the most common kind of critical response to them reminds one of the behavior of the whooping crane during the mating season. Possibly this overemphasis is due to our inveterate habit of interpreting the plays in terms of the characters: we applaud Rosalind as an extremely acceptable dream girl and Touchstone as a very droll jester, and let it go at that.

Far be it from me to deny the romantic attractiveness of these plays; I am concerned only to point out that it rests on a rather meager and possibly equivocal basis in the plays themselves, and may loom larger to our view than to that of Shakespeare and the more judicious of his contemporaries. I am even more concerned to point out that the comic element is at the very least as palpable, as pervasive as the romantic. In other words, when we call these plays romantic comedies, the stress is on the noun rather than the adjective. And in fact—what should be no surprise at all—the comic view of life in these plays is largely a comic view of love.

For in these plays what is said about love and lovers is mostly by way of disparagement, and this is the richest vein of comic interest in them. Shakespeare's comic characters, including some of his heroes and heroines, not only fail in the romantic lover's duty to suffer love's bondage proudly and to rationalize it as dedication to a service that will eventually be rewarded or as a form of supersensuous idealism, but they are regularly exposed by their romantic susceptibilities to ridicule, they become illustrations of the text that all nature in love is mortal in folly. Indeed sometimes they themselves protest vigorously against it and hold it up to ridicule and derision. Instead of kissing the rod they laugh at it, and the laughter is sometimes a horse laugh. From first to last, love is treated to a steady shower of badinage which points up not its ecstasy but its folly. Love leads to happiness, but only through a series of freakish mischances. And the happiness is not heaped up full and overflowing after the common fashion of romantic story; its complexion is a little mottled. In Shakespeare's comedies love is the prime joke.

From Berowne's exasperated denigration of Cupid and his comparison of a woman to a German clock to Rosalind's characterization of love as a madness deserving of the dark house and the whip, this chorus of witty disparagement and comic raillery is kept up. Incidentally, the same kind of aspersions are cast upon love even in *Romeo and Juliet,* where, for example, Mercutio speaks of "this sir-reverence love" as a mire out of which Romeo must be drawn and describes "this drivelling love" as "a great natural that runs lolling up and down to hide his bauble in a hole." In *A Midsummer Night's Dream* we hear that "The course of true love never did run smooth" almost as soon as the play begins, together with much other complaint about love's capriciousness. It is the sight of the young lovers in the woods, baffled and sore, that moves Robin Goodfellow to exclaim "Lord, what fools these mortals be!" The duke's epithet for the lover is "frantic." And the play ends with a grotesque parody of one of the most famous stories of romantic love from ancient times. *Much Ado about Nothing,* with two loquacious characters who are professed skeptics about love, is particularly full of abusive comment. To Benedick a "man is a fool when he dedicates his behaviors to love," marriage is thrusting one's neck into a yoke, and no woman is to be trusted. When Claudio asks for his opinion of Hero and Benedick asks, "Would you buy her, that you enquire after her?" Claudio exclaims, "Can the world buy such a jewel?" Benedick's reply is brutal: "Yea, and a case to put it into." Beatrice says she had rather hear her dog bark at a crow than a man swear he loves her and that she is at God upon her knees every morning and evening to beg the blessing of not being sent a husband. And the song of the play declares that "Men were deceivers ever." Even after his conversion, Benedick goes on sniping at the behavior prescribed for lovers. He suffers love—"I do suffer love indeed, for I love thee against my will." He cannot write the verses expected of a lover: he has tried, but he can find out no rime to *lady* but *baby,* for *scorn, horn*—a hard rime. "Leander, the good swimmer, Troilus the first employer of panders, and a whole book full of these quondam carpetmongers, whose names yet run smoothly in the even road of a blank verse—why, they were never so truly turn'd over and over as my poor self in love." And his conclusion is that "man is a giddy thing" and his vagaries as a lover are to be expected. In *As You Like It* this gibing at love reaches a peak, for Rosalind's undertaking to cure Orlando of his infatuation, to wash his liver as clean as a sound sheep's heart, that there shall not be one spot of love in it, affords an unparalleled opportunity to canvass the affectations of lovers. She describes the marks of a lover—his lean cheek, his sunken eye, his unsociableness, his neglect of his dress—and the changeableness of women, "longing, and liking, proud, fantastical, apish, shallow, inconstant, full of tears, full of smiles." She admonishes Orlando that "Men have died from time to time, and worms have eaten them, but not for love," that love lasts not "for ever and a day" but a day without the "ever," that the wiser a woman is, the waywarder. She pays her respects to the god of love as "that same wicked bastard of Venus that was begot of thought, conceiv'd of spleen, and born of madness, that blind rascally boy that abuses every one's eyes because his own are out." The indictment is quite comprehensive. And as if this were not enough, Touchstone travesties the excesses of lovers throughout. "We that are true lovers run into strange capers," he says, and he owns up to having kissed Jane Smile's batler for her sake, "and the cow's dugs that her pretty chopt hands had milk'd." He utters devastating home truths: "As the ox hath his bow, sir, the horse his curb, and the falcon her bells, so man hath his desires; and as pigeons bill, so wedlock would be nibbling." In *Twelfth Night* there is much less acid comment of this kind, the exposure of the capriciousness of love being effected chiefly by means of the plot, but the sentimental vaporizings of the duke and Viola's amused reflections on the susceptibility of women provoke smiles. In short, throughout these comedies love is subtly and grossly caricatured; its pretentions are transposed from the key of the sublime to that of the ridiculous.

In these plays there is also some disparagement of marriage, though not very much. It appears in Benedick's rueful observations on the inevitable fate of husbands to "sigh away Sundays"; in

Beatrice's remarks on the inevitability of the sequence of wooing, wedding, and repentance; in Touchstone's courageous acceptance of the fact that "as horns are odious, they are necessary" and his proof that the forehead of a married man is more honorable than the bare brow of a bachelor; in Rosalind's assurance to Orlando that "Maids are May when they are maids, but the sky changes when they are wives" and that the use of a woman's wit is to find the way to her neighbor's bed; in the clown's aphorism, in *Twelfth Night,* that "many a good hanging prevents a bad marriage," in the refrain of the spring song at the end of *Love's Labour's Lost,* " 'Cuckoo, cuckoo!' O word of fear, / Unpleasing to a married ear." This is a horse of a different color. The discommodities of marriage are the oldest joke in the world and comic writers had been exploiting them since the beginning of time. The surprising thing is that Shakespeare made no more capital out of them than he did. For a man who made as wretched a marriage as Shakespeare is reputed by some to have made, his attitude toward it seems simple and straightforward: he is all for it. This is especially true if we can accept the episode of Phebe and Silvius in *As You Like It* as a clue to his feelings, and certainly it is hard to account for some parts of this subplot if it is not monitory. Phebe, like the marble-hearted ladies of Petrarchan poetry, delights in tyrannizing over her lover and capriciously holding off his suit; Silvius, like the Petrarchan lover, absorbs his punishment meekly and asks for more. Rosalind's brutal comments on Phebe's unwomanliness in temporizing with a good man's offer of marriage seem to deflate thoroughly the romantic extravagance of which Phebe is the exemplar. Perhaps this helps us to single out precisely the form of romantic love which Shakespeare's comedies laugh at. It is not the desire for marriage nor the hazards of marriage itself. It is not that less brutal form of concupiscence which also passes under the name of love, the kind that abounds in Latin comedy, for instance, though the follies into which it betrays us are often the same as those encouraged by romantic love. But romantic love is quite different. It is not simply the desire for one woman rather than any woman or all women. It is also the disposition to worship her as well as to desire her, even to worship her without desiring her, and to abase oneself accordingly. The crucial test of its genuineness is always the willingness to sacrifice one's life for the sake of the beloved or the preference for death rather than life without her. Its most exquisite expression is the courtly-love poetry of the Renaissance. It is above all the exercise of a refined sensibility, which unbinds the imagination and tempts it to lapse into extravagance and eccentricity. It is love-in-idleness, love as the yearning of sensitive spirits for the quintessence of sensation, a luxury much too bright and good for human nature's daily food.

Shakespeare's, I submit, is a really detached view of love, the product of a real sense of humor. Shakespeare neither tries to correct the aberrations to which lovers are prone nor erects these aberrations into a cult which invests them with an inflated value. He is neither shocked nor disgusted nor taken in. Romantic love is, to its votaries, a form of devotion only a little less intense and absolute than religious devotion; to those not under its spell it is a truancy from reason—as Bottom says, "reason and love keep little company together nowadays." In this discrepancy Shakespeare finds the material of comedy; he finds love, as both blessing and curse, amusing.

This amusement, I think, is all the deeper because it is not based simply upon a rejection of romance and the illusions which support it. The cream of the jest is the juxtaposition of the disparagement of love and a romantic interest to which all but the most obstinately unromantic respond warmly. The cream of the jest is not that lovers are prone to folly and that Cupid is a prankish lad: that is really no news at all, and any number of detractors and humorists had pointed it out abundantly ever since the gods raised the first laugh at lovers' perjuries. The cream of the jest is that the comic aspect of love and the romantic are two sides of one thing, that they are inseparable, that neither is valid—neither is possible —to the total exclusion of the other. Shakespeare's comic view of love is based on the acceptance of it—on the acceptance of all of it, its component of folly as well as its component of glory. In the disparity between these two aspects, between its highest pretensions and all-conquering force and its Circean power to convert its devotees into laughingstocks, Shakespeare finds matter for endless amusement, amusement of the heartiest but the most genial and sympathetic kind.

I have said so much about Shakespeare's comic view of love that I need say little about his comic view of life as we find it applied to other matters. The story is much the same. Like Fielding, Shakespeare sets up affectation as his target and cleaves the pin neatly with his raillery. The exposure of affectation is sometimes brought off by plot devices, as in the confounding of Malvolio, but more often by the derisive comments of the characters. But as all the world knows, this exposure is rarely complete, the comment rarely scathing. The *saeva indignatio* of the satirist or self-appointed censor is far to seek. Shakespeare suffers fools gladly; indeed, sometimes it may seem that he loves them. Their limitations are clearly enough set forth, but they are not divested of all dignity or of all humanity. Sir Nathaniel is no doubt a simpleton, but he is also "a marvelous good neighbor, faith, and a very good bowler." Holofernes is an abominable pedant, but he has the sincere respect of Nathaniel, and even when he is hooted out of the part of Judas, he makes his exit gathering a few remnants of his dignity about him—"This is not generous, not gentle, not humble." Even Armado, though a fantastic travesty of fashionable affectations, is made human enough to fall in love with Jaquenetta. When Berowne disclaims the use of "figures pedantical," he disclaims what he and everybody else in the play—and quite obviously Shakespeare, too—take honest delight in. It is the same in all these plays. The stupid and the affected are almost never merely stupid and affected; they are not mere laughingstocks. We are shown also, as the reverse side of their stupidity and affectation, some human quality which makes them more than laughingstocks. The egregious Bottom would not be half so funny if he were merely stupid; it is the disparity between his stupidity and his immense self-possession, his inexhaustible good nature that makes him delightful, makes him infinitely more amusing than a mere comic butt. Jaques, Sir Andrew Aguecheek, and Malvolio are more uniformly held up to scorn, but at least Jaques is allowed to be consistent (he does not abandon the trees and their tongues, the stones and their sermons at the first opportunity to return to the pompous court), Malvolio is given the last word of retort against his tormentors and something like a dignified exit, while Sir Andrew, though pitiably bird-brained, is too harmless to arouse complete contempt. Shakespeare never mistakes invective for the full range of comedy. His attitude is critical but also compassionate. In *As You Like It,* he marks very plainly the affectation that exalts country life above court life and also that which exalts court life above country life, but he does not stack the cards in favor of either. This suspension of judgment is usually called Shakespeare's tolerance. It could just as well be called his sense of humor. What is comical in the plays is not something that fills us with disgust but something that we can cherish at the same time as we note its shortcomings, and our laughter is our recognition of the incongruity between its value and its limitations. Indeed, our laughter may express an even deeper perception, that value is never or rarely absolute, that however we may yearn for perfection, it is available only in a form diluted by imperfection; our laughter is our acquiescence in a settlement for fifty or seventy or ninety cents on the dollar.

Notes

Notes

1. See Brandes, *William Shakespeare* (New York, 1898), II, 55; Bradley, *Shakespearean Tragedy* (1904; reprint ed., London, 1950), p. 415; Tolman, *The Views about Hamlet and Other Essays* (New York, 1904), p. 42; S. L. Bethell, *Shakespeare and the Popular Dramatic Tradition* (London, 1944), p. 146; G. B. Harrison, ed., *Shakespeare: The Complete Works* (New York, 1952), p. 907, n.; F. E. Halliday, *The Enjoyment of Shakespeare* (London, 1952), p. 110; Cecile de Banke, *Shakespearian Stage Production* (London, 1954), p. 122; Michael Redgrave, "Shakespeare and the Actors," in *Talking of Shakespeare,* ed. John Garrett (London, 1954), p. 146; and B. L. Joseph, "Elizabethan Stage and Acting," in *The Age of Shakespeare,* ed. Boris Ford (Harmondsworth, Middlesex, 1956), p. 155.

2. *English Literary Criticism: The Renaissance* (London, 1947), p. 247.

3. *Shakespeare's "Hamlet": A New Commentary* (London, 1913), pp. 149-50.

4. J. Dover Wilson, *What Happens in Hamlet,* 3d ed. (New York, 1956), pp. 301-2, thinks Shakespeare intended the First Player as a caricature of Edward Alleyn, the leading actor in the company which competed with Shakespeare's and had in its repertory *The Spanish Tragedy* and Marlowe's plays. Bethell (*Shakespeare,* p. 148) calls the speech a conscious burlesque by Shakespeare of the "salient characteristics of Senecan tragedy: rant, Latinity, the stock emotive word; classical reference; extended conceit; the classical simile." Bradley had objected that if the speech is palpably bad, we must credit Hamlet with bad taste. Bethell tries to get around this by postulating that the audience would sympathize with Hamlet's "serious" view of the speech until the ranting begins, then would tune out to enjoy Shakespeare's takeoff of a rival company known for its older type of tragedy, then would switch back to Hamlet without crediting Hamlet with bad taste. Yet this explanation tells us no more than does Wilson's how the passage is relevant to the tragedy of Prince Hamlet.

5. M. A. Bayfield, in *A Study of Shakespeare's Versification* (Cambridge, 1920), pp. 103-6, is much perplexed by the fact that Hamlet here talks like a Stratford yokel, using the vulgar "woo't" instead of the correct *wilt.* To absolve Shakespeare of such writing, Bayfield conjectures that *woo't* found its way into the play-copy because it happened to fall from the lips of the actors in unguarded moments, thus corrupting the true text. I would reply that unguarded moments are exactly what Shakespeare saw the role of Hamlet as requiring.

6. *What Happens in Hamlet,* p. 213.

7. This principle applies, of course, in other of Shakespeare's plays as well. An actor who plays the jealous Othello must at one point (at the passage beginning, "Lie with her! Lie on her!" in IV.i) completely abandon verse speech for a whirling mode of utterance which ends in his falling like an epileptic.

8. *The Question of Hamlet* (New York, 1959), p. 150.

9. *The Meaning of Shakespeare* (Chicago, 1951), p. 367.

10. " 'Miching Malicho' and the Play Scene in *Hamlet*," *Modern Language Review*, XXXI (1936), 515.

11. Since Shakespeare is here imitating Italianate tragedy, we may note how Wolfgang Clemen has recently described the kind of tragedy written by the Italian tragic dramatists of the sixteenth century. Its personages, he says, "have no clear outlines, and no humanity; they are soulless puppets who are made to express well-worn and constantly reiterated sentiments and reflections." *English Tragedy Before Shakespeare* (London, 1966), p. 30.

12. See "Shakespeare's 'Small Latine and Less Greeke,' " in *Talking of Shakespeare*, pp. 210–11.

13. "The Basis of Shakespearian Comedy," in *Essays and Studies by Members of the English Association*, n.s. III (1950), 1–28.

14. *Shakespeare and the Rival Tradition* (New York, 1952), p. 115.

15. *Shakespeare as Dramatist* (London, 1935), p. 203.

16. Alvin Kernan ably discusses *Histriomastix* and *Satiromastix* in *The Cankered Muse* (New Haven, 1959), pp. 143–49, 163.

17. See O. J. Campbell, *Shakespeare's Satire* (Oxford, 1943), p. 55. Arthur Gray, however, in *How Shakespeare "Purged" Jonson* (Cambridge, 1928), has argued that Jaques was a portrait of Jonson specifically.

18. *Discoveries*, ed. G. B. Harrison (London, 1923), p. 33.

19. *Ben Jonson*, ed. C. H. Herford and Percy Simpson, 16 vols. (Oxford, 1925–52), II, 21.

20. Ibid., pp. 25–27.

21. *Discoveries*, p. 44.

22. See *Englische Studien*, XLIII (1910–11), 379.

23. In *Shakespearean Tragedy* (p. 415), Bradley calls it Marlovian, and reasons that Shakespeare must have liked this style and "despised the million for not approving it." J. M. Robertson (*Shakespeare and Chapman* [London, 1917], p. 215) considers the versification Marlovian but the vocabulary characteristic of Chapman— e.g., in the words "coagulate," "repugnant," and "fellies."

24. Kernan (*The Cankered Muse*, pp. 66–67) describes the philosophical continuity.

25. See Harrison's edition, p. 88; also O. J. Campbell, *Comicall Satyre and Shakespeare's "Troilus and Cressida"* (San Marino, 1938), pp. 39–40.

26. Campbell so interprets (ibid., pp. 60–62).

27. *The Cankered Muse*, pp. 162–63.

28. "The Structural Experiment in Hamlet," *Review of English Studies*, XXII (1946), 282–88.

29. *What Happens in Hamlet*, pp. 323–24.

30. See, e.g., C. S. Baldwin, *Renaissance Literary Theory and Practice* (New York, 1939), esp. p. 179; Marvin T. Herrick, *The Fusion of Horatian and Aristotelian Literary Criticism, 1531–1555* (Urbana, 1946), esp. pp. 2, 106; and R. S. Crane, *The Languages of Criticism* (Toronto, 1953), p. 94.

31. *Ben Jonson*, I, 379.

32. Nevill Coghill, in "The Basis of Shakespearian Comedy" (p. 7) remarks that the neoclassicist comedy of ridicule "offers no antithesis to Tragedy as such, and indeed the ends of either form are often alike." In illustration of this, one could cite Preston's *Cambises* (1569), which is called on its title page a "lamentable tragedy" but named a "comedie" in the running title.

33. *"Catiline* and the Nature of Jonson's Tragic Fable," *PMLA,* LXIX (1954), 274.

34. *Discoveries,* p. 42.

35. *The Oration in Shakespeare* (Chapel Hill, 1942), p. 223.

36. Clarence Mendenhall (*Our Seneca* [New Haven, 1941], p. 195) has remarked that Shakespeare, like Sophocles, handled *plots* in drama "with an economy of means quite foreign to the genius of Seneca."

37. I have treated other aspects of the play in my *Shakespearean Tragedy: Its Art and Its Christian Premises* (Bloomington, 1969), chap. 4.

38. Shakespeare may have been familiar with Augustine's critique of the Stoic ideal, in *City of God* ix.4–5, xiv.2–4, and xix.4.

"MELEAGER" AND "ULYSSES REDUX"

1. For a valuable account of William Gager's life and career, see C. F. Tucker Brooke, "The Life and Times of William Gager (1555–1622)," *Proceedings of the American Philosophical Society,* XCV (1951), 401–31. See also Frederick Samuel Boas, *University Drama in the Tudor Age* (Oxford, 1914), pp. 165–219 et passim.

2. Francis Meres, *Palladis Tamia* (London, 1598), sig. Oo3ᵛ.

3. Boas, *University Drama,* pp. 165, 192.

4. Ibid., p. 197, n., Boas made an error of one day in dating the play. See E. K. Chambers's review of Boas, *University Drama in the Tudor Age,* in *Modern Language Review,* XI (1916), 358–60.

5. See the list of university plays and their dates as given by Boas, pp. 385–90.

6. In my quotations from Gager's Latin works, I have expanded abbreviations, modernized the long *s,* adopted the modern usage of *v* and *u,* printed *j* as *i* throughout, separated ligatures, and removed diacritical accents.

7. *Metamorphoses* vi.193–95.

8. *University Drama,* pp. 170, 174.

9. Catullus lxii.42–54.

10. For full details of this controversy, see Karl Young, "William Gager's Defence of the Academic Stage," *Transactions of the Wisconsin Academy of Sciences, Arts and Letters,* XVIII (1916), 593–638. Young gives the text of Gager's important letter to Rainolds of 31 July 1592, in which Gager writes: "What resemblance is there betweene owre *Hippodamia* only singing, *Eurymachus* only sayinge, *Phemius* bothe singinge and sayinge . . . and betweene *Nero*" (Young, p. 615).

11. Gager's stage directions are discussed by David Greenwood, "The Staging of Neo-Latin Plays in Sixteenth Century England," *Educational Theatre Journal,* XVI (1964), 311–23.

12. Rainolds, letter to Gager of 30 May 1593, printed in Rainolds, *Th' Overthrow of Stage-Plays* ([Middleburgh], 1599), p. 102. The long *s* has been modernized in this quotation.

13. E. K. Chambers, *The Elizabethan Stage* (Oxford, 1951), I, 186.

"KING HENRY IV," PART I

1. Percy is but my factor, good my lord,
   To engross up glorious deeds on my behalf;

And I will call him to so strict account
That he shall render every glory up. . . .

[III.ii.147–50]

2. How now, my Lord of Worcester? 'Tis not well
That you and I should meet upon such terms
As now we meet. . . .
. . . .
. . . Will you again unknit
This churlish knot of all-abhorred war,
And move in that obedient orb again
Where you did give a fair and natural light,
And be no more an exhal'd meteor,
A prodigy of fear, and a portent
Of broached mischief to the unborn times?

[V.i.9–21]

3. One may compare the prophecy of Elizabeth's greatness that ends *Henry VIII.* Is it not possible that Hotspur's dying "O, I could prophesy, / But that the earthy and cold hand of death / Lies on my tongue" (V.iv.83–85) also refers to Hal's future greatness?

4.   but let me tell the world,
If he outlive the envy of this day,
England did never owe so sweet a hope,
So much misconstrued in his wantonness.
To this, Percy replies,
be he as he will, yet once ere night
I will embrace him with a soldier's arm,
That he shall shrink under my courtesy.

[V.ii.66–69, 73–75]

5. This account of the Francis incident condenses the larger analysis of it in my "Hal and Francis in *King Henry IV, Part 1*," *Renaissance Papers 1965,* pp. 15–20.

6. *Action* means, substantially, a battle, an encounter, or some course that would lead to an important conflict. It is in this sense that Hotspur in the preceding scene abuses himself for trying to win to his party a cautious lord, "O, I could divide myself and go to buffets for moving such a dish of skim milk, with so honourable an action" (II.iii.34–36). Hal's words to Poins are intended to repeat Hotspur's phrase as a form of parody. "Action" is also on Falstaff's lips. As he enters at III.iii, he enquires of Bardolph, "Am I not fall'n away vilely since this last action? Do I not bate? Do I not dwindle?" Here in the cant of the highway is another parody of the word, one that demotes its honorable and warlike connotations to the farcical engagement at Gadshill. Falstaff may not be wholly serious (certainly he rolls the word under his tongue), but Hal's use of *action* (as of *honor*) is clearly ironic and turned against himself, even though Poins is too stupid to recognize the fact, as Hal well knows. The heir to the throne has put himself into a position where his "action" can be only a drinking bout with the tavern boys. Thus his irony is a form of self-disgust and accusation, which sets the tone for the second "action"— although this is not so named—the individual encounter (single combat?) with Francis.

7. No one can take seriously Falstaff's promise to purge and live cleanly if he is rewarded for the alleged slaying of Percy (V.iv.166–68).

8. "The famous 'I know you all' soliloquy, at the very beginning of the play, effectively disposes of any dramatic suspense that might have developed from a genuine inability in the Prince to make up his mind about his future. From the start of the play, therefore, Shakespeare has deliberately cast off the legitimate suspense that might have been generated by a lack of Hal's firm commitment. The soliloquy shows Hal to be plain enough. He is amusing himself for the nonce. When an emergency arises he will break through the clouds like the sun and show himself in his true majesty. He is not in the least deceived by Falstaff, nor does he have more than a partial interest in their tavern life. . . . It is not a character speech at all, as Kittredge has observed, but a time-saving plot device, rather on the clumsy side, deliberately to remove from the audience any suspense that Hal was actually committed to his low-life surroundings" (Bowers, "Shakespeare's Art: The Point of View," *Literary Views: Critical and Historical Essays,* ed. Carroll Camden [Chicago, 1964], p. 56). To this, one may perhaps add the incentive Hal felt to remove himself from court during the critical time before he is to inherit the throne. That Hal amuses himself genuinely in the taverns is clear enough, but that he also chafes under the necessity is indicated in the Francis episode. Finally, Shakespeare goes to extraordinary lengths to keep Hal blameless. Falstaff's sly suggestion of sexual incontinence is promptly rejected (I.ii.53–54), and it is clear that before Gadshill Hal had gone on no highway-robbery expeditions. In short, we hear talk about a dissolute life, but we see none of it except of the most harmless variety.

9. The moment the words are uttered, Bardolph runs in with the announcement of the arrival of the sheriff. Falstaff, who is surely in danger from this approach, is so concerned with answering Hal, also directly, though maintaining the fiction of the play, that he shouts him off. The Hostess then brings the same news. At this point Falstaff gives up the fiction of play-acting and addresses Hal without pretense: "Dost thou hear, Hal? Never call a true piece of gold a counterfeit. Thou art essentially mad without seeming so." These words can refer only to Hal's abuse of Falstaff in the role of the King, but particularly to the seriousness of "I do, I will," which Falstaff recognizes. (I must reject Kittredge's preferred alternative that they mean, "Believe what the hostess is telling you.") I am genuine gold, says Falstaff, not a sham. If you are serious in your proposal to reject me, you are truly insane, even though your surface demeanor would not suggest it. This is followed by Falstaff's direct challenge to Hal to let the sheriff come in and arrest him, the result being his execution as a highwayman. Hal does not accept this challenge (II.iv.540 ff.).

10. "Shakespeare's Art: The Point of View," pp. 54–58: "In terms of the plot the climax can only be Act III, scene ii, in which, seemingly, King Henry weans Hal from his dissolute life and sets him on the road to Shrewsbury, the conquest of Hotspur, and the acceptance of his duties as Prince of Wales. By himself, it is implied, King Henry cannot subdue the rebels. By himself, Hal can have no national forces to lead. A scene of high drama can be anticipated in which the father pleads with his son to join him against a common danger; and, on the surface, Shakespeare gives us just that. . . . Every indication points to Henry's having prepared this interview with particular care, as was his way, leaving nothing to chance. . . . Are we to believe, then, that the King has truly won over his son by this contrivance, has broken down Hal's indifference, detached him from Falstaff and the idle tavern life that was corrupting him, and returned the Prince to the great world of affairs that was to be the training for the hero-king Henry V? If we are to believe so, then we must take it that a real conflict of wills was present and

that it was resolved in classic fashion in a turnabout of motive and action, a true peripeteia. The King would have been right, and Hal wrong. Hal would have been convinced of the error of his ways by the force of his father's speech and would have been, in a manner of speaking, converted. Such a scene might well have been an exciting and significant one; but Shakespeare did not write it so. The true point of the climax is that no peripeteia takes place. Hal makes no decision that he had not previously planned. . . . What kind of a play is it in which the Prince from the start reveals to the audience his whole future course of action and therefore destroys the pleasurable uncertainty the audience would feel in the development of the suspense and its resolution? . . . What kind of a play is it in which the climax goes through all the motions of a decision, but no decision is actually made, for none is needed? The answer is an obvious one. . . . Once we learn to read the plot, we see what Shakespeare intends to convey to us through the action. . . . King Henry may think he has converted his erring son, but Shakespeare tells us the contrary in his plot. That the climax is no climax, in respect to any decision not made before, should alert us to Shakespeare's clear intentions. [Hal] is not influenced in any way by the attempts of others to engage him, because from the start he knows the synthesis that lies ahead for him in the ideals of kingship, chivalry, and the proper use of materialism. This is what Shakespeare tells us through the plot, and we should pay attention to its evidence."

11. For an examination of the Elizabethan code in this matter, see my "Middleton's *A Fair Quarrel* and the Duelling Code," *Journal of English and Germanic Philology*, XXXVI (1937), 40–65.

IAGO'S "IF"

1. The Kittredge edition of *Othello* (Boston, 1941) has been used for reference.

2. I am not attempting character interpretation for its own sake; my position is that of Stoll in putting dramatic necessity before completeness or consistency of character. What Shakespeare does is to create within the dramatic framework an illusion of credible action, convincing as long as one abides by his terms. My study of the movement of the syntax is meant to account in part for this credibility.

3. For an excellent example of this, see in Roderigo's speech to Brabantio (I.i.120–38) a logical sequence of conditional sentences ending in a false conclusion based on the argument from sign; dramatically at this moment Iago and Roderigo are acting as one. On the use of the enthymeme in rhetoric, see Aristotle's *Rhetoric,* in *Rhetoric and Poetics,* ed. Friedrich Solmsen (New York: Modern Library, 1954), esp. 1355^a6 ff., 1356^b1 ff. (definition), 1357^a14 ff. (basis in the contingent), 1357^b1 ff. (type based on sign), 1394^a26 ff. (relation to maxims), 1397^a7 ff. (examples in conditional form), 1400^b35 ff. (spurious kinds, esp. 6, arguments from consequence; 7, causes which are not causes).

4. On Iago's destructive role put in other terms (i.e., as slanderer) see the present writer's "Good Name in Othello," *Studies in English Literature,* VII (Spring 1967), 195–217.

5. Many others, reinforcing or varying these, are left as riches for the exploring reader.

6. In Evanthius, iv. 5, and Donatus, vii. 1–4 (*Comicorum graecorum fragmenta,* ed. G. Kaibel [Berlin, 1899], vol. I, fasc. 1, pp. 67, 69), familiar through Renaissance

editions of Terence and commentaries on him; see especially Erasmus's school edition (Basel: Froben, 1532, 1534).

TRAGEDY IN THE SPANISH GOLDEN AGE

1. In *Classical Drama and Its Influence: Essays Presented to H. D. F. Kitto,* ed. M. J. Anderson (London, 1965), pp. 193–228.

2. In "Some Observations on *Tragedia* and *Tragicomedia* in Lope," *Hispanic Review* (1943), pp. 185–209. The quotation is from a summary of Morby's argument by Mr. Victor Dixon, contained in a review of my edition of Lope's *El castigo sin venganza* (Oxford, 1966) published in the St. Andrew's *Forum for Modern Language Studies,* III (1967), 188–91.

3. "escrita al estilo Español, no por la antigüedad Griega, y Seueridad Latina, huyendo de las sombras, Nuncios y coros." Prologue to the 1634 *Suelta* edition of the play, produced at Barcelona.

4. ". . . comedia no es otra cosa sino vn artificio ingenioso de notables y finalmente alegres acontecimientos, por personas disputado." Torres Naharro, *"Propalladia" and Other Works* (Bryn Mawr, 1943), I, ed. J. E. Gillet, p. 142.

5. Morby discusses also the term *tragicomedia* as used by Lope, but his observations are not strictly relevant here.

6. *Francisco de Rojas Zorrilla and the Tragedy* (Albuquerque, 1958).

7. "porque el deleyte viene a la tragedia de la compassion del oyente, y no la podrá tener si el agente no parece estar muy apassionado." *Philosophia Antigua Poética,* ed. A. Carballo Picazo (Madrid, 1953), II, 320.

8. "Brecht y el drama del Siglo del Oro," *Segismundo* (1967), pp. 39–54.

THE COMEDIES OF CALDERON

1. The traditional view, as G. W. Ribbans reminds me, is that most of Calderón's plays were lacking in tragic emotion. But several recent critics have sought to redress the balance. See, e.g., A. A. Parker, "Towards a Definition of Calderonian Tragedy," *Bulletin of Hispanic Studies,* XXXIX (1962), 222–37.

2. A translation of *Una casa con dos puertas mala es de guardar* ("A House with Two Doors") was published in the *Tulane Drama Review,* VIII (1963), 1–157.

3. Bertrand Evans, *Shakespeare's Comedies* (New York, 1960), passim.

4. *Calderón: Four Plays* (New York, 1961), pp. xxii–xxiv. But I doubt whether Mr. Honig is right in suggesting that Luis is guilty of incestuous desires: Luis does not know that he is pursuing his own sister.

5. If the intention is to show that the sword has been damaged, this is not made clear in the dialogue.

"LA VENEXIANA"

1. *Storia della letteratura italiana,* 8th ed. (Milan-Messina, 1965), p. 173. *"La Mandragola* . . . è la più potente commedia del nostro teatro."

2. Actually, as a careful examination of the manuscript reveals, the correct spelling

is *La Veniexiana* but since this has not appeared in any publication before 1967, I adhere to the old spelling, for the sake of uniformity.

3. "... è tornata da pochi anni alla luce una commedia anonima, *La Venexiana*, ... l'unica commedia appassionata del secolo, l'unica—insieme con *La Mandragola* —che esuli affatto dagli schemi convenzionali." Momigliano's history of Italian literature first appeared in 1934 but the phrase "da pochi anni" remains in the 1965 edition.

4. *"La Venexiana": Commedia di ignoto cinquecentista*, ed. Emilio Lovarini (Bologna, 1928), no. 1 in Nuova scelta di curiosità letterarie inedite o rare. Le Monnier in Florence published a reprint in 1947; in the modified introduction Lovarini tackled a problem he had gingerly side-stepped in 1928: when was the play written?

5. "la vaghissima commedia che qui pubblichiamo," in the first sentence of the introduction.

6. *"La Venexiana": A Sixteenth Century Venetian Comedy*, ed. and trans. Matilde Valenti Pfeiffer (New York, 1950).

7. "oramai nota e celebre," in Ruzzante, *"La Pastorale,"* ed. E. Lovarini (Florence, 1951), p. vii. This play and *La Venexiana* stem from the same manuscript, hence the reference to the latter in this context.

8. The anonymous author of *La Venexiana*, not plagued by modesty, was quite sure to have created *the* comedy of the Venetian society of his day. The title is not derived from either one of the leading ladies of the play.

9. (Milan, 1966), 288 pp.

10. "D'altra parte, ho ritenuto di dover escludere dalla mia indagine una commedia come *La Venexiana*, in quanto essa mi è sembrata legata meglio, per il linguaggio anche formalmente dialettale, all'altro tipo di drammaturgia—quella popolare—la cui caratterizzazione può avvenire, a mio avviso, unicamente sull'elemento linguistico."

11. *"La Venexiana* è il primo componimento in solo dialetto veneziano, ma il suo contenuto e i suoi personaggi non risultano che in minima parte popolari." One could similarly contrast Marvin T. Herrick with Benedetto Croce. Herrick, on p. 56 of his *Italian Comedy of the Renaissance* (Urbana, 1960), makes the following astonishing statement: "[*La Venexiana*] has several features of the farce, such as Venetian and Bergamask dialects, a straightforward plot devoid of elaborate intrigues, disguises, mistaken identities, and recognition scenes." Croce, sensitive to the sad and potentially tragic currents in the play, prefers to call it a drama. See "La 'Commedia' del Rinascimento," in *Poesia popolare e poesia d'arte* (Bari, 1946); pp. 299–301 deal with *La Venexiana*. These points seem worth mentioning, even before the discussion of the play.

12. When Bartolomeo Gamba compiled his bibliography, *Serie degli scritti impressi in dialetto veneziano*, the discovery of *La Venexiana* was still over one hundred years away. In the second edition, prepared by Nereo Vianello and published in 1959 by the Istituto per la Collaborazione Culturale, Venice-Rome (Fondazione Giorgio Cini), the play makes its entry in a footnote on p. 59.

13. *Teatro italiano*, ed. Silvio d'Amico (Milan, 1955), I, 503–52.

14. (Milan, 1959), II, 493–553.

15. *Teatro veneto*, vol. VI, in the series La Fenice del teatro, ed. Vito Pandolfi (Parma, 1960), xcviii + 1268 pp.

16. Ignoto veneto del Cinquecento, *La Venexiana*, Collezione di teatro, no. 63

(Turin, 1965). The success of this edition was such that it became quickly unavailable, but a reissue has been announced.

17. (Bologna 1966). In the title "minore" should not be taken too seriously, with such authors as Castiglione, Cellini, and Michelangelo represented.

18. "Pur nella abbondantissima produzione del teatro comico italiano del Cinquecento, non sono molte le commedie che, come *La Venexiana,* si possono sicuramente collocare accanto alla *Mandragola;* fiorite in due situazioni culturali profondamente diverse . . . nella *Mandragola* [il proposito] è l'aspra denuncia della corruzione nei diversi individui della società . . . mentre nella *Venexiana* è lo spettacolo delle passioni che dominano l'animo dell'uomo e che merita non reprimere ma soddisfare" (*Cinquecento minore,* p. 218).

19. The volume will be published by the Unione Tipografico-Editrice Torinese.

20. "Pinxero ingenuamente gli antichi Cupido, figliuol de Venere, un fanciul cieco, nudo, alato et pharetrato." The quotations in the original are taken from the Zorzi text which in turn is based upon the Lovarini edition of 1947. As for the translations, the English version of M. V. Pfeiffer has helped me with my own.

21. "in sottintesa polemica antibembesca," i.e., against Bembo's exaltation of idealized love. G. Padoan, *"La Veniexiana;* 'non fabula non comedia, ma vera historia,' " *Lettere italiane,* XIX, no. 1 (1967), 41. The article, the most important recent study of the play, comprises pp. 1–54. Padoan transcribes correctly *Veniexiana,* a spelling that is corroborated by other sources pertaining to the first half of the sixteenth century (see n. 2 above).

22. "Oggi lo cognoscerete chiaro, o spectatori, quando lo amor smisurato de una nobile conterranea vostra odirete posto in un forestiero giovenetto; . . . parimenti lo amor de una altra, pur in quel medemo [medesimo] già posto. . . . Di che, la letizia de una et il dolor de l'altra comprehendendo, vederete quanto Amor in donna sii potente. . . ."

23. ". . . oggi di nostri mimi senza vergogna serà publicato." The references to the spectators, to the actors, and to the fact that the female roles were actually taken by males (mentioned elsewhere in the Prologue) all suggest a performance of the play. But Lovarini hedges on this issue, admitting only the possibility. The crudity of certain passages may have been too much—but was Aretino's Venice really that sensitive? (1928 ed., pp. 19–20). A much more serious matter was the implication of families living in Venice at the time, a question which G. Padoan has pretty much removed from the realm of conjecture.

24. In the manuscript we find the abbreviation "for." Lovarini explains with subtlety that the author perhaps wanted to be understood also by those who were weak in Latin and would not have understood the classical *advena;* and that at the same time the author was reluctant to write out, "quella barbara voce," *foresterius* (1928 ed., p. 24).

25. "One would say that he is a budding Casanova" ("Si direbbe un Casanova in erba"). Lovarini, 1928 ed., p. 15.

26. "che xè [è] un viso de anzolo [angiolo], un musin d'oro, vegnuo [venuto] qua dal Paradiso." Here I cannot agree with Pfeiffer who has "a countenance of gold" for "un musin d'oro." This is hardly Angela's language, and surely not at this moment.

27. "Stè indrío, ché me sofeghè. . . . Vu no v'arecordè che sun dona . . . perché vu fe matieríe."

28. "Cara Nena, fa' un puoco el sbisao [il bullo] per mio amor." To Diego Valeri

it seems that ladies of good families really don't talk (or shouldn't talk) like that. Therefore he says of Valeria and Angela, "due donne (quasi gentildonne)." "Caratteri e valori del teatro comico," in *La Civiltà veneziana del Rinascimento* (Florence, publ. for the Fondazione Giorgio Cini, 1958), p. 12.

29. Some traits of the Roman *servus* of the better type are still recognizable in our *baiulus:* he provides most of the humor, he is a faithful servant when the occasion requires it, he is not beyond self-glorification, and he is fond of moralizing. But he is not impudent and surely not indiscreet. And he is no buffoon, despite his favorite exclamation, "cacasangue!" It is equally interesting to insert Bernardo into the Zanni-Arlecchino tradition of the *commedia dell'arte.*

30. "Volíu che 'l marío la maze? Ché la xè noviza."

31. "Vedí, se m'volí dà la fed da om da be' e fà com dico mi, af menarò sta not in *gloria in eselcis.*" In modern Italian: "Vedete, se mi volete dar fede di uomo dabbene e fare come dico io, vi menerò stanotte in *gloria in excelsis*" (Zorzi). In English: "Look here, if you want to trust me like a gent and do as I tell you, I will take you tonight to the top of the scale" (Pfeiffer; this passage points up some of the weaknesses of this translation).

32. "Colei, se questa non è, non sapendo tal cosa, me averà excusato." This remark suffices to illustrate that Iulio talks from a much higher linguistic plateau than the others.

33. "A' no gh'ho dit vergot, s'a no che a'l vòi menà int'un lugh, in sta not, a dormí."

34. "El xè tropo belo per mi." This single remark could serve as a preamble to a broader comment by Diego Valeri: "The moment of happiness towards which they [Angela and Valeria] rush, in a different spirit but with the same impulsive desire, cannot give them peace of mind: in the half consciousness which they have of this fate, something bitter wells up which tinges the entire comedy with tragedy." ("L'attimo di felicità, verso cui esse corrono con diverso animo ma con pari impeto di desiderio, non potrà dar pace alle anime loro: dalla mezza coscienza che esse hanno di questa fatalità *surgit amari aliquid,* che insapora di dramma tutta la commedia.") It is obvious that Valeri agrees with Croce on these tragic implications (see n. 11 above). The above quotation comes from an opuscule of 40 pages by Valeri, *Il Teatro comico veneziano,* Venice, 1949. Published by the Gruppo Editoriale Veneziano, this has had a very small distribution, but as one might expect, it is available in the Biblioteca Marciana.

35. "Sastu che? . . . Qualche morosa che vul dormir co esso."

36. I am referring to the veiled identity of Signora Ponza in Pirandello's *Così è, se vi pare* ("It Is So if You Think So").

37. "Fio dolçe, quanto t'ho desiderao!"

38. "Questo non pàtio. Vostra Signoria se svesta, che io la adiutarò lei."

39. I cannot share in the high opinion Mario Apollonio has of the language used by the lovers: "Thus the courtly mannerisms of the lovers have the freshness of something new before they become the abstract and technical formulary of the actors of the *Commedia dell'arte*" ("E così i lezi cortigiani degli innamorati hanno la freschezza della novità, prima che diventino il formulario astratto e tecnico degli attori dell'Arte"). *Storia del teatro italiano* (Florence, 1958), I, 457. I feel that Iulio knows how to apply the varnish, with little substance underneath. As for Angela, the shift from "donna" to "gentildonna" is too abrupt to be convincing.

40. "Le mie carne brúsciano. Moro de doia."

41. "Anima mia dolçe, credea che ti avessi portao aqua per amorzar el foco del mio peto, ma ti ha portao legna e carbon per farlo pí arder."

42. *Lenguina,* Venetian for *linguina,* diminutive of *lingua,* "tongue"; *boca,* "mouth"; *dàme,* Venetian for *dàmmi,* "give me."

43. "Lo amor mio in voi non accade piú arecordarlo, però che, e morto e vivo, Iulio è vostro."

44. "però che è nobilissima vidua o coniugata."

45. "Lo experimentar è cosa bellissima, per aver avvantaggio in cognoscer." This sentenious statement has been interpreted as *the* key to both Iulio's and the author's character, first by Franca Angelini in her article *"La Venexiana"* in the *Enciclopedia dello Spettacolo.* Iulio is considered to be a typical man of the Renaissance who declares his hedonism and fondness of experimentation with complete lucidity. Through his intelligence and willingness to experiment (away from books and abstract idealism) he will succeed in the realm of possibilities. (The point has been picked up and elaborated by G. Padoan, *"La Veniexiana,"* p. 42.)

46. "Questa xè la magagna! Basta, intendo ben."

47. "Basta! Anzola e vu m'avè assassinàa."

48. "E possa che costei è suspiziosa, saría suttil cosa che li manifestassi l'odio; et quella, accorgendosi, se me ama, se accenderà piú."

49. Lovarini has carefully used all the references to elapsed time in the play and added up a total of four days for the action (1928 ed., p. 4).

50. These are other examples of parallel or linear action which are characteristic of the play.

51. "Perché gera tropo zelosa."

52. "Non vorrei poi, venendo, esser causa de maggior male suo. Lei è collerica et non mi crede. Come me veggia, se adirerà tanto, che gli nocerà poi."

53. "A' la va mal, quat ol puza li rusi" (Bergamask dialect). In Italian: "La va male, quando puzzano le rose" (Zorzi). The English version used here is Pfeiffer's again. This is another example of the proverbial language Bernardo likes to use.

54. "Vu avè guadagnà un corpo e un'anima che gera persa."

55. "Signora, non volio aver guadagnato piú che la grazia de Vostra Signoria, ché Quella se degna avermi in servitore suo."

56. "Oria, fia, sera la camera e va' su a Misser Grando, che no çiga. E se 'l dise gnente de mi, di' che ho mal e che, per questa sera, non voio che nissun me rompa la testa."

57. Croce points out that the sensuality in the play has altogether serious aspects that are far removed from Boccaccio's jocular handling of similar situations; a sensuality that could lead "to revenge, to blood, to tragedy" ("alla vendetta, al sangue, alla tragedia"). *Poesia popolare,* p. 300 (see n. 11 above).

Apollonio feels that in the fourth and fifth acts the author shows the greatest skill, employing an extremely well-handled decrescendo, and then ending the play sottovoce with the same theme that had been set forth in the prologue (*Storia del teatro italiano,* I, 456).

Mortier sees two possibilities: either that matters end badly, in violence characteristic of the Venetian Renaissance, or that they end in what Mortier considers an amusing situation, with Iulio finding himself in the presence of both women and having to squirm with embarrassment so that they will forgive him his double infidelity. But would the second alternative really be so amusing? I see in it a serious misconception of the three persons involved. ("Une comédie vénitienne de la Renaissance," *Etudes italiennes,* n.s. II [1932], 273. The entire article, which depends heavily upon Lovarini for the summary of the play, comprises pp. 265–75.)

Zorzi, while not denying the serious undercurrents of the comedy, considers Croce's gloomy prognosis exaggerated. "Scheda per *La Venexiana,*" p. 107 (see n. 16 above).

58. *The Freedom of French Classicism* (Princeton, 1950), p. 160.

59. The very pale ink has suffered even further from the chemical reagent Lovarini applied in order to make it more legible. Modern photographic processes can, however, heighten the contrast a little and the director of the Biblioteca Marciana wants to preserve the entire manuscript in this form.

60. In the introduction to Ruzzante (i.e. Beolco), *"La Pastorale,"* pp. vii–x (see n. 7 above).

61. Beolco contrasted in this juvenile effort the ideal pastoral world with the crude and cruel reality of the peasant's world.

62. *"La Bulesca": Commedia cinquecentesca inedita,* ed. Gildo Meneghetti (Venice, 1952); the play can also be found in Cibotto's anthology, *Teatro veneto,* pp. 351–76.

63. Lovarini restored the distichs to an intelligible reading (in an appendix to the 1947 ed., "I due distici latini della *Venexiana,*" pp. 157–58). I am reproducing the Latin with Lovarini's emendations, e.g., "resculptus" for "res stuptus" in the manuscript.

64. The alliance against the Venetians concluded in 1508 between Pope Julius II, the emperor Maximilian, Louis XII of France, and Ferdinand V of Aragon.

65. I repeat here the title of Padoan's revolutionary study, *"La Veniexiana:* 'non fabula non comedia, ma vera historia,' " *Lettere italiane,* XIX, no. 1 (1967), 1–54. This is the first in a projected series of studies dealing with problems of the Venetian theater of the sixteenth century. The second of these has already appeared, "Angelo Beolco de Ruzante a Perduoçimo," *Lettere italiane,* XX, no. 2 (1968), 121–200.

66. It is impossible to avoid an awkward translation of *duchesco,* a subject of the duchy of Milan.

67. There is no tangible proof that the passage from Sanudo quoted by Lovarini (1928 ed., p. 20) refers to *La Venexiana.*

68. "I fatti narrati nella *Veniexiana* sono ambientati dunque nell'inverno 1535–36, o nel successivo" (*"La Veniexiana,"* p. 19).

69. Both spellings occur in the manuscript.

70. Lovarini thought in 1928 that the "title" used by Valeria indicated that her husband was chief of police, adding in 1947 that Valeria may have said "Misser Grando" merely in order to make fun of her older husband. Padoan points out that the position referred to would have been completely out of the question for a nobleman. But, I wonder, would Valeria have threatened Iulio so quickly with court proceedings and deportation if she had not been conscious of considerable legal power "upstairs"?

71. *Nuova Antologia* LXIV, no. 1381 (Oct. 1929), 273–81.

72. Sanesi's attitude, definitely an example of "old" criticism on *La Venexiana,* infuriated Croce, and a sharp altercation between the two men followed. The arguments on both sides are summarized in Sanesi, "Chiosa intorno alla *Venexiana,*" *Rendiconti del R. Istituto Lombardo di Scienze e Lettere,* 2d ser. LXV (1932), 694–96. We can understand why Croce did not take kindly to one remark (among

others he didn't like): "Certainly, also its esthetic value is not exceptional" ("Certo, anche il suo valore estetico non è eccezionale").

73. Short of reading the plays themselves, we get a much better idea of their contents and import in Herrick, *Italian Comedy*, pp. 16–17, 22–23 (see n. 11 above).

74. Giustinian's range of interests and accomplishments is suggested in the title of the two most important studies that deal with him: Berthold Fenigstein, *Leonardo Giustiniani, venezianischer Staatsmann, Humanist und Vulgärdichter* (Halle, 1909), and Manlio Dazzi, *Leonardo Giustinian, poeta popolare d'amore* (Bari, 1934).

75. For the text, see Cibotto, *Teatro veneto*, pp. 188–94; for the chief biographical and bibliographical data, see also Cibotto, pp. 165–67.

76. Oria addresses her mistress also as "Madona Valiera," and when things begin to go really well, in Act V, as "Magnifica Madona."

77. Fenigstein comments, on p. 108 of his *L. Giustiniani:* "We are no longer dealing with types, but with characters" ("Wir haben es nicht mehr mit Typen zu tun, sondern mit Charakteren"). Padoan, on p. 43 of his article: "In the *Veniexiana* there really live personalities, not types" ("Nella *Veniexiana* infatti vivono personaggi, e non tipi").

78. See Zorzi edition, pp. 104–5.

79. The writing of the *Novelle* was spread over a long period, from 1510 to 1560.

80. "Girolamo Zarello—chi lo conosce?—sarebbe stato l'autore di questa originalissima operetta?" (p. 21).

81. In "Letteratura del Cinquecento: Una commedia in cerca d'autore," *Nuova Antologia* LXXXI, no. 1749 (Sept. 1946), 92–96.

82. Actually, Dazzi only speaks of the same intellectual climate without ever committing himself outright. Cf. p. 13 of his edition of *Il libro chiuso di Maffìo Venier (La tenzone con Veronica Franco),* a supplement "non venale" ("not for sale") to his four-volume anthology, *Il Fiore della lirica veneziana* (Venice, 1956). Cibotto, *Teatro veneto*, p. 201 agrees with Dazzi that the play should probably be ascribed to Maffìo Venier but I have not been able to find where Dazzi said that much.

83. The much discussed "Ci falt la geste, que Turoldus declinet." Turoldus, the author, the redactor, the scribe? And who was Turoldus? Not to mention the various interpretations of *declinet*.

SHAKESPEARE THE IGNORAMUS

1. An abridged version of this paper was read at the Shakespeare section of the Modern Language Association meeting in December 1967.

2. Thomas Carlyle, *On Heroes, Hero-Worship and the Heroic in History,* in *Works,* 17 vols. (London, 1885–88), III, 85, 87; see also p. 89.

3. E. K. Chambers, *William Shakespeare: A Study of Facts and Problems* (Oxford, 1930), II, 224.

4. Ibid.

5. Ibid., p. 232.

6. *Some Account of the Life &c. of Mr. William Shakespear,* in *Eighteenth Century Essays on Shakespeare,* ed. D. Nichol Smith (2d ed.; Oxford, 1963), p. 8.

7. Chambers, *William Shakespeare,* II, 249, 250.

8. *The History of the Worthies of England* (London, 1662), p. 126 ("Warwickshire").

9. Chambers, *William Shakespeare*, II, 254.

10. *Enquiry into the Learning of Shakespeare* (London, 1748), pp. iv–v (Preface).

11. *Critical, Historical, and Explanatory Notes on Shakespeare* (London, 1754), I, vi–vii (Preface).

12. Ibid., II, 146.

13. *Essay on the Learning of Shakespeare,* in *Eighteenth Century Essays on Shakespeare,* ed. Smith, p. 201.

14. James Northcote, *The Life of Sir Joshua Reynolds* (2d ed.; London, 1819), I, 152.

15. *The Essential Shakespeare* (Cambridge, 1932), p. 6.

16. Alfred Harbage, *Conceptions of Shakespeare* (Cambridge, Mass., 1966), p. 11.

17. *The Works of William Shakespeare,* ed. James O. Halliwell[-Phillipps] (London, 1853), I, 230.

18. *Outlines of the Life of Shakespeare* (5th ed.; London, 1885), pp. 137–38. As early as 1848 Halliwell[-Phillipps] described the subject of money as "not a very poetical theme, but one in which the dramatist evidently took a lively interest, having seen, perhaps, that 'if money go before, all ways do lie open,' and that it is 'a good soldier, and will on' " (*The Life of William Shakespeare* [London, 1848], p. 175). His subsequent writings on Shakespeare contain a number of variations on this unpoetical theme.

19. *A Life of William Shakespeare* (London, 1899), pp. 278–79. Lee expanded this statement when he enlarged his biography, but his view did not change.

20. Ibid., p. 279.

21. See Gerald Eades Bentley, "Shakespeare and the Blackfriars Theatre," *Shakespeare Survey 1* (Cambridge, 1948), 38–50. This is surely one of the most important articles on Shakespeare to be published in the past quarter century.

22. *Cymbeline,* ed. J. M. Nosworthy, The Arden Shakespeare (London, 1955), p. xi (Introduction).

23. "The Dramatists' Independence," *Research Opportunities in Renaissance Drama,* X (1967), 17–23.

24. ". . . he made a simple identification, being no intellectual, of Machiavellianism with what ordinary people had always called Evil. . . . he knew instinctively the uselessness of much speculation" (*William Shakespeare: A Biography* [New York, 1963], p. 120). William Empson refers to "the assertively unlearned Shakespeare (the case seems pretty well proved)"; see "Donne and the Rhetorical Tradition," *Kenyon Review,* XI (1949), 571.

SHAKESPEARE'S COMEDIES

1. *The Anatomy of Melancholy* III.2.2.4 (ed. Holbrook Jackson, 3 vols., Everyman's Library [1932], III, 112).

2. "Amor formae, rationis oblivio est" (*Adversus Jovinianum* i.49 [*Patrologia Latina,* XXIII, 293]).

Bibliography

Bibliography of Leicester Bradner

1921 "Ninigret's Fort: A Refutation of the Dutch Theory." *Rhode Island Historical Society Collections*, XIV, 1–5.

1925 "Ninigret's Naval Campaigns." *Rhode Island Historical Society Collections*, XVIII, 14–19.

1927 *The Life and Poems of Richard Edwards*. New Haven: Yale University Press.
"A Test for Udall's Authorship." *MLN*, XLII, 378–80.
"Dr. Wharton's Translation of Gray's Latin Poems." *Modern Philology*, XXV, 124–27.

1928 "Forerunners of the Spenserian Stanza." *Review of English Studies*, IV, 207–8.

1929 "A Finding List of Anglo-Latin Anthologies." *Modern Philology*, XXVII, 97–102.

1930 "The First English Novel: A Study of George Gascoigne's *Adventures of Master F. J.*" *PMLA*, XLV, 543–52.
Review of *The Latin Poems of John Milton*, edited and translated by Walter MacKellar. *Modern Philology*, XXVIII, 116–17.

1932 "Milton's *Epitaphium Damonis*." *The Times Literary Supplement*, 18 August, p. 581.

1933 "The Growth of *Wuthering Heights*." *PMLA*, XLVIII, 129–46.
"A Verse Translation by John Quincy Adams." *New England Quarterly*, VI, 361–63.

1934 Review of *Christopher Marlowe in London*, by Mark Eccles. *Modern Philology*, XXXII, 209–10.
"An Allusion to Bromley in *The Shepheardes Calendar*." *MLN*, XLIX, 443–45.
"Henry Cheke's *Freewyl*." *PMLA*, XLIX, 1036–40.

1935 "The Latin Translations of Spenser's *Shepheardes Calendar*." *Modern Philology*, XXXIII, 21–26.
Review of *Two Poems by Emily Brontë: With the Gondal Background of Her Poems and Novel*, by Fannie E. Ratchford. *Modern Philology*, XXXIII, 209–10.

1936 "References to Chaucer in Campion's *Poemata*." *Review of English Studies*, XIV, 322–23.

1938 "An Earlier Text of Addison's *Ode to Dr. Hannes*." *MLN*, LIII, 279–80.
"The Composition and Publication of Addison's Latin Poems." *Modern Philology*, XXXV, 359–67.
"The Authorship of *Spenser Redivivus*." *Review of English Studies*, XIV, 323–26.

1939   Review of *Lateinische Dichtung in England vom Ausgang des Frühhumanismus bis zum Regierungsantritt Elisabeths,* by W. Mann. *Modern Philology,* XXXVII, 98–99.

1940   *Musae Anglicanae: A History of Anglo-Latin Poetry, 1500–1925.* New York: Modern Language Association of America.

Review of *Studies in Iconology,* by E. Panofsky. *Modern Philology,* XXXVIII, 103–4.

1941   Review of *Elizabethan Music and Musical Criticism,* by Morrison C. Boyd. *MLN,* LVI, 242.

1942   Review of *The Brontës' Web of Childhood,* by Fannie E. Ratchford, and of *The Complete Poems,* by Emily Jane Brontë, edited by C. W. Hatfield. *MLN,* LVII, 304–5.

1943   Review of *George Gascoigne,* by C. T. Prouty. *Journal of English and Germanic Philology,* XLII, 120–21.

"A Check-List of Original Neo-Latin Dramas by Continental Writers Printed before 1650." *PMLA,* LVIII, 621–33.

Review of *Hundreth Sundrie Flowres,* by G. Gascoigne, edited by C. T. Prouty. *Journal of English and Germanic Philology,* XLII, 586–87.

1944   "Poems on the Defeat of the Spanish Armada." *Journal of English and Germanic Philology,* XLIII, 447–48.

1945   "Spenser's Connections with Hampshire." *MLN,* LX, 180–84.

1946   Review of *England and the Mediterranean Tradition,* edited by the Warburg and Courtauld Institutes. *Modern Philology,* XLIV, 61–62.

1948   *Edmund Spenser and "The Faerie Queene."* Chicago: University of Chicago Press.

(Ed.) *Essays on Shakespeare and Other Elizabethans,* by Tucker Brooke. New Haven: Yale University Press.

Review of *The Epigram in the English Renaissance,* by H. H. Hudson. *MLN,* LXIII, 577–78.

1950   " 'The Renaissance'—1939–1945: A Bibliographical Survey." *Medievalia et Humanistica,* V, 62–72.

Review of *The Life of Sir Thomas More, Knight,* by William Roper, edited by J. M. Cline. *Renaissance News,* III, 44–45.

1951   "Sixteenth Century Poems on Columbus," in *Essays Honoring Lawrence C. Wroth.* Portland, Maine: Anthoensen Press.

1953   (Ed., with C. A. Lynch.) *The Latin Epigrams of Thomas More.* Chicago: University of Chicago Press.

(Ed.) *A Contribution to a Union Catalogue of Sixteenth-Century Imprints in Certain New England Libraries.* Providence: Brown University Library.

"From Petrarch to Shakespeare," in *The Renaissance: A Symposium.* New York: Metropolitan Museum of Art.

Review of *Elizabethan Poetry,* by H. Smith. *MLN,* LXVIII, 425–26.

Review of *The Sphera of George Buchanan (1506–1582),* translated by James R. Naiden. *Classical Weekly,* XLVI, 247–48.

1954   "Renaissance Scholarship in America." *Renaissance News*, VII, 1–5.

"The Neo-Latin Epigram in Italy in the Fifteenth Century." *Medievalia et Humanistica*, VIII, 62–70. Translated by Josefa Nünning as "Das neulateinische Epigramm das fünfzehnten Jahrhunderts in Italien," in *Das Epigramm*. Darmstadt, 1969.

1955   "The First Cambridge Production of *Miles Gloriosus.*" *MLN*, LXX, 400–403.

Review of *English Literature in the Sixteenth Century*, by C. S. Lewis. *Renaissance News*, VIII, 19–22.

1956   "The Rise of Secular Drama in the Renaissance." *Studies in the Renaissance*, III, 7–22.

"Some Unpublished Poems by John Leland." *PMLA*, LXXI, 827–36.

1957   *Incarnation in Religion and Literature*. New York: The National Council of the Episcopal Church.

"The Latin Drama of the Renaissance." *Studies in the Renaissance*, IV, 31–70.

1958   Review of *Complaint and Satire in Early English Literature*, by John D. Peter. *MLN*, LXXIII, 57–58.

1960   Review of *The Sir Thomas More Circle*, by Pearl Hogrefe. *MLN*, LXXV, 707–8.

1962   (With C. A. Lynch.) "On St. Thomas More, an Epitaph of Uncertain Origin." *Renaissance News*, XV, 1–2.

"New Poems by George Herbert: The Cambridge Latin Gratulatory Anthology of 1613." *Renaissance News*, XV, 208–11.

1963   "Desiderata for the Study of Neo-Latin Drama." *Renaissance Drama*, VI, 17–20.

1964   (Ed.) *The Poems of Queen Elizabeth I.* Providence: Brown University Press.

"The Xenophon Translation Attributed to Elizabeth I." *Journal of the Warburg and Courtauld Institutes*, XXVII, 324–26.

1965   "Point of View in George Gascoigne's Fiction." *Studies in Short Fiction*, III, 16–22.

Review of *The Latin Poetry of George Herbert*, by Mark McCloskey and Paul Murphy. *Renaissance News*, XVIII, 348–49.

1966   Review of *Samuel Johnson: Poems*, edited by E. McAdam, Jr., and George Milne. *Modern Philology*, LXIII, 269–70.

Review of *Acolastus*, by G. Gnaphaeus, edited by W. E. D. Atkinson. *English Language Notes*, III, 222–23.

1967   "*Musae Anglicanae*: A Supplemental List." *Library*, 5th ser. XXII, 93–103.

WITHDRAWN